Way Home

Way Home

· ·

Journeys through Homelessness

JOSEPHINE ENSIGN

JOHNS HOPKINS UNIVERSITY PRESS

Baltimore

© 2024 Johns Hopkins University Press
All rights reserved. Published 2024
Printed in the United States of America on acid-free paper
9 8 7 6 5 4 3 2 1

Johns Hopkins University Press
2715 North Charles Street
Baltimore, Maryland 21218
www.press.jhu.edu

Library of Congress Cataloging-in-Publication Data

Names: Ensign, Josephine, author.
Title: Way home : journeys through homelessness / Josephine Ensign.
Description: Baltimore : Johns Hopkins University Press, [2024] |
    Includes bibliographical references and index.
Identifiers: LCCN 2024010357 | ISBN 9781421450230 (hardcover) |
    ISBN 9781421450247 (ebook)
Subjects: LCSH: Homelessness—Washington (State)—Seattle—
    History. | Homeless persons—Health and hygiene—Washington
    (State)—Seattle—History.
Classification: LCC HV4506.S43 E58 2024 |
    DDC 362.1086/942—dc23/eng/20240426
LC record available at https://lccn.loc.gov/2024010357

A catalog record for this book is available from the British Library.

*Special discounts are available for bulk purchases of this book.
For more information, please contact Special Sales at
specialsales@jh.edu.*

To my granddaughters, Hazel Elise and Chloe Calliope,
for the continuous joy and sense of hope they give
to both my life and work.

Contents

Acknowledgments

I have had the great fortune of talking with many people, groups, and organizations about the history of homelessness in Seattle and how those historical precedents reverberate today. This book is in conversation with my 2021 book, *Skid Road*, which launched during the prolonged COVID-19 pandemic. Living and working in Seattle through the pandemic, the heat domes of the summers of 2020 and 2021, and the CHAZ/CHOP protests (occupation protests in Seattle's Capitol Hill neighborhood), I saw the rippling effects of these events on homeless systems of care, service providers, and people experiencing homelessness. This experience led to the questions that guided me in researching and writing this book. I refined the ideas and questions through conversations with colleagues, friends, and groups of people in communities throughout Washington State through the Humanities Washington Speakers Bureau. I thank the journalists at the *Seattle Times* and its Project Homelessness, especially Anna Patrick and Sydney Brownstone, for sharing ideas and resources integral to my research and writing of *Way Home*.

My editor at Johns Hopkins University Press, Robin Coleman, helped shepherd this project throughout its development, from a wildly ambitious book proposal, thought up during the surreal early days of the pandemic, through chapter drafts, and on to what has become this book. The anonymous reviewers through the Press provided me with valuable feedback and suggestions that helped shape my writing. Copyeditor Jeremy Horsefield did a superb job with final edits of the book manuscript. Historian and colleague Lorraine McConaughy has been my long-term mentor, especially for the oral history interviews that inform my writing.

I thank all the people who graciously gave their time and expertise to allow me to interview them about their lives, viewpoints, and work related to homelessness. I extend special thanks to Derrick Belgarde, Anitra Freeman, and Jenn Adams for reading drafts of the chapters pertinent to them and providing feedback. Penny Miller has served as my steadfast transcriptionist for all my oral history interviews.

A 4Culture Heritage Award and a Jack Straw Artist Support grant provided funding and studio recording time for the oral history interviews and the educational components of this project. Assistance from Joe Lambert and Armand Jayne at the StoryCenter provided design coaching for developing my ArcGIS StoryMap of place-based stories of the history and contemporary landscape of homelessness in Seattle and King County. Containing videos and excerpts from my oral history interviews, "Skid Road: Stories of Homelessness in Seattle" is available at the ArcGIS StoryMap site under that title. My Skid Road oral history project is ongoing, and I will add content, including podcasts of my interviews and related content, to this StoryMap site and to my "Medical Margins" website.

I wrote this book with the time, space, and hospitality of various people and places. People who provided grounding support include my partner, Peter Kahn; my son, Jonathan, and daughter-in-law, Lily; my granddaughters, Hazel and Chloe; and my step-daughter, Margaret. They are my family, my home.

Acknowledgments

The caring staff members at Elizabeth Gregory Home (EGH), a day shelter for women and female-identified people experiencing homelessness, welcome groups of our University of Washington (UW) medical and nursing students through the student-run University District Street Medicine Project (UDSM). Working as a UDSM and a UW School of Nursing faculty preceptor at EGH is hands down the most rewarding part of what I do as a nurse practitioner and UW faculty member. It provided an essential and ongoing grounding to the research and writing of this book.

Writing residencies and self-directed retreats featured prominently in the support of my research and writing of this book. The residencies and retreats took me away from a challenging academic year and gave me the peace, encouragement, and enrichment required to complete this book project. I wrote it through the generous gift of time, space, and the community of writers afforded by the residencies.

A three-week writing fellowship at the Virginia Center for the Creative Arts (VCCA) in the late summer of 2022 allowed me to write and sleep in the converted milk room of an old kudzu-draped dairy barn in the foothills of the Blue Ridge Mountains. My time at VCCA in a rural Virginia setting reminiscent of the one of my childhood helped me make more peace, if not completely settled peace, with "the complexity, the offbeat rhythm of the South that has formed me."[1] My understanding of the nuances of home, of the contributors and consequences of being unhomed, grew in this familiar, yet uncannily unfamiliar, landscape.

Being in the company of a group of talented, accomplished, and generous writers, musicians, composers, and artists while I recovered coherent thoughts and proper word choices in the foggy aftermath of my first bout of COVID-19 guided me through the writing of one of the more emotionally demanding and ethically challenging chapters of this book—that of the life and death of Charleena Lyles.

My time at VCCA was followed by a two-week winter writing residency at Centrum, Fort Warden, on the Olympic Peninsula, where I wrote and lived in a moss-covered World War I army barracks with deer sleeping outside. Another two-week winter writing retreat saw me in a wood-stove-heated log cabin on the shore of the Salish Sea on my beloved Orcas Island. Since moving to the Pacific Northwest thirty years ago, the Doe Bay Resort and Beach Haven Resort (both blessedly unpretentious and funky) have been places I retreat to for writing and restoration. I am thankful for the magic of these places, full of frolicking families of otters, orcas, ravens, and deer, as well as fir-covered mountains and agate-strewn beaches.

For a week in the spring of 2023, I found myself among the majestic red rocks and painted desert of New Mexico, writing, hiking, and horseback riding at Ghost Ranch. I was coached by one of my longtime narrative nonfiction writing mentors, Wendy Call, in the company of other writers and one flexible yoga instructor and writer, Yael Flusberg. While in that high desert landscape, I had a glimpse of what Terry Tempest Williams means when she writes of the desert as being a sacred, healing place.

And finally, I am grateful for a two-week Mesa Refuge writing residency at Point Reyes Station, California, and for being named their 2023 May and Jack Elinson Public Health Fellow. The Mesa Refuge gave me the time, space, support, and inspiration from two excellent nonfiction social justice journalists, Margaret Lee and Molly O'Toole, to complete the writing of this book.

They say that writing is a solitary affair. While there is truth to that, I find that deeper writing is a communal affair. In gratitude to my growing community of writers. In gratitude to you, my readers.

Note

1. Josephine Ensign, *Catching Homelessness: A Nurse's Story of Falling through the Safety Net* (Berkeley, CA: She Writes Press, 2016), 32.

Prologue

· · · · · · · · · · · · · · · · · · ·

Having a home stabilizes you. A home grounds
you, and that's how you build a life.

—MANNY LOLEY

SUPPOSE YOU ARE THE COACH for your son's Little League team
in Seattle and arrive for a Saturday game at your local city park's
baseball field to find a man camped out in the dugout. What
would you do? Would you offer to buy him pizza and help move
his tent and belongings off the field so the children can play? If
he refuses to leave, do you call the police, your elected officials,
or the people at Seattle Parks and Recreation from whom you
reserved and rented the field? Is there a more compassionate and
skilled team of outreach workers you could call? Would they even
respond? Generally speaking, what can we do about "those
people" who don't seem to want any help? Why do we allow people
to live in tent encampments in our parks and on our sidewalks?
What is causing such an increase in homelessness in Seattle–
King County, and what are some possible solutions?

These are just some of the questions people ask me, most often with a palpable mixture of compassion and frustration: compassion for people experiencing homelessness and frustration at city officials over the lack of progress toward ending homelessness, or at least the most extreme and visible forms of homelessness.

People ask me about ways to help a friend, colleague, or family member experiencing homelessness who lacks access to needed health care, especially when they have recently lost their job or their health insurance, have cycled in and out of jail for an outstanding warrant, or are on an endless waiting list for substance use treatment. "How can I help them get a case manager?" "They need surgery, but the surgeon won't do the procedure unless they have a place to stay afterward, and medical respite won't take them, so what are their options?" "I know someone who has terminal cancer and is homeless. What exists in our community in terms of palliative and hospice care for homeless people?"[1]

Then there are questions that people experiencing or having experienced homelessness ask me. "Why do they make it so hard to get to talk to a counselor?" "Why do I have to be living out on the streets a lot longer to be able to qualify for housing?" "Why did they cut off my Medicaid and food stamps because my disability payment increased just a little bit, but I'm still homeless?" "How come the police or community vigilantes can come take our tents and stuff when that's considered stealing for anyone else?" "Why do people not get it that harm reduction saves lives, including the lives of their children and grandchildren, their brothers and sisters?"

People ask me these questions because I have worked with people experiencing homelessness for close to forty years, with thirty of those years working and living in Seattle. I have done this work as a nurse, a researcher, and a program and policy designer, and as someone with the lived experience of home-lessness and severe depression as a young adult.[2]

I recognize my privileges as a white, educated woman from a middle-class, primarily intact family, who had access, eventu-ally, to competent mental health treatment. My experience of homelessness was within these privileges, was relatively brief (six months), and was one time only. I know that a disproportionate number of people experiencing homelessness are persons of color and are from more resource-constrained, chaotic childhoods and educational lives than my own. Nevertheless, I know that my lived experience of homelessness as a young adult informs my research, writing, advocacy, and care provision as a nurse. My experience is an essential element of my moral compass. It helps me be aware when people use othering, stigmatizing, socially exclusionary, and derogatory language and actions toward people experiencing homelessness. "Those people" include me. "Those people" could be you, your neighbors, coworkers, friends, or family members. "Those people" are all of us.

SEATTLE PRIDES ITSELF on being a progressive, forward-thinking community. Perhaps this is a mythology of place, but its reputation is part of what drew me to Seattle from the much older and more conservative East Coast city of Baltimore. Seat-tle has the enviable position of being one of the best places in the United States for the upward socioeconomic mobility of children in many of its high-opportunity neighborhoods.[3] At the same time, Seattle has had one of our nation's highest rates of homelessness since the founding of the settler-colonial town in the early 1850s.[4] It continues to have one of the highest rates of homelessness, as does King County, in which Seattle is located.

In November 2015, King County executive Dow Constantine and Seattle mayor Ed Murray declared a state of emergency for homelessness in Seattle–King County. Since then, homelessness has continued to grow despite the work of people on multiple renditions of committees to end homelessness.

In January 2020, according to Housing and Urban Development's (HUD) Point-in-Time (PIT) count of homelessness in Seattle–King County, there were 11,751 people in King County experiencing homelessness, 8,166 of whom were living homeless in Seattle on the night of the count.[5] City, county, and federal officials curtailed the annual PIT count in January 2021 as a result of the COVID-19 pandemic. The newly formed King County Regional Homelessness Authority (RHA) revised the parameters of the altered January 2022 PIT count. The RHA's leaders claimed that its affiliate community partners did not have the capacity to participate in the annual count given the continuing pandemic and resulting staffing shortages. They also claimed that the previous methodology severely undercounted homelessness, especially in suburban and rural areas, areas they hoped would contribute more funding support for their efforts.[6] Instead, they planned to conduct a smaller, multimodal qualitative study of regional homelessness in collaboration with community partners. HUD required them to add a "head count" of people experiencing unsheltered homelessness.[7]

The RHA for Seattle and King County conducted two separate homelessness counts. Using a methodology modified from the previous labor-intensive PIT, the RHA reported that there were 13,368 individuals experiencing homelessness in King County on the January night of the national HUD PIT.[8] In a separate study using multiple data collection points, the RHA reported that there were a total of 40,800 homeless people during the twelve-month time period of 2022.[9] As of May 2, 2023, the

RHA had updated its five-year plan to end homelessness in King County. It now says that there were 53,000 people who experienced homelessness in King County in 2022 and states that ending homelessness in the county would require more than $8 billion in capital costs and an additional $3.5 billion in operating costs.[10]

Seattle has long had many transient people, and this continues today, from the seasonal people working in the fishing industry to construction workers who come from many parts of our country and live here temporarily. I've led a King County PIT count in previous years in the University District in Seattle and have noted many construction workers living in their vehicles. Are they homeless? The official answer was yes.

Even though the vast majority of homeless people in Seattle and King County are originally from this region or at least from Washington State, some people move here from other US locations in the hopes of finding jobs and better living conditions. They might have a job offer that then falls through when they arrive, and, without friends or family members locally, they end up precariously housed, if not outright homeless. They do not anticipate the high cost of housing in our city.

The reintegration of people exiting our nation's prolific prisons, complicated by the link between a felony conviction in certain states and laws limiting access to housing, food assistance, jobs, and even voting rights, can be difficult.[11] Advocates for reforms to our carceral system call restrictions on ex-felons a form of "double punishment."[12] The risk of homelessness and re-offending is highest during the month after release from prison; supportive housing and employment services help prevent this.[13] A recent study found that former prison inmates are ten times more likely to become homeless than the general population; persons of color and women are at the highest risk.[14]

Beth Macy, in her book *Dopesick*, wonders about the fate of Ronnie, a Black man in prison for the third time in Virginia for drug-related crimes: "What if Ronnie's reentry had been managed not by an overburdened and apathetic system but instead by workers from Bryan Stevenson's Equal Justice Initiative, which sends clients to felon-friendly cities like Seattle?"[15] People with felony convictions, even for nonviolent drug charges, from Washington State or elsewhere can end up homeless in Seattle. Former prison inmates face fewer barriers in Seattle than they would if they stayed in states like Virginia or South Carolina. Although this fact is fodder for right-wing reactionaries claiming that progressive—and in their view overly permissive—Seattle attracts ex-felons, I would rather live in a compassionate city that gives people a chance of reintegrating into the community and not ending up homeless.

Native American and Native Alaskan people—Indigenous people—are the most overrepresented subpopulation of people experiencing homelessness in Seattle, followed by Black people, highlighting the effects of historical trauma from settler colonialism, slavery, and racism. Seattle has fallout from our history of racial housing covenants, redlining, and racist single-family zoning laws. Of note, many rural and suburban areas of King County are more conservative than Seattle, and partisan political conflicts over approaches to regional homelessness echo those around our nation.

People living unsheltered in vehicles and tent encampments increased visibly during the pandemic, creating humanitarian, public health, policing, and political controversies. From City Hall Park encampments in downtown Seattle, to the Capitol Hill Organized Protest (CHOP) encampments on Capitol Hill after the police killing of George Floyd, to encampments in Green

Lake Park and adjacent to Bitter Lake Elementary School, conflicts have deepened. These conflicts have arisen between advocates for homeless people, those experiencing homelessness, business leaders, government officials, homeowners, and renters on land adjacent to encampments.

Homelessness was the top issue for Seattle voters in the November 2021 elections, with moderate and business-backed candidate Bruce Harrell winning the Seattle mayoral race over the more progressive candidate Lorena González.[16] In addition, the worsening of visible homelessness factored in the contentious race for Seattle's next city attorney general, with "Law and Order Republican" candidate Ann Davison winning decisively over the progressive former public defender and "police abolitionist" Nicole Thomas Kennedy.[17] Kennedy has called for an end to misdemeanor prosecutions, "crimes of survival" numbering among them, which fall disproportionately on homeless people and persons of color.[18]

Visible homelessness in our city and county is at a level not seen since the Great Depression, when Seattle had our country's largest and longest-lasting tent city, Hooverville, south of Pioneer Square.[19] With the ending of nationwide, state, and local moratoriums on foreclosures and residential evictions, confusion over the Emergency Rental Assistance Program and housing vouchers, and phasing out of Medicaid continuity during the pandemic, most people working on the front lines of health and social services in Seattle–King County and elsewhere expect to see another surge in homelessness.[20] This is especially problematic in the Seattle area, with its rapidly escalating cost of housing.[21]

The Seattle area was the first in our country to identify the community-wide spread of the novel coronavirus. Early in the

COVID-19 pandemic, when we were asked to shelter at home, and congregate living spaces such as emergency shelters were known to hasten the spread of the virus, public health officials locally and nationally moved to limit shelter capacity. They placed moratoriums on both evictions from housing and homeless encampment clearances. The city and county worked quickly to acquire hotels and motels—even Harborview Hall, the former nurses' residence at Harborview Medical Center—to safely house homeless people and others who could not safely isolate and recover from the infection. Public Health–Seattle & King County and its Health Care for the Homeless (HCH) program, along with Harborview Medical Center, provided nursing and public health support staff at these isolation and quarantine facilities. They implemented a harm reduction approach to engage with clients experiencing homelessness. Several of my students who are nurses worked there throughout the pandemic, so I learned about the challenges and innovations of such programs from the perspective of nurses.

As our country contends with the new reality of post-pandemic individual and community life, there is clear evidence of deepening economic and racial inequities, as well as breakdowns in our already frayed health and social care safety nets. Any walk or drive through our urban areas, from Washington, DC, to Los Angeles, reveals a steep rise in visible poverty, suffering, and homelessness, especially for persons of color. Deaths, disabilities, and economic fallout from COVID-19 have disproportionately fallen on the elderly, the medically vulnerable, the disabled, frontline workers, and Black, Indigenous, and persons of color (BIPOC) communities.[22] The COVID-19 pandemic accelerated an already steep rise nationally in mortality rates for people experiencing homelessness. Recent studies show a 77% rise nationally in mortality for homeless people over the five years from

2016 to 2022.[23] Causes of death include exposure to heat or cold, worsened by weather extremes from climate change; overdose and suicide (the so-called diseases of despair); and, more recently, COVID-19. King County marked a record-breaking 310 deaths of people experiencing homelessness in 2022, an increase of 65% from 2021, with fentanyl overdoses and homicides as leading causes.[24] The numbers of these deaths in King County continue to rise, with 415 deaths recorded in 2023.[25]

Here in Seattle, which had a high rate of homelessness and stark income disparities even before the pandemic, tents and other temporary living structures made of cast-off materials line the hillsides along Interstate 5, appear on sidewalks, and fill green spaces such as ravines and city parks. Cars, RVs, and trucks with screened-off and fogged-up windows and windshields—the temporary homes of vehicle residents—dot the landscape. A house next door to my own home in a mixed-income neighborhood near the university where I work has changed from an informal refuge for homeless squatters to a "flipped" single-family home that recently sold for $1.3 million to a young couple working in the local tech industry. An unofficial count of unsheltered people experiencing homelessness found a more than 50% increase in people living in encampments from summer 2019 to summer 2020.[26]

HOW DO WE reconcile the fact that Seattle is both a progressive, hopeful city and a place in which homelessness is such a large, growing, and deeply entrenched problem? I asked a version of this question in my book *Skid Road: On the Frontier of Health and Homelessness in an American City*, which traces the history of homelessness and safety-net health care in Seattle–King County. People wonder whether our high rate of homelessness stems from our progressive politics. Some people liken it to overly permissive parenting at a civic level, similar to what has happened in San Francisco.[27] More conservative voices come to the conclusion that homelessness in Seattle is a "drug problem" or a "mental health problem" and even recommend locking up homeless people beside violent criminals at the nearby McNeil high-security prison.[28] Elsewhere along the political spectrum, people ask me why we do not apply a Marxist analysis of homelessness and recognize that capitalism requires an underclass; to solve homelessness would require getting rid of capitalism.

I realize how contentious and politically polarizing many issues, including homelessness, have become in our country. Homelessness is a wicked problem, meaning it is complex, is multifaceted, and causes a high degree of public conflict because no one can agree on its causes, much less its solutions.[29] We need ways to provide more constructive civil discourse to find paths forward. We need to cultivate a deeper, more nuanced understanding of homelessness. We need to elevate the voices and stories of people with the lived experience of homelessness, including people who have overcome homelessness. All of this led me to write *Way Home*.

A WORK OF NARRATIVE NONFICTION, *Way Home: Journeys through Homelessness* is set in Seattle–King County, Washington, and explores the contemporary landscape of homelessness with an emphasis on innovative local solutions. From safe parking lots for vehicle residents, early adoption of the Housing First model of care, consumer-led programs, and reforms of single-family zoning to changes spurred by the COVID-19 pandemic, Seattle–King County is a leader in its diversity of ways to address homelessness. Amplifying the voices and stories of people with the lived experience of homelessness, I weave in the positive and negative impacts of various policies and programs. In this book, I address the often overlooked and undervalued role of health issues and our frayed public health and health care safety net in contributing to poverty and homelessness. Alongside *Skid Road*, *Way Home* deepens our understanding of the historical roots of homelessness and the current public policy and program efforts at the national, state, and local levels that attempt to address it.

Besides extensive ethnographic research, archival research, and reading of published sources, I conducted more than sixty audio- and videotaped oral history interviews. These professionally transcribed interviews are with people who have firsthand knowledge of the intersection of health and homelessness, both locally in Seattle–King County and nationally. These interviews are with politicians, policymakers, and program directors, as well as with people with the lived experience of homelessness. I purposely interviewed people who not only survived homeless but also overcame systemic and personal challenges to become stably housed. They are thriving, giving back to their communities, and helping to shape policies and programs addressing homelessness. I draw on these interviews and additional focused interviews with a variety of people in *Way Home*.

My ethnographic research includes participant observations made over the past five years through my ongoing volunteer work in various Seattle homeless shelters, in policymaking work groups, and as a board member for a Seattle faith-based philanthropy that supports community-based services for homeless families, children, and youths. In addition, my observations and interviews include time spent in and with people involved with the King County Regional Mental Health Court and the King County Adult Diversion Drug Court, King County Juvenile Detention, Seattle's Navigation Team, various sanctioned and unsanctioned tent encampments, tiny house villages, and vehicle residency programs. During the CHOP protests, I worked with nursing students who volunteered as street medics and other students who worked as National Guard troop members alongside Seattle police at the protests. These experiences inform *Way Home*, and in drawing on them, I have upheld professional standards for privacy and confidentiality of source material.

I intentionally did not approach my participant observation as immersive research or stunt journalism, such as by living in a homeless encampment. While there are examples of this approach that resulted in excellent and influential books, including Jessica Bruder's *Nomadland* and Matthew Desmond's *Evicted*, I question the ethics of this approach. My concerns are not only about researchers using resources intended for people in need. Having experienced homelessness as a young adult, I know that "real homelessness" is just not the same as "pretend homelessness" for extractive purposes, no matter how well intentioned.

As to terminology, I am aware of and agree with the move of advocates and even government agencies like the Centers for Disease Control and Prevention (CDC) to replace the term "homeless people" with "people experiencing homelessness" to support person-first language. Throughout this book, I use this term whenever possible. Another proposed change of terminology is replacing "homeless" with "houseless." Although I understand the motivation behind an increasing number of advocates using this alternative, I disagree with the change. Homelessness is about social exclusion and disaffiliation as much as it is about not having an adequate, safe, affordable, and stable place to live.

"TODAY, I FEEL homeless. I woke up this morning and thought, *it's a homeless sort of day*," said a young man standing in the rain with a small group of his friends outside a homeless youth shelter, a stone's throw from the university campus where I teach. I was at the shelter recently as a faculty preceptor with a group of our University of Washington (UW) medical, nursing, and dental students for what we call a "Teeth and Toes Clinic" for the provision of basic foot and dental care. One of the young man's friends asked him, "How do you define homeless?" He replied, "I don't know. I like to think of myself as a traveler, but today I am homeless."

This conversation stayed with me all morning as we cared for the young people who had come just for the clinic services. It continues to haunt me. Reflecting on the fact that I have lived in Seattle for thirty years, working as a nurse practitioner, researcher, and advocate for people experiencing homelessness, I wondered, *what progress have we made, have I made in terms of solving homelessness? How can we make it so that no one has to wake up to a homeless sort of day?*

Amid the rapidly evolving public health and political landscape accelerated by the COVID-19 pandemic, policies were enacted by the nation, by states, and by municipalities to provide social and economic support for people. These supports included child tax credits, Medicaid expansion subsidies, rental subsidies, eviction moratoriums, congregate shelter deintensification, isolation and quarantine units for people without adequate housing options, and the establishment of group motels with colocated medical and social support services. Researchers documented the effects of these policies on improving health outcomes, preventing new homelessness, and shortening homelessness for individuals and families. With eviction moratoriums and Medicaid expansion subsidies ending, including in Washington State, concerns are growing over a possible wave of newly homeless people.

The people of Seattle–King County have frequently found innovative ways to provide compassionate care to people living on society's margins and to address upstream causes of social exclusion. The long-standing progressive political beliefs of many of the city's citizens and elected officials are in tension with more centrist and conservative beliefs. These contrasting views affect how we frame, talk about, and address homelessness. *Way Home* contributes to deeper conversations about homelessness and health care by exploring their historical intersections and challenges while highlighting innovative local solutions. This book increases ways to amplify diverse voices, including those of people with the lived experience of homelessness, within contemporary health care and public policy debates. It challenges us as individuals, residents, health and social care providers, and government workers to learn from the past in order to make more informed choices affecting our present and future lives together.

Notes

1. Sydney Brownstone, "She Didn't Want to Die Homeless. But in Seattle, There Were Few Places to Turn," *Seattle Times*, January 9, 2022, https://www.seattletimes.com/seattle-news/homeless/she -didnt-want-to-die-without-a-home-but-even-with-cancer-she-had -few-options-in-seattle/.
2. Josephine Ensign, *Catching Homelessness: A Nurse's Story of Falling through the Safety Net* (Berkeley, CA: She Writes Press, 2016).
3. "Creating Moves to Opportunity in Seattle–King County," Abdul Latif Jameel Poverty Action Lab, accessed July 25, 2021, https://www .povertyactionlab.org/evaluation/creating-moves-opportunity-seattle -king-county.
4. Josephine Ensign, *Skid Road: On the Frontier of Health and Homelessness in an American City* (Baltimore: Johns Hopkins University Press, 2021).
5. "Count Us In," KCRHA, accessed July 1, 2020, https://kcrha.org/king -county-point-in-time-count/.

6. martensesq, "FAQ: Point in Time Count," KCRHA, accessed November 22, 2021, https://kcrha.org/2021/11/22/faq-point-in-time-count/.

7. Erica C. Barnett, "King County Will Forego Annual Count of Homeless Population," South Seattle Emerald, November 29, 2021, https://southseattleemerald.com/2021/11/29/king-county-will-forego-annual-count-of-homeless-population/.

8. "How Many Homeless People Are in King County? Depends Who You Ask," *Seattle Times*, July 4, 2022, https://www.seattletimes.com/seattle-news/homeless/how-many-homeless-people-are-in-king-county-depends-who-you-ask/.

9. "Spurning Old Way of Counting Homeless People, King County Says Number Is Much Higher Than Previously Reported," *Seattle Times*, December 16, 2021, https://www.seattletimes.com/seattle-news/homeless/spurning-old-way-of-counting-homeless-people-king-county-says-number-is-much-higher-than-previously-reported/; "America's First Homelessness Problem: Knowing Who Is Actually Homeless," *Washington Post*, August 24, 2022, https://www.washingtonpost.com/dc-md-va/2022/08/24/homeless-seattle-hud-statistics/.

10. martensesq, "An Update on Our 5-Year Plan," KCRHA, May 2, 2023, https://kcrha.org/news-an-update-on-our-5-year-plan/.

11. "From Prisons to Communities: Confronting Re-entry Challenges and Social Inequality," American Psychological Association, accessed May 7, 2023, https://www.apa.org/pi/ses/resources/indicator/2018/03/prisons-to-communities; Melissa Li, "From Prisons to Communities: Confronting Re-entry Challenges and Social Inequality," Tarrant Cares, accessed March 13, 2024, https://tarrant.tx.networkofcare.org/ps/library/article.aspx?id=3135.

12. "No More Double Punishments: Lifting the Ban on SNAP and TANF for People with Prior Felony Drug Convictions," CLASP, accessed May 7, 2023, https://www.clasp.org/publications/report/brief/no-more-double-punishments/.

13. "From Prisons to Communities," American Psychological Association.

14. Lucius Couloute, "Nowhere to Go: Homelessness among Formerly Incarcerated People," Prison Policy Initiative, August 2018, https://www.prisonpolicy.org/reports/housing.html.

15. Beth Macy, *Dopesick: Dealers, Doctors, and the Drug Company That Addicted America* (New York: Little, Brown, 2018), chap. 12; Beth

Macy, email to the author, May 6, 2023. Macy said that Brian Stevenson told her that in a phone interview.

16. "How Would Mayoral Candidates Bruce Harrell and M. Lorena González Tackle Homelessness in Seattle?," *Seattle Times*, September 28, 2021, https://www.seattletimes.com/seattle-news/homeless /how-would-mayoral-candidates-bruce-harrell-and-m-lorena -gonzalez-tackle-homelessness-in-seattle/; Anne Christnovich, "Seattle Elections 2021: Digging Deeper into Voters' Top Priorities," Crosscut, June 22, 2021, https://crosscut.com/inside-crosscut/2021 /06/seattle-elections-2021-digging-deeper-voters-top-priorities.

17. Mike Baker, "Seattle's Choice: A Police Abolitionist or a Law-and-Order Republican?," *New York Times*, sec. U.S., October 30, 2021, https://www.nytimes.com/2021/10/30/us/seattle-city-attorney -election.html.

18. "Seattle's New City Attorney to Expedite Prosecution Decisions, Focus on Misdemeanors, Backlog," *Seattle Times*, February 6, 2022, https://www.seattletimes.com/seattle-news/politics/seattles-new-city -attorney-to-expedite-prosecution-decisions-focus-on-misdemeanors -backlog/.

19. Ensign, *Skid Road*.

20. Claire Cain Miller and Alicia Parlapiano, "The U.S. Built a European-Style Welfare State. It's Largely Over," *New York Times*, sec. The Upshot, April 6, 2023, https://www.nytimes.com/interactive/2023 /04/06/upshot/pandemic-safety-net-medicaid.html.

21. Gene Balk, "It's Not Just Housing—Almost Everything Is More Expensive in Seattle," *Seattle Times*, June 14, 2021, https://www .seattletimes.com/seattle-news/data/toothpaste-and-olive-oil-its-not -just-housing-almost-everything-is-expensive-in-seattle/.

22. Latoya Hill and Samantha Artiga, "COVID-19 Cases and Deaths by Race/Ethnicity: Current Data and Changes over Time," *KFF* (blog), August 22, 2022, https://www.kff.org/racial-equity-and-health-policy /issue-brief/covid-19-cases-and-deaths-by-race-ethnicity-current -data-and-changes-over-time/.

23. Erin McCormick, "'Homelessness Is Lethal': US Deaths among Those without Housing Are Surging," *Guardian*, sec. US news, February 7, 2022, https://www.theguardian.com/us-news/2022/feb/07 /homelessness-is-lethal-deaths-have-risen-dramatically.

24. Associated Press, "Fentanyl Fuels Record Number of Homeless Deaths in the Seattle Area," *Los Angeles Times*, January 17, 2023, https://www.latimes.com/world-nation/story/2023-01-17/fentanyl-fuels-record-homeless-deaths-seattle-area.

25. "King County Setting Records for Homeless Deaths Is Becoming Awfully Routine," Seattle Times, January 10, 2024, https://www.seattletimes.com/seattle-news/king-county-setting-records-for-homeless-deaths-is-becoming-awfully-routine/.

26. "Tents in Seattle Increased by More Than 50% after COVID Pandemic Began, Survey Says," *Seattle Times*, April 3, 2021, https://www.seattletimes.com/seattle-news/homeless/tents-in-seattle-increased-by-more-than-50-after-covid-pandemic-began-survey-says/.

27. Thomas Fuller and Shaila Dewan, "San Francisco Mayor Declares State of Emergency to Fight 'Nasty Streets' of the City," *New York Times*, sec. U.S., December 17, 2021, https://www.nytimes.com/2021/12/17/us/san-francisco-state-of-emergency-crime.html; Michael Shellenberger, *San Fransicko: Why Progressives Ruin Cities* (New York: HarperCollins, 2021).

28. Eric Johnson, "KOMO News Special: Seattle Is Dying," KOMO, updated March 20, 2019, https://komonews.com/news/local/komo-news-special-seattle-is-dying.

29. Edward P. Weber, D. Denise Lach, and Brent Steel, *New Strategies for Wicked Problems: Science and Solutions in the Twenty-First Century* (Corvallis: Oregon State University Press, 2017).

CHAPTER 1

Prelude to Compassion

. . . .

The prelude to compassion is the willingness
to see.

—SUNITA PURI, "WE MUST LEARN TO LOOK AT GRIEF,
EVEN WHEN WE WANT TO RUN AWAY"

ON FOURTH AVENUE, at the foot of the cascading staircase of
Seattle City Hall, the site of thousands of wedding photographs,
lies a bronze maple leaf embedded in the sidewalk. It bears the
inscription "Lisa Vach, 1983–2020." This and the growing number of "leaves of remembrance" scattered nearby are easy to
miss unless you know to look for them. The leaves of remembrance are for people who have died outside or while living
homeless in Seattle. The group Women in Black began this city-
sanctioned volunteer project through the self-governed group
Women's Housing Equality and Enhancement League (WHEEL).
WHEEL has its own fascinating story, one that we return to
later. This is Lisa's story. And unfortunately, it is the story of the
deeply troubled and proudly violent man who killed her, Travis

Berge. It is the story of multiple systems failures, especially the messy, ineffective, and oftentimes abusive amalgam of our behavioral health and criminal justice systems. It is the story of the tensions over who has the right to be in public spaces. It is the story of how distorted media exacerbated the problems—for Lisa, for Travis, for all of us. It is the story of how we see what we want to see and the costs of that selective vision.

THE DAY THAT LISA was killed in Cal Anderson Park, September 17, 2020, was an oppressively warm day, with an ominous orange glow in the sky. Air quality measures hovered over red and dark-purple alerts in the "unhealthy for all" and "very unhealthy" categories, respectively. Starting on September 11, King County officials closed all city parks and beaches owing to the smoke. They opened up "healthy air" shelters for people experiencing homelessness or who otherwise lacked adequate housing.[1] Since July, wildfires had burned out of control in Eastern Washington, Oregon, California, and British Columbia, with their collective plumes of smoke hovering over Seattle and the surrounding area. Thick smoke obliterated views of the tops of downtown skyscrapers. It resembled reports of the experience of living through the Great Smog of London in 1952, but instead of it lasting a few days as it had in London, it extended for weeks in Seattle. People were on edge from the continuing COVID-19 pandemic, with the first diagnosed cases in the United States being in the Seattle area in January of that year. Health reports cautioned the public about the double threat of COVID and smoke inhalation. There was a documented link between exposure to the fine particulates of wildfire smoke and increased risk of severe complications and death from COVID-19.[2] Data showed a disproportionate burden of disease and death from COVID-19 for Black, Indigenous, and Hispanic people, a disproportionality that continued to grow.[3]

People in Seattle were anxious about this apocalyptic landscape combined with the disorienting, disruptive, and isolating effects of the ongoing COVID-19 pandemic. People were also on edge from the continuing protests over racial justice and police violence from the killing of a Black man, George Floyd, by a white male police officer in Minneapolis. The widely viewed video footage of Floyd's killing in late May added to the urgency of this issue. It resurfaced the names, faces, and stories of other Black, Brown, and Indigenous people killed by police, including Breonna Taylor and Ahmaud Arbery. Locally, this list included the following people. On August 30, 2010, on a downtown Seattle street, a Seattle police officer shot and killed the well-known Indigenous woodcarver John T. Williams, a homeless man with severe hearing loss and mental illness. Williams was unarmed, carrying only his small woodcarving knife and not threatening anyone. In June 2017, police killed Charleena Lyles, a thirty-year-old pregnant Black woman with a history of domestic violence and homelessness, living with her four children in permanent supportive housing in North Seattle. On May 31, 2019, a white Auburn police officer fatally shot the unarmed homeless Black and Cambodian American twenty-six-year-old Jesse Sarey.[4] The police killings of Williams, Lyles, Sarey, and others contributed to federal oversight of the Seattle Police Department (SPD) under a consent decree. This consent decree was set to expire in the summer of 2020.[5] Floyd's killing grew support for the Black Lives Matter (BLM) movement, including BLM Seattle–King County (BLMSKC). The Seattle protests began in the downtown business district. They coalesced in and around the East Precinct of the SPD, spreading into the nearby Cal

Anderson Park in the Capitol Hill district, just east of downtown Seattle.

EMERGING IN EARLY JUNE 2020, a purposefully leaderless, de-
centralized, consensus-driven governance group calling their
area the Capitol Hill Autonomous Zone (CHAZ) set up protests.
The BLMSKC group made clear early on that they were not involved in the street protests, and they even issued a warning calling for BIPOC communities to avoid crowded protests for public health reasons.[6] These protests spread to a six-block radius
around the East Precinct of the SPD on the corner of Twelfth and
Pine Streets.[7] Built in an old auto repair shop sharing walls with
an adjacent large apartment building with street-level businesses, the East Precinct employed many officers identifying as
BIPOC and LGBTQ. They were conflicted over the racial and police brutality protests. "They are Pine Street, the lefty precinct,
many of them Black and brown and female and queer."[8]

Beginning on June 1, in confrontations between Seattle police, the SWAT team, and National Guard members on one side
and protestors on the other side in front of the East Precinct, police used tear gas, pepper spray, flash-bang devices, and rubber
bullets to disperse the crowds. A woman protestor holding a pink
umbrella as protection had it wrestled out of her hands by a
police officer, captured on video by the Black citizen journalist
Omari Salisbury.[9] The pink umbrella became a symbol of the
protests.[10] This excessive use of force to dispel largely peaceful
protests led a federal judge to extend oversight of the SPD under
the consent decree.[11] Former Seattle police chief Carmen Best,
in her memoir of this time, *Black in Blue: Lessons on Leadership, Breaking Barriers, and Racial Reconciliation*, defended
the actions of the police, stating, "These protestors were taking

over a neighborhood, destroying property, attacking officers."[12] She added that the fire chief was worried that protestors would burn down the East Precinct police building, as protestors had done in Minneapolis, and that a fire in the old building would be difficult to control and could spread rapidly to adjacent apartment buildings.[13]

Thousands of physicians, nurses, and other health care providers gathered outside Harborview Medical Center on First Hill near Capitol Hill on June 6 for a Health Care Workers for Justice March to City Hall. The co-organizers for this event were the surgeon Dr. Estell Williams and her partner Edwin G. Lindo, lawyer and critical race theory lecturer at the UW School of Medicine. At the rally, Lindo spoke out against racism and police violence, including what was happening to Capitol Hill protesters and the disproportionate effects of the COVID-19 pandemic on persons and communities of color. Calling this a double public health crisis, he added, "Nothing in this country that has ever changed or seen progress has ever occurred without going into the streets. And so the answer is to be in the streets."[14]

On June 8, police abandoned the Capitol Hill police precinct when the situation became too volatile. Ecstatic protestors took over the area around the building, hanging homemade signs reading "No Justice, No Peace, No Racist Police" and "Seattle People Department" over the SPD sign, claiming that the area was now a police-free zone.[15] Protestors did not burn down the precinct building as many had feared. Although many protestors continued to use the name CHAZ, the group renamed themselves "Capitol Hill Organized Protest" (CHOP). Protestors included BLM-related activists and people supporting racial justice and other progressive and leftist causes such as universal health care, Indigenous land rights, and taxing wealthy people and corporations. Some also protested homeless encampment sweeps.

Mutual-aid groups, including street medics composed of nurses, emergency medical technicians, and health science students, simultaneously participated in the protests and supported the protestors. It is worth noting that mutual-aid groups have their roots in socialist movements and proliferated during the pandemic in many urban areas of the United States.[16] From the beginning, Seattle City Council member and Socialist Alternative party member Kshama Sawant, a coleader of the Occupy Seattle protests in 2011 and now council member for the district including Capitol Hill, was a vocal and visible supporter of the CHAZ/CHOP protests. In an evening speech at Cal Anderson Park on June 8, Sawant stated, "You can never have zero police and an elimination of racism and oppression on the basis of capitalism." The next evening, Sawant led protestors downhill and into City Hall, where she spoke about defunding the police and taxing Amazon, headquartered in Seattle. A Black protestor spoke up, accusing her and other speakers of trying to co-opt BLM and CHAZ/CHOP for their own agendas.[17]

ONE OF THE PEOPLE drawn to the CHAZ/CHOP protests and its community-building atmosphere was Lisa Vach. Originally from the Southern California towns of Pomona and Pasadena, Lisa had moved to Seattle in 2017 in search of more opportunities. Her maternal aunt, Nina Morris, lived and still lives in Seattle. Lisa was a self-trained artist and free spirit with long red hair and green eyes. In a letter from her mother, Stella Morris, to her Seattle aunt postmarked March 1, 2001, her mother described Lisa as "a mother earth type."[18] A recovering alcoholic since Lisa was nine years old, Stella worked as a drug and alcohol dependency counselor in Pasadena until her death not long after she had sent this letter to her sister.

According to her Facebook postings, Lisa had lived in the Regenerative Cooperative of Pomona ("Regen") in the Kingsley House for ten years. Started in 1999 by environmentalist and electric car early adopter William R. Korthof, the Regen Cooperative was solar-powered, gray-water-landscaped, consensus-driven shared housing. Former residents described what they called "Will-fare," saying that if anyone was broke but willing to work, "Will would find them work." Lisa's best friend, Shade Falcon Remelin, who lived in Regen at the same time as Lisa, said after her death that "it was the place she felt safest, in her all too brief time here."[19]

Lisa loved animals and enjoyed traveling and going to music festivals and art museums. One of her favorite authors was Jeannette Winterson, author of the memoir *Why Be Happy When You Could Be Normal?* Lisa joined social justice rallies like the 2019 Women's March in Seattle. During Brett Kavanaugh's Supreme Court confirmation hearings before the US Senate Judiciary Committee in fall of 2018, with the sexual assault accusations against him, Lisa wrote on her Facebook page that it was breaking her heart. "Do these men know the damage they are doing? Much love to everyone who is reliving their trauma with this story so much in the news. Wounds heal best with air."

Lisa had various jobs in Seattle, mainly located in the Pioneer Square area downtown. She worked as a housekeeper at the bed and breakfast above the historic Merchant's Café and Saloon.[20] Her last job, or at least the last one she wrote about, beginning in the winter of 2018, was through a temp agency. She worked in the gift shop of Bill Speidel's Underground Tour in the heart of Pioneer Square. Lisa posted Facebook photos of a wall of the gift shop that she helped restore, and she wrote of liking her coworkers and her job. She commented that she wanted to get over her "stage fright" to apply for a permanent position as one of the guides for the underground tours. It seems she never did. She restored wood furniture and used reclaimed pieces of wood to paint a Loteria set. Her card no. 46 was El Sol (The Sun), which she called "the blanket of the poor."

By the start of the COVID-19 pandemic, Lisa had lost her job and housing. She became homeless, from all indications for the first time in her life. From one of her last Facebook postings and photographs from March 5, 2020, it appears that she was inside one of the Downtown Emergency Service Center (DESC) permanent supportive housing units at the old Morrison Hotel in Pioneer Square. DESC is one of Seattle's largest and longest-running service providers for people experiencing homelessness. Lisa's photograph is taken from inside a room at the Morrison Hotel and includes a close-up of a seagull sitting on an open window ledge. Outside, in the background, is City Hall, where her bronze leaf of remembrance would be placed in less than a year. It is unclear whether she was living in a DESC supportive housing unit at the Morrison or she was visiting someone who lived there.

Around this time, when COVID-19 cases and deaths were accelerating in Seattle and King County, DESC staff closed their large congregant shelter in the former ballroom of the Morrison. DESC relocated people to hotels and other spaces less conducive to the rapid spread of infections and disease. DESC maintained, but at a reduced capacity, their permanent supportive housing units on the upper floors of the Morrison, where Lisa's photograph of the seagull on the windowsill appears to have been taken. Seattle and King County moved swiftly to establish isolation and quarantine (I & Q) units in unused hotels, with staffing by nurses and social workers. The I & Q units were for people who were homeless or inadequately housed with known exposure to COVID-19 and for people mildly ill with the disease and not needing hospitalization. With a nod to the enduring legacy of the founding of Seattle as a settler-colonial port town, fishing crew members stayed at the I & Q units as COVID-19 outbreaks plagued the local commercial fishing industry.[21]

Images and stories of Japanese creatures, both real and mythological, resonated with Lisa, having spent several of her childhood years with her family in Yokosuka, Japan, at the US naval base where her father worked. In her Facebook "Intro" section, she identifies as "Tanuki Troubadour," with tanuki being Japanese raccoon dogs. Tanuki, in Japanese folklore, is a shape-shifting animal. On March 20, 2020, Lisa posted her drawing done on cardboard of Amabie, a mythological creature from Japanese folklore. Amabie is depicted as half-human, half-fish with a bird's beak and shimmering scales on its body. The folklore story is that Amabie appeared out of the sea and told people to make and share depictions of it to help ward off a plague.[22]

It is difficult to know what Lisa's state of mind was during this time, mainly based on her increasingly sparse Facebook posts, but these are all that remain publicly of what she wrote and the images she shared. Like many people, especially women, who are oriented toward helping other people, Lisa may have found it difficult to ask for help, even to her own detriment. Having been the daughter of an alcoholic mother likely contributed to this problem. It is unclear what, if any, mental health therapy Lisa had received.

At this point in her life, if she had seen a social worker or intake counselor at DESC and they had screened her using their Vulnerability Assessment Tool (VAT), she would have been deemed high-risk, at least in the domain of survival skills. One of the examples on the VAT for evidence of severe vulnerability in survival skills is "disregard for personal safety, e.g., walks into traffic."[23]

On March 21, Lisa posted that the day before she had walked through intersections downtown without first looking for traffic, adding, "Today I walked smack-dab in the middle of the street for blocks. Howling like a wolf." Several of her friends responded on Facebook about how cool that was. But, in retrospect, was this literally a cry for help? As her life spiraled deeper into homelessness, support services were strained beyond capacity because of the pandemic. Like her former Underground Tour coworker, Sirena Ross, and her longtime friend, Shade Falcon Remelin, who lived in Seattle, Lisa's friends were likely dealing with their own job, housing, and other disruptions caused by the pandemic.

On April 9, Lisa superimposed "I am a pre-existing condition" over her drawing of Amabie. Her last Facebook post was on May 11, 2020, and included photographs of squirrels in what appears to be a Seattle park. She wrote, "Tried making squirrel 'friends.' I suggested they respect social distancing. They refused to wear masks. I DEFINITELY heard one sneeze, and then the other dude jumped in my purse and robbed me of my cookies I wanted to share with them. This is why I have so few friends." By the time she joined the CHAZ/CHOP protests, she lived in her truck and then in a tent encampment in Cal Anderson Park.

CAL ANDERSON PARK is in the heart of the bustling bar and restaurant section of Capitol Hill, an area long established as the center of LGBTQ culture and life in Seattle.[24] The park, named for Washington State's first openly gay state legislator, is adjacent to Seattle Central College, sometimes called Little Berkeley, a public community college with roots in the civil rights movement of the 1960s. Cal Anderson Park and Seattle Central College have long been a center of protests, including the civil rights and Vietnam War issues of the 1960s and 1970s, the 1999

World Trade Organization "Battle of Seattle," Occupy Seattle in 2011, and the recurring May Day demonstrations for workers' and immigrants' rights.[25] Cal Anderson Park had the city's first water reservoir, contained in an underground vault in 2005, and an old pumphouse and wading pool. The water was cut off to the aboveground water features at the start of the COVID-19 pandemic, when city parks were closed to prevent the spread of the coronavirus. In the 1990s, Cal Anderson Park was often called Needle Park for the level of drug use and visible homelessness, and it underwent a revitalization in the late 1990s based on the original 1909 John Olmstead designs for the park as part of Seattle's City Beautiful movement.[26] Banks of trees were planted around the playfields. By the summer of 2020, Cal Anderson Park was one of the city's most popular parks.[27] Even though Seattle and King County had closed this and all other parks at the beginning of the pandemic, Cal Anderson Park became the central gathering place for the CHAZ/CHOP protest. The baseball field was where people congregated every day in a large circle for the People's Assemblies, gatherings intended to work through issues that arose, ostensibly using a participatory democracy model begun in the Occupy protests.

A videotape dated June 24, 2020, by a white male Amazon employee and resident of a Capitol Hill apartment who goes by the YouTube name of "Earthworm" included an entire hour-long People's Assembly in Cal Anderson Park.[28] There is a palpable and visual division between mainly young white people on one side of the circle and an all-Black BLM contingent calling themselves the Collective for CHOP on the other side. People use a megaphone to vie for speaking time.

An older Black man, Mark Anthony, wearing a bulletproof vest with what appears to be a gun and a baton strapped to his waist, identifies himself as being part of the ad hoc CHAZ/CHOP security team known as the Sentinels.[29] He strides across the open area in the middle of the circle, accompanied by several other Black men. When a young Black woman holding a second microphone calls for a more structured People's Assembly based on the principles established during the Occupy Wall Street protests, Mark quickly walks toward her and yells, "Do you represent the Black Community?" She replies, "No," backs up, and sits down in the bleachers, adding, "My voice is being silenced by Mark Anthony!" Mark hands the microphone to a young Black woman, Angelica Campbell, who identifies herself as a leader of the BLM Collective for CHOP. She states, "We are here to occupy and protest, not to camp," disassociating their group from the "tent people" who she claims are not part of the BLM movement. She points toward the tent encampment in the wooded area of the park behind her, indicates that a sexual assault and shootings have happened there recently, and states, "That is not occupying. That is camping." Lisa lived in the tent encampment in Cal Anderson Park by this time. Both Mark and Angelica refer to the People's Assembly the day before, calling it a "shit show."

At the People's Assembly in Cal Anderson Park the day before, a meeting mainly led by women and videotaped in its entirety by the man calling himself Earthworm, a Black woman speaks of the need for more people with trauma-informed and crisis training to take the lead in maintaining peace in the occupied zone.[30] She indicates that the ad hoc, male-led CHAZ/CHOP security team carrying assault rifles creates more trauma. She laments "the mental health issues that go unnoticed as well and the fact that we're occupying a space that unhoused people have been living at prior to the creation of CHAZ and CHOP." A white woman speaks up and indicates that the street medics have left the protest area because they were targeted with increasing threats of violence. She adds that when the street medics were present at CHAZ/CHOP, they helped monitor safe injection zones. She says, "I think we need to remember that a lot of homeless people live here; they're going to use drugs here because there's nowhere else for them to go." A middle-aged white woman speaks passionately at the end of the meeting about the multiple instances of sexual assault of women associated with CHAZ/ CHOP, especially in and around the tent encampments.

THE TENSION BETWEEN protestors and homeless people living within the areas of protest movements was an ongoing issue, having arisen during the Occupy Wall Street and spin-off Occupy movements emerging across the United States in September 2011. The Occupy movement, begun in the wake of the Great Recession and lasting from 2007 to 2009, was against corporate control of government and the growing wealth inequities within the United States. The Occupy movement introduced the now well-known concept of the 99% versus the 1% to emphasize income and power inequities. "We are the 99%" became the rallying cry, one that resonated for many Americans negatively affected by the Great Recession, from seniors seeing their retirement funds precipitously decline with the falling stock market to families evicted from their homes as a result of the housing bubble caused by the subprime mortgage crisis. Despite federal stimulus programs, many people, disproportionately persons of color, fell into homelessness.[31]

Beginning in September 2011, with the Occupy Wall Street protest centering in Zuccotti Park in New York City, there was pushback from protestors against people experiencing homelessness who were drawn to the Occupy protest areas across the country. With newspaper headlines such as "Dissenting, or Seeking Shelter? Homeless Stake a Claim at Protests,"[32] "Anti-

Wall Street Camps Lure U.S. Homeless,"[33] and "Homeless Find Home at Occupy Seattle, So Is It Still a Protest?,"[34] debates occurred about the presence of homeless people in the Occupy movement spaces. Some protestors complained about homeless people drawn to the protests because of the free food, medical care, and relative protection from the police, public harassment, and violence. Others complained about the increase in severe mental illness, substance use, disruptions, and violence they felt accompanied the presence of chronically homeless people. There was a perennial debate about whether homeless people were more prone to commit acts of violence or whether they were more likely to be victims of violence.[35] Other protestors pointed out that homeless people in the protest camps helped increase the numbers and visibility of their protest movement and "highlighted the very economic disparities in American society that the Occupy movement is protesting against."[36]

Organizers of Occupy San Francisco reminded people that their city had struggled with homelessness long before the Occupy movement came along and "that the camps have simply forced the mainstream public to confront an uncomfortable issue long overlooked or hidden from sight."[37] This was also true in Seattle at the CHAZ/CHOP protests in the summer of 2020. Homelessness has long been a significant problem in Seattle and King County, being deemed a public health and civil emergency in 2015, only to increase in subsequent years, along with deepening racial disproportionality.[38] Of note, Lisa Vach was both a protestor, participating in the marches and mutual-aid activities at CHAZ/CHOP, and homeless, becoming one of the "tent people" derided by at least some of the protestors and leaders of the BLM Collective for CHOP.

These tensions and debates about the presence of people experiencing homelessness within protest spaces highlighted ongoing problems with criminalizing homelessness. Beginning with the Occupy Seattle protests and extending into CHAZ/CHOP, city officials tried to distinguish between people whose actions were deemed to be part of a legitimate peaceful protest, protected under the First Amendment, and those people involved in criminal activities, not just acts of violence but also illegal activities like camping and urinating in public spaces such as Cal Anderson Park. As Barbara Ehrenreich wrote, "What Occupy Wall Streeters are beginning to discover, and homeless people have known all along, is that most ordinary, biologically necessary activities are illegal when performed in American streets—not just peeing, but sitting, lying down and sleeping."[39] She adds, "It is illegal, in other words, to be homeless or to live outdoors for any other reason. It should be noted, though, that there are no laws requiring cities to provide food, shelter or restrooms for their indigent citizens."[40]

Criminalizing poverty and homelessness has a long history in our country. Our various state-level poor laws, including those first enacted by the Washington Territorial Legislature in 1854, were based on the Elizabethan Poor Laws adopted by the thirteen British colonies.[41] The Poor Laws treated paupers, especially the "undeserving poor," which included able-bodied men and children, as criminals who could be locked away in prisons, where they were forced to work. Paupers who were not from a particular parish or county were undeserving and "warned out," banished from the area or even the country.[42] British social historian David Hitchcock points out that "Christian charity and proper punishment were delicately connected in English culture," a connection reflected in the English Poor Laws.[43] English paupers were sent to the colonies, including the Virginia Company at Jamestown, as punishment, in what Hitchcock terms "welfare colonialism."[44] What became the United States was built, in part, on this welfare colonialism.

Benjamin Franklin, the vocal proponent of the "pull yourself up by your bootstraps" American metaphor of personal transformation through hard work, openly despised poor people and advocated for sending them to the western frontier, which at that time was Western Pennsylvania.[45] Franklin viewed this practice as a survival-of-the-fittest sort of endeavor that would simultaneously rid East Coast cities of urban blight and disease, force the assimilation of immigrants, and improve the character and hardiness of Americans.

Beginning with the economic depression starting in 1873 and continuing through the Great Depression, with its burgeoning homelessness and the presence of Hoovervilles in US urban areas, punitive anti-vagrancy laws known as Tramp Acts were enacted in response to a "tramp scare" and "tramp evil" fomented by newspapers.[46] The Tramp Acts and other anti-vagrancy laws highlighted "the struggles between the propertied and the unpropertied over the use of public space, fears about the growth of a propertyless proletariat, and anxieties about the loss of traditional social controls in American cities."[47] People with physical disabilities or anyone appearing repulsive to the general public, including many homeless people, were banned from public spaces in many cities through the so-called "Ugly Laws."[48] During the Dust Bowl and Great Depression years of the 1930s, many western states enacted anti-Okie laws to prevent indigent former farmers and other people living in poverty from migrating to their states. The evil legacy of slavery, especially in the American South, led to the post–Civil War Jim Crow laws. Racist and xenophobic laws were enacted in the form of sundowning laws, where towns across the country banned all "colored people," Chinese Americans, and Hispanics from living or even being in town after dark.[49]

The westering, frontier mentality has reverberations today in Seattle, from the increase in tiny house villages looking eerily like the shacktown Hoovervilles of the Great Depression to the increase in vehicle residents similar to the Dust Bowl's Rubber Tramps who lined city parks, as well as the RV residents depicted in *Nomadland: Surviving America in the Twenty-First Century.*[50] More recently, a team of human rights lawyers invoked the frontier-era Homestead Act of 1862 in King County Superior Court. They were representing a homeless construction worker who lived in his truck parked near the downtown sports arenas in a case against the city of Seattle for impounding his truck and charging him $557 in impound fees.[51]

Tent encampment clearances or "sweeps" have long been controversial, including in Seattle–King County. Advocacy groups, such as the American Public Health Association, highlight the deleterious public health consequences of encampment clearances.[52] In sweeps, homeless people have their few belongings taken, including necessary medications, identification, health insurance, and medical and court appointment papers. On September 4, 2018, the Ninth Circuit Court of Appeals, in the case of Martin V. Boise, ruled that homeless persons cannot be punished for sleeping outside on public property in the absence of adequate shelter alternatives.[53] The US Supreme Court upheld it.[54] At the beginning of the COVID-19 pandemic, the CDC issued a statement of interim guidance calling for a pause on all homeless encampment clearances.[55] The rationale was to help prevent infection among people experiencing homelessness and to allow outreach services for health, safety, and hygiene.[56] Despite this CDC guidance, homeless encampment clearances continued in Seattle–King County.[57]

Misdemeanor crimes like trespassing and theft of food and basic necessities, dubbed "survival crimes" in Seattle, were not prosecuted by the office of the former city attorney Pete Holmes even before the pandemic. During the pandemic, prosecutions of survival crimes were reduced further when the city and county moved to decrease the King County Detention Center population. Inmates who were nearing completion of their jail time and who were not violent offenders were released early to reduce the spread of COVID-19 among inmates and staff. Travis Berge was one of the people released from jail at the beginning of the pandemic. He had been in the King County jail for 240 days for vandalizing a county building. Travis was released from jail in late February 2020. His life would soon intersect with that of Lisa Vach's, with tragic consequences.

Notes

1. "During Dual Crises of COVID-19 and Wildfire Smoke, City and County Partner to Open New Healthy Air Center in SoDo for People Experiencing Homelessness," King County, September 11, 2020, https://kingcounty.gov/elected/executive/constantine/news/release/2020/September/11-smoke-shelter.aspx.
2. Xiaodan Zhou et al., "Excess of COVID-19 Cases and Deaths due to Fine Particulate Matter Exposure during the 2020 Wildfires in the United States," *Science Advances* 7, no. 33 (August 2021), https://doi.org/10.1126/sciadv.abi8789.
3. Eric B. Brandt, Andrew F. Beck, and Tesfaye B. Mersha, "Air Pollution, Racial Disparities, and COVID-19 Mortality," *Journal of Allergy and Clinical Immunology* 146, no. 1 (July 2020): 61–63, https://doi.org/10.1016/j.jaci.2020.04.035; Latoya Hill and Samantha Artiga, "COVID-19 Cases and Deaths by Race/Ethnicity: Current Data and Changes over Time," *KFF* (blog), August 22, 2022, https://www.kff.org/racial-equity-and-health-policy/issue-brief/covid-19-cases-and-deaths-by-race-ethnicity-current-data-and-changes-over-time/; Monica Webb Hooper, Anna María Nápoles, and Eliseo J. Pérez-Stable, "COVID-19 and Racial/Ethnic Disparities," *JAMA* 323,

no. 24 (June 23, 2020): 2466–67, https://doi.org/10.1001/jama.2020
.8598.

4. Sara Jean Green, Mike Carter, and Asia Fields, "Auburn Police Officer
Charged with Murder in 2019 Shooting," *Seattle Times*, August 20,
2020, https://www.seattletimes.com/seattle-news/law-justice/auburn
-police-officer-charged-with-murder-in-2019-shooting/.

5. Merrick Bobb, "A Long Wait for SPD Reform," *Seattle Times*, February 4, 2022, https://www.seattletimes.com/opinion/a-long-wait-for
-spd-reform/.

6. "Black Lives Matter Seattle–King County," Facebook, June 2, 2020,
https://www.facebook.com/blmseattle.

7. Becca Savransky, "How CHAZ Became CHOP: Seattle's Police-Free
Zone Explained," Seattle Post-Intelligencer, updated June 22, 2020,
https://www.seattlepi.com/seattlenews/article/What-is-CHOP-the
-zone-in-Seattle-formed-by-15341281.php.

8. Isolde Raftery, "We Know Who Made the Call to Leave Seattle
Police's East Precinct Last Summer, Finally," KUOW, July 9, 2021,
https://www.kuow.org/stories/we-know-who-made-the-call-to
-seattle-police-s-east-precinct-last-summer-finally.

9. Converge, "The Pink Umbrella Seattle Protest First Person Perspective," YouTube video, 2020, https://www.youtube.com/watch?v
=D5sQt_bQS4A.

10. Elise Takahama, "Seattle Police Chief Overturns Watchdog's Discipline Recommendation in 'Pink Umbrella' Protest Clash," *Seattle
Times*, May 12, 2021, https://www.seattletimes.com/seattle-news
/politics/seattle-police-chief-overturns-watchdogs-discipline
-recommendation-in-pink-umbrella-protest-clash/.

11. Bobb, "Long Wait for SPD Reform."

12. Carmen Best, *Black in Blue: Lessons on Leadership, Breaking
Barriers, and Racial Reconciliation* (New York: HarperCollins
Leadership, 2021), 107.

13. Best, *Black in Blue*, 109.

14. Hannah Weinberger, "Seattle Health Workers March to Expose Racism
as a Health Crisis," Crosscut, June 10, 2020, https://crosscut.com/2020
/06/seattle-health-workers-march-expose-racism-health-crisis.

15. Marcus Harrison Green, "What Really Happened in CHOP?," *Seattle
Met*, June 8, 2021, https://www.seattlemet.com/news-and-city-life
/2021/06/history-of-chop-capitol-hill-protests-seattle.

16. Jia Tolentino, "What Mutual Aid Can Do during a Pandemic," *New Yorker*, May 11, 2020, https://www.newyorker.com/magazine/2020 /05/18/what-mutual-aid-can-do-during-a-pandemic; Rebecca Solnit, "'The Way We Get through This Is Together': The Rise of Mutual Aid under Coronavirus," *Guardian*, sec. World news, May 14, 2020, https://www.theguardian.com/world/2020/may/14/mutual-aid -coronavirus-pandemic-rebecca-solnit.

17. Jake Goldstein-Street, "Sawant and Protesters—Briefly—Occupy Seattle City Hall as Capitol Hill Autonomous Zone Grows— UPDATE," *Capitol Hill Seattle* (blog), June 10, 2020, https://www .capitolhillseattle.com/2020/06/sawant-and-protesters-briefly -occupy-seattle-city-hall-as-capitol-hill-autonomous-zone-grows/.

18. Lisa Vach, "Lisa Vach," Facebook, September 9, 2018, https://www .facebook.com/bruce.cat.35.

19. "Regen Co-Op," Facebook, accessed April 30, 2022, https://www .facebook.com/groups/346553219022/about/.

20. jseattle, "Remember Lisa Vach," *Capitol Hill Seattle* (blog), September 23, 2020, https://www.capitolhillseattle.com/2020/09/remember -lisa-vach/.

21. Hal Berton, "Trawl Fishing in the Age of the Coronavirus: First, You Make It through Quarantine," *Seattle Times*, May 16, 2020, https:// www.seattletimes.com/seattle-news/trawl-fishing-in-the-age-of-the -coronavirus-first-you-make-it-through-quarantine/.

22. "Plague-Predicting Japanese Folklore Creature Resurfaces amid Coronavirus Chaos," *Mainichi Daily News*, March 25, 2020, https:// mainichi.jp/english/articles/20200325/p2a/00m/0na/021000c ?fbclid=IwAR32GfzBvc _hGld1vzs5YYYjmdGEB9Ax0C6Ck_q_iW3CN51tpeG4sXiJhMc.

23. Downtown Emergency Services Center, "Vulnerability Assessment Tool for Determining Eligibility and Allocating Services and Housing for Adults Experiencing Homelessness" (DESC, April 2022).

24. Chrystie Hill, "Queer History in Seattle, Part 2: After Stonewall," HistoryLink.org, November 28, 2003, https://www.historylink.org /File/4266.

25. Katherine Long, "Seattle Central College Turns 50, Celebrates History of Social Activism," *Seattle Times*, September 22, 2016, https://www.seattletimes.com/seattle-news/education/seattle-central -college-turns-50-celebrates-history-of-social-activism/.

26. Josephine Ensign, *Skid Road: On the Frontier of Health and Homelessness in an American City* (Baltimore: Johns Hopkins University Press, 2021).

27. "Cal Anderson Park: The Park behind CHAZ/CHOP," *Historic Seattle* (blog), July 1, 2020, https://historicseattle.org/cal-anderson-park-the-park-behind-chaz-chop/.

28. Earthworm, "Seattle CHOP (Formerly CHAZ) Day 10—Speeches and Organizing," YouTube video, 2020, https://www.youtube.com/watch?v=cNXvKlyuMnY.

29. Arun Gupta, "Seattle's CHOP Went Out with Both a Bang and a Whimper," Intercept, July 2 2020, https://theintercept.com/2020/07/02/seattle-chop-zone-police/.

30. Earthworm, "Seattle CHOP (Formerly CHAZ) Day 9—'All Gas No Brakes,' Shooting, and Mother Losing Child," YouTube video, 2020, https://www.youtube.com/watch?v=YK7q-Zskl8w.

31. David B. Grusky, Bruce Western, and Christopher Wimer, *The Great Recession* (New York: Russell Sage Foundation, 2011).

32. Adam Nagourney, "Dissenting, or Seeking Shelter? Homeless Stake a Claim at Protests," *New York Times*, sec. U.S., November 1, 2011, https://www.nytimes.com/2011/11/01/us/dissenting-or-seeking-shelter-homeless-stake-a-claim-at-protests.html.

33. Laird Harrison, "Anti–Wall Street Camps Lure U.S. Homeless," Reuters, sec. U.S. News, December 2, 2011, https://www.reuters.com/article/us-usa-protests-homeless-idUSTRE7B10YU20111202.

34. Paula Wissel, "Homeless Find Home at Occupy Seattle, So Is It Still a Protest?," KNKX Public Radio, October 10, 2011, https://www.knkx.org/other-news/2011-10-10/homeless-find-home-at-occupy-seattle-so-is-it-still-a-protest.

35. Molly Meinbresse et al., "Exploring the Experiences of Violence among Individuals Who Are Homeless Using a Consumer-Led Approach," *Violence and Victims* 29, no. 1 (February 1, 2014): 122–36, https://doi.org/10.1891/0886-6708.VV-D-12-00069.

36. Harrison, "Anti–Wall Street Camps Lure U.S. Homeless."

37. Harrison, "Anti–Wall Street Camps Lure U.S. Homeless."

38. Alexa Peters, "CHAZ Is Becoming a Refuge for Homeless People as Well as Protestors in Black Lives Matter Movement," Converge, accessed June 8, 2022, https://www.whereweconverge.com/post/chaz

-is-becoming-a-refuge-for-homeless-people-as-well-as-protestors-in
-black-lives-matter-movement.

39. Barbara Ehrenreich, "Occupy Wall Street Brings Homelessness into
the Open," *Guardian*, sec. Opinion, October 24, 2011, https://www
.theguardian.com/commentisfree/cifamerica/2011/oct/24/occupy
-wall-street-homelessness-us.

40. Ehrenreich, "Occupy Wall Street."

41. Ensign, *Skid Road*.

42. Ensign, *Skid Road*; Walter I. Trattner, *From Poor Law to Welfare
State: A History of Social Welfare in America*, 6th ed. (New York: Free
Press, 1999).

43. David Hitchcock, "'Punishment Is All the Charity That the Law
Affordeth Them': Penal Transportation, Vagrancy, and the Chari-
table Impulse in the British Atlantic, c. 1600–1750," *New Global
Studies* 12, no. 2 (2018): 195–215, https://doi.org/10.1515/ngs-2018
-0029.

44. Hitchcock, "'Punishment Is All.'"

45. Nancy Isenberg, *White Trash: The 400-Year Untold History of Class
in America* (New York: Viking, 2016).

46. Tim Cresswell, *Tramp in America* (London: Reaktion Books, 2001);
Todd DePastino, *Citizen Hobo: How a Century of Homelessness
Shaped America* (Chicago: University of Chicago Press, 2003).

47. DePastino, *Citizen Hobo*, 8.

48. Susan Schweik, "Kicked to the Curb: Ugly Law Then and Now,"
Harvard Civil Rights–Civil Liberties Law Review 46 (2012): 16.

49. Javier Ortiz, Matthew Dick, and Sara Rankin, "The Wrong Side of
History: A Comparison of Modern and Historical Criminalization
Laws" (Social Science Research Network, May 4, 2015), https://
papers.ssrn.com/abstract=2602533.

50. Jessica Bruder, *Nomadland: Surviving America in the Twenty-First
Century* (New York: W. W. Norton, 2017).

51. "City of Seattle v. Steven Long," *Columbia Legal Services* (blog),
accessed January 18, 2022, http://columbialegal.org/impact
_litigations/city-of-seattle-v-steven-long-2/.

52. "Housing and Homelessness as a Public Health Issue: Policy Number
20178," American Public Health Association, November 7, 2017,
https://apha.org/policies-and-advocacy/public-health-policy

-statements/policy-database/2018/01/18/housing-and-homelessness
-as-a-public-health-issue.

53. Martin v. City of Boise, 902 F.3d 1031, 1035 (9th Cir. 2018).

54. Karianna Barr, "Supreme Court Lets Martin v. Boise Stand," *National Homelessness Law Center* (blog), December 16, 2019, https://homelesslaw.org/supreme-court-martin-v-boise/.

55. "Community, Work, and School," Centers for Disease Control and Prevention, February 11, 2020, https://www.cdc.gov/coronavirus/2019-ncov/community/health-equity/race-ethnicity.html; Joshua Barocas, Samantha Nall, and Sarah Axelrath, "Population-Level Health Effects of Involuntary Displacement of People Experiencing Unsheltered Homelessness Who Inject Drugs in US Cities," *JAMA* 329, no. 17 (April 10, 2023): 1478–86, https://jamanetwork-com.offcampus.lib.washington.edu/journals/jama/fullarticle/2803839?guestAccessKey=f321ceca-78d6-4d55-bcc5-e7a775ce1152&utm_source=For_The_Media&utm_medium=referral&utm_campaign=ftm_links&utm_content=tfl&utm_term=041023.

56. Alyse D. Oneto and Samantha Batko, "Why Homeless Encampment Sweeps Are Dangerous during COVID-19," Urban Institute, May 12, 2020, https://www.urban.org/urban-wire/why-homeless-encampment-sweeps-are-dangerous-during-covid-19.

57. "Cities Cut Back Homeless Sweeps during Crisis. Activists Hope They'll Stop for Good," HuffPost, April 14, 2020, https://www.huffpost.com/entry/homeless-encampment-sweeps-coronavirus_n_5e947646c5b6ac981514147f; Teresa Wiltz, "Against CDC Guidance, Some Cities Sweep Homeless Encampments," Stateline, April 28, 2020, https://pew.org/2W4sXhq; Dae Shik Kim Jr. and Guy Oron, "Seattle Destroyed Homeless Encampments as the Pandemic Raged," *Nation*, April 2, 2020, https://www.thenation.com/article/society/seattle-homeless-sweeps-coronavirus/.

CHAPTER 2

Seattle Is Dying

· · · · · · · · · · · · · · · · · · ·

> *Life is about another chance, and while we are*
> *alive, till the very end, there is always another*
> *chance.*
>
> —JEANNETTE WINTERSON, *WHY BE HAPPY WHEN*
> *YOU COULD BE NORMAL?*

IF LISA VACH WAS NEWLY homeless in Seattle during the summer of 2020, at least in part because of the effects of the COVID-19 pandemic, with further fraying of the health and social support networks, Travis Berge was chronically homeless, for a variety of personal and systemic reasons. Understanding more of Lisa's and Travis's individual stories and their intersecting story when they became a couple on Seattle's streets helps shed light on missed opportunities and missteps that they and we as a community made, contributing to their tragically early, violent, and avoidable deaths.

Travis Berge, who went by the street name Travel Tron, was both a creative and deeply troubled person who craved an audience. He moved to Seattle from his hometown of Reno, Nevada, sometime in late 2013 when he was around thirty years old.

From an older Facebook page when he was living in Reno, he chronicled his road travels throughout the United States as a paid signature gatherer for the Green Party. He posted frequent photographs and videos of himself, often shirtless, playing an accordion or flute and wearing jumping stilts, which he said made him feel like he had superpowers.[1] In one post from March 26, 2012, he includes a photograph of a petition to legalize marijuana. In a June 11, 2012, Facebook post accompanied by yet another selfie of him shirtless, suntanned, and with long, uncombed auburn hair, he states, "I'm sexy and I'm homeless."

In Seattle, Travis worked as a busker, a street performer, and a musician, working around Pike Place Market. He continued living in homelessness, staying in encampments and emergency shelters, including the one run by DESC at the Morrison. He boasted of engaging in mutual combat with people on the street, including with police officers. In invoking the legal term "mutual combat," he likely was simultaneously trying to justify his aggressive, combative tendencies and imagining himself as part of the bizarre group of Seattle-based street vigilantes dressed as superheroes and engaged in combat. The Rain City Superhero Movement was started by the Black martial arts fighter Benjamin Fodor, who goes by the Superhero name Phoenix Jones.[2] Despite having been charged with selling MDMA (street name Molly or Ecstasy) to an undercover SPD officer in January 2020, Phoenix Jones announced on social media on June 12, 2020, "The CHAZ army is a group exercising their right to free speech and to open carry arms. I'm only going to stop crimes that put people in danger. . . . See you in the streets."[3] At that point, Washington State law allowed open carry of firearms even at demonstrations. Washington State gun laws were tightened in the 2022 legislative session.[4] Travis likely bought into the misinterpretation of Seattle Municipal Code 12A.06.025, on fighting in public.[5]

Some people, including Travis, have interpreted this municipal code section to mean that they can openly fight in public as long as they do not injure a person not directly involved in the fight or harm someone's property.

It is plausible to surmise that Travis was attracted to Seattle in late 2013, at least in part, because Washington State legalized recreational marijuana use for people ages twenty-one and older. Initiative 502, approved by voters in the November 2012 election, made Washington State the second US state, following Colorado, to legalize recreational marijuana.[6] Travis was a proud and unabashed user of multiple legal and illegal substances, but his drug of choice was the highly addictive stimulant methamphetamine. Meth use, especially chronic meth use, causes long-term irreversible damage to the cardiovascular and central nervous system. Meth use causes psychotic episodes and aggressive, violent behavior, and people can, and do more often than commonly thought, die of a meth overdose.[7]

IN MARCH 2019, Travis became more widely known when he was featured in an hour-long documentary titled "Seattle Is Dying," produced by the local Seattle ABC-affiliate news station KOMO-TV. It aired nationally and was narrated by Emmy-award-winning reporter Eric Johnson. The conservative Sinclair Broadcasting bought KOMO-TV in 2013. Then, in 2019, the station became controversial when Donald Trump supporter and CEO of Sinclair Broadcasting Chris Ripley mandated the inclusion of conservative talking points, such as other mainstream news sources being "fake news."[8]

In "Seattle Is Dying," the opening shot is an aerial view over a sprawling tent encampment along Interstate 5 just south of downtown Seattle, panning from it to a shot of the downtown skyline, including Harborview Medical Center. The background sound is of a heartbeat speeding up and then stopping. It breaks to close-up video segments of homeless people sitting or lying on sidewalks and pedestrians walking past them. Eric Johnson asks, "What if Seattle is dying and we don't even know it?" He adds, "This story is about a seething, simmering anger that is now boiling over into outrage. It is about people who have felt compassion, yes, but who no longer feel safe, no longer feel like they are heard, no longer feel protected."

The documentary then shows footage of a contentious Town Hall meeting in the Ballard neighborhood of Seattle in May 2018, where angry residents and business owners assailed the council members present, especially after council members told people in attendance to call 911 in cases of trespassing or property damage caused by people experiencing homelessness. A white woman stood up and yelled, "Don't tell us to call 911! The cops have told us to vote you out of office so they can do something!" It cuts to video footage of a man talking to himself on a downtown Seattle sidewalk and then eating from a garbage can. Johnson asks, "How can this be who we are? How did the word 'compassion' get twisted into this sickening reality?" Johnson shows police body cam footage of a shirtless and disheveled Travis Berge as he throws heavy electric bicycles at the windows of a downtown Seattle business, strips to his underwear, and then jumps into a metal trash can on the sidewalk, spitting at police officers as they attempt to arrest him.

In "Seattle Is Dying" and the December 2020 follow-up KOMO documentary "Fight for the Soul of Seattle," Johnson points to statistics compiled by the Downtown Seattle Association on the top 100 repeat criminal offenders in and around downtown Seattle.[9] Travis is on this list. At age thirty-five and only having lived in Seattle for five years, he already has one hundred encounters with police and thirty-four criminal cases in the city and county. These cases include disturbance, assault, trespass, and, his most serious offense, the attempted rape in 2015 of a homeless teen female who was asleep in a doorway on Capitol Hill. The King County Superior Court charge was amended to second-degree assault, in part because the young female victim did not want to go further with the proceedings. Unfortunately, this was likely due to a court system's failure in King County, which has long wait times from arraignment of the defendants to a court date. The experience can be retraumatizing to victims, and very few cases result in prosecution. Many victims simply give up.[10] As of June 2022, SPD officers have stopped investigating cases of adult sexual assault altogether, due to staffing issues.[11] Travis was sentenced to three months in King County Detention Center for the sexual assault but was released after two months.

In multiple case reports of arrests made by SPD officers and King County sheriffs, Travis is identified as having mental illness and a substance use disorder. It is unclear what mental illness he had. An accurate psychiatric assessment and diagnosis would have been difficult with Travis since he was deep into a severe substance use disorder. Was his erratic behavior due to a mental illness like bipolar disorder or caused by long-term meth use? Travis had a court-ordered mental health evaluation that he defied and seemed never to have received. He also had court-mandated substance use treatment that he refused. The SPD flagged Travis in their system with an officer safety caution, being a threat to officers and the general public owing to his instability and aggression, especially when using meth.[12] They comment on his propensity for mutual combat. In several police reports, they note that Travis told officers that he had just swallowed an opiate so that they would have to take him to

Harborview Medical Center for observation instead of to the King County Detention Center. In the documentary, when told by Johnson that he is on the list of top offenders, Travis jumps up and down and says, "They've really exalted me and shown deference and love towards me. I have conquered the criminal justice system."[13]

Eric Johnson contends that Seattle does not have a homelessness problem; it has a drug problem made worse by a too-lenient criminal justice system, progressive politics, and a distorted sense of compassion in Seattle. In a blatant form of criminalizing homelessness, he concludes the documentary by recommending that Seattle round up all the homeless drug addicts and lock them in the former McNeil Island Corrections Center, now the McNeil Island special commitment center and home of 214 men deemed to be sexually violent predators.[14] The producers of "Seattle Is Dying" make no pretense of having a balanced approach to the issues of homelessness, crime, mental illness, and substance use disorder. They also go against basic journalistic ethical guidelines. They show close-up, identifiable shots of people in distress on city streets and sidewalks, people who exhibit signs of psychosis, from mental illness, substance use, or both. "Seattle Is Dying" reinforces public fear of homeless people.

Tim Harris, the founder and former director of *Real Change*, Seattle's anti-poverty street newspaper, described "Seattle Is Dying" as "misery porn."[15] Catherine Hinrichsen, then head of Seattle University's Gates Foundation–funded Project on Family Homelessness, wrote, "The KOMO special, by reporter Eric Johnson, definitely appeals to the 'I don't want to have to look at homelessness' viewer. It's a call to punish, rather than help, people in need, and it seeks to divide them into the 'real homeless' (or 'deserving poor') and all the others."[16] Yet "Seattle Is

Dying" had traction locally and nationally and "catalyzed vigorous debate about the nature and future of the city."[17] It hit a nerve in Seattle, with people across the sociopolitical spectrum discussing the problem of homelessness in their city. As the Crosscut news opinion writer John Carlson states, "The reason 'Seattle is Dying' so angers critics anchored to the status quo is that it confirms what many people who live and work here see and believe."[18]

A focus on the subversive elements of homelessness and its attendant ills made visible—the dirty undergarments of a society—catalyzes the human urge either for sympathy or for repulsion and anger. "Seattle Is Dying" fanned the flames of revulsion and anger toward people experiencing homelessness. Perversely and disturbingly, "Seattle Is Dying" and other news coverage featuring Travis Berge grew a fan base for his image as a free-spirited renegade.

THROUGHOUT THE TIME of the CHAZ/CHOP protests, Travis Berge made himself known and displayed increasingly outlandish attire and behaviors. He wove flowers and entire tree branches into his long hair, went shirtless, and often wore a long skirt shredded to the waistband with nothing underneath.[19] He seemed to relish touching and exposing his genitals in public. Travis talks about his charismatic Pentecostal Christian upbringing and how he was taught that drugs were sinful, his current lifestyle the work of the devil. At times he sings Christian hymns while digging through trash at CHAZ/CHOP, collecting and licking used needles, claiming, "Diseases, for me, are like Pokémon, I gotta' catch 'em all."[20] He makes himself the focus of several of the CHAZ/CHOP videos posted by Earthworm, literally jumping in front of the video camera, hissing, and insisting that Earthworm, also identified as Seth by Travis, film him. In Earthworm's videos of Travis, Seth calls him a "cool dude" and a "friend of the police."

In one of Earthworm's videos titled "Introducing Travis Berge, Diogenes of the CHOP," dated June 23, 2020, Travis is in front of the videographer as they walk through Cal Anderson Park after dark. In Seattle, true darkness does not occur until close to 11:00 P.M. for that time of year. At one point, Travis yells, "Anyone want to give me some drugs for this?" Earthworm stops filming what appears to be the beginning of a drug deal. The video resumes, showing a small group of protestors walking on the park's edge chanting, "Whose lives matter? Black lives matter!" Travis yells, "Black lives matter! We all matter together!"

Lisa Vach appears to be with the protestors. Travis yells to Lisa, "Babe! Babe! Would you come here for a second? Will you bring a lighter, please?" Lisa replies, "That's what you called me over for?" and curses at him ("suck my dick"). She adds, "You can't call me your girl. That's fucking bullshit!" She walks away back toward the protestors. Travis then says to Earthworm, "Look at my girlfriend real quick. On Facebook, it says we are boyfriend and girlfriend for like so many months, dude. I just want you to be able to see her beauty." Earthworm refuses to film Lisa directly, saying he only films people with their permission. After leaving Travis and CHOP, Earthworm ends this video, voicing his views on Travis: "I don't think he's nuts, but he is on a different wavelength. He's extremely socially perceptive."[21]

It is unclear when, where, and in what context Travis met Lisa. Did they meet at DESC's Morrison Hotel around the time of Lisa's Facebook posting on March 5, 2020, of a seagull on the windowsill of the Morrison's permanent supportive housing units? Did they meet on the downtown Seattle streets when Lisa had become homeless, and when Travis was sleeping on the floor of City Hall after having been released from King County jail in late February 2020?[22] Did they meet in a Seattle homeless service center or feeding program after Travis was, yet again, jailed for felony harassment on May 5, 2020, and then released just two days later?[23] Or did they meet at CHAZ/CHOP?

Sirena Ross, a friend of Lisa's and a coworker at the Underground Tour, thinks that Lisa may have been attracted to Travis because of his creativity and because Lisa had a "rescue personality." "When it comes to domestic violence, once the person is through being charming, they're like a bomb attached to you and they're gonna detonate."[24] Besides appearing together briefly in Earthworm's nighttime videotaped walk with Travis, they are videotaped together outside of the King County Detention Center on July 2, 2020, both just released from jail for failure to disperse at the CHAZ/CHOP encampment clearance by police the day before.[25]

CHAZ/CHOP, AS A semiorganized protest zone and social experiment in police-free communal living, began to fall apart in the wake of multiple sexual assaults, shootings, and deaths in the area. A street medic intervened before a deaf woman was raped in a tent by a man she did not know who lured her in.[26] In another case of a woman being raped in Cal Anderson Park, the Black citizen-journalist Omari Salisbury was asked by police officers to help locate the woman so they could take her to the sexual assault center at Harborview Medical Center. Salisbury recounts how he searched for her but did not videotape any of it, "because it wasn't about that. And I was thinking that was somebody's daughter that was assaulted there, and we couldn't find her, which means we couldn't help her."[27]

Early in the morning of June 20, a nineteen-year-old young man, Horace Lorenzo Anderson, was shot and killed in the protest zone, and a thirty-three-year-old man was shot and injured.[28] Horace Lorenzo Anderson, who went by the name Lorenzo, had graduated from a local south King County special needs alternative high school on June 19. He was shot in the back by an eighteen-year-old Black man with whom he had a long-standing feud over a fight that his assailant had lost, a fight that was videotaped and shared on YouTube.[29] Lorenzo was shot next to the street medics station, creating a chaotic scene where protestors and bystanders were yelling at the medics to help save a profusely bleeding Lorenzo.[30] The Seattle Fire Department Medic One unit was less than two blocks away but was prevented from entering the CHAZ/CHOP zone until the SPD arrived to provide an escort as per their protocol.[31] By the time the Medic One unit reached the scene, Lorenzo had been loaded into the back of a volunteer medic's pickup truck and taken to Harborview Medical Center, where he died.

The next day, again at night, a sixteen-year-old homeless young Black man, Antonio Mays Jr., was shot and killed, and a fourteen-year-old young man was shot and injured. Mays had run away from his home in California to come to Seattle, likely because of the CHAZ/CHOP protests. In reflecting on Antonio's death, Salisbury states, "People up here were sending him live-streams. And so, when people say I saw your live streams that's what sits in the back of my mind."[32] People spoke of a "Tale of Two CHOPS," one in the daytime that was relatively peaceful and one at night, which was increasingly chaotic, drug fueled, and dangerous.[33] In response to then President Trump tweeting, "Domestic terrorists have taken over Seattle," Fox News called CHAZ/CHOP an "Antifa-led insurrection" and ran digitally altered images of the protestors.[34] Conservative commentators equated CHAZ/CHOP with "the latest symbol of failed progressive politics and the unchecked rise of anarchy and protests."[35] Michael Solan, president of the Seattle Police Officers Guild, said that CHAZ/CHOP was the closest thing he had seen in our country and in Seattle "to becoming a lawless state."[36] He added, "This could metastasize across the country."[37]

Besides the escalating violence, CHAZ/CHOP was weighed down by a lack of clear leadership and the in-fighting between various groups, as highlighted by the increasingly contentious and dysfunctional People's Assemblies. On July 1, Mayor Jenny Durkan issued an executive order for the clearance of CHAZ/CHOP and for the SPD to regain control of the East Precinct.[38] She dispatched hundreds of riot police and assault vehicles to the area, and they arrested dozens of protestors who refused to leave the area, including Lisa Vach and Travis Berge.[39] Smaller BLM protests continued in the area through the rest of the summer and into the autumn of 2020.[40]

IN SEATTLE–KING COUNTY, as across the United States, the pandemic caused breakdowns in an already frayed health and social support safety net. The double pandemic of COVID-19 and social isolation increased throughout the United States, but it was especially acute for the elderly, incarcerated people, and people living in homelessness and poverty.[41] The pandemic worsened the already severe crises in mental illness, substance use disorders, overdose deaths, and domestic violence.[42] These diseases of despair, combined with COVID-19 deaths and disabilities, contributed to high morbidity and mortality.[43] The further fraying of the safety net adversely affected many people, including Lisa Vach.

Converge, an independent Black media group in Seattle, reported on the link between the CHAZ/CHOP protests over racism and the combined homeless and COVID crises, saying that "protestors assert that CHAZ is showing up for the city's homeless population as part of a comprehensive and multi-pronged approach to address systemic racism and bring more money to community organizations that can help minority communities, the homeless, mentally ill and more."[44] On July 20, 2020, BLMSKC called for an end to homeless encampment sweeps during COVID and beyond, citing the CDC community guidance on encampment sweeps and other public health evidence that sweeps are ineffective and harmful.[45] Calling on Governor Inslee, Mayor Durkan, King County executive Dow Constantine, the Seattle City Council, and the Washington Department of Health, they issued this statement: "We demand the cities and state redirect all funds currently spent to sweep people without shelter towards more effective responses that address the true needs of people, disproportionately Black, Indigenous, and other people of color who bear the brunt of the crisis of homelessness and lack of affordable housing."[46]

In early August, in response to increasing calls to defund the police by 50%, Seattle City Council voted to eliminate the Navigation Team, an SPD program of outreach to and clearances of homeless encampments that was begun in 2017.[47] Given increasing pressure to defund the SPD from advocacy groups like Decriminalize Seattle and King County Equity Now, the council made additional cuts to the SPD budget, overriding a veto by the then mayor Jenny Durkan.[48] In response to this vote, Seattle police chief Carmen Best resigned, effective September 2, 2020.[49] Best ended her thirty-year career with the SPD as the city's first Black female chief. Although she claimed in her book and public statements that she did not know about or authorize the abandonment of the East Precinct by SPD officers in the early part of the CHAZ/CHOP protests, recent evidence indicates that she did have this knowledge at the time.[50]

MUTUAL-AID GROUPS ENLISTED during CHAZ/CHOP spun off to provide food, clothing, and support. This support included rudimentary medical, behavioral health, and domestic violence counseling for homeless people who had returned to an encampment at Cal Anderson Park.[51] The mutual-aid group broke into and occupied a park building called the Shelterhouse to heat food in the small kitchen and provide services, including medical care and domestic violence counseling by volunteers.[52] Under orders by Mayor Durkan, the SPD cleared the encampment and mutual-aid group from Cal Anderson Park twice in August, but they returned.[53] In mid-August, Travis Berge was videotaped and photographed in front of the Shelterhouse, eating food provided by the mutual-aid group. In the video footage, he is near a woman wearing a hoodie who is sitting at a table outside, eating dinner. Although the hoodie partially covers her face, she appears to be Lisa Vach.[54]

On August 21, according to body cam footage, SPD officers Mika Harmon and Patrick Walters arrested a man for shoplifting shoes and toiletries from several downtown stores. During the interaction, Officer Harmon complains about the lack of basic support services with which to connect him. She recommends that he go to Cal Anderson Park for clothes and food.[55] She is later recorded in her police car as she looks for the man in the area around Cal Anderson Park. She curses when she refers to the protestors and the mutual-aid group in the park. Despite the SPD's repeated encampment clearances at Cal Anderson Park, people experiencing homelessness returned to the area to camp, and people who were remnants of the CHAZ/CHOP movement continued to distribute food, clothing, and other basic necessities to homeless people. Among these activists were the ones who began the Stop the Sweeps Seattle group, who continue to provide mutual aid to people living in encampments throughout the city and monitor and protest ongoing sweeps.[56]

On September 11, 2020, Travis posted on Facebook about Lisa, saying they were still camping at what was left of CHAZ/CHOP in Cal Anderson Park. "She's a little untalkative right now. She's still recovering from me beating the shit out of her the other night (stfu liberal lassel femme nazi personnel: we got our declaration of mutual combat consent and reciprocal indemnification and liability release notarized yesterday) ima be posting all her blackeyes with triumphant pride."[57] His post had seven thumbs-up and laugh emojis. Despite this public posting and the fact that KOMO news reporters, mutual-aid workers, and other people in the homeless encampment knew that Travis and Lisa had frequent and escalating physical fights in Cal Anderson Park, no one intervened to help Lisa, or if they intervened, it was not effective.[58]

The mutual-aid group had been forced out of the Cal Anderson Park Shelterhouse by the SPD and Seattle Parks and Recreation in early September. When Travis was high on meth and churned into one of his violent rampages, it is unlikely that any mutual-aid volunteer, no matter how well-intentioned and trained in de-escalation techniques, would have been able to stop Travis from beating Lisa. After all, it had taken a group of trained and armed police officers to subdue Travis in multiple other documented meth-fueled episodes. It is possible that Lisa had become so psychologically enmeshed with Travis in a cycle of intimate partner violence that she refused all offers of help.

Just after sunset on the smoke-filled day of September 17, people staying in Cal Anderson Park called 911 to report that they had found an unresponsive woman in a fort-like tent amid trees. When a Seattle Fire Department Medic One unit arrived and tried to resuscitate the woman, they were unsuccessful. They called in the SPD homicide unit, which arrived at around 8:00 P.M.[59] Lisa Vach died of blunt force trauma from being beaten with a hammer, as well as likely asphyxiation from choking. Travis Berge murdered her. He ran from the scene, throwing trash at police officers and barricading himself inside the pump house. SPD negotiators worked for hours to convince Travis to come out of the pump house. He rebuffed their efforts and then went quiet. The SWAT team arrived. When they entered the pump house at 12:30 A.M., they found Travis dead at the bottom of a ten-foot open tank containing fifty gallons of a 12% bleach solution. Accidental or intentional, Travis's ending in that tank of bleach solution was a strange sort of baptism, one that does not absolve him of guilt for the murder of Lisa, or for the spate of escalating crimes and their victims in Seattle that he left behind.

AS MANY PEOPLE POINTED OUT when news of this murder-suicide spread, there were multiple systems failures in the lives and deaths of Lisa Vach and Travis Berge. The new interim Seattle police chief Adrian Diaz said, "That right there is such a sad thing for us in this city. There's so many systems that have been broken, whether they didn't serve him properly, and we've got to figure out how we actually make that better."[60] Sirena Ross, Lisa's former coworker, echoed this sentiment. She added, "I know there are other Travis Berges out there. I know there are other Lisas out there . . . and this needs to end."[61]

Distorted media coverage of Travis by KOMO and other news sources likely worsened Travis's mental illness—including his grandiosity—and the severity of his substance use disorder. It is worth asking whether this contributed to his downward spiral, his murder of Lisa, and his own death. Travis's mother, Paula Schaeffer, a real estate agent in Reno, Nevada, told a KOMO News reporter after she was notified of Travis's death, "I tried and tried and tried to talk to him about coming back here, you know (and) finding work, staying off the meth and he just would not do it. He made that choice and he's just gotten worse and worse."[62] She added, "You know I always hoped that one day I would get him back. And you know, where there's life, there's hope, but there's no more hope left for that." Local news stories about what was called the murder-suicide in Cal Anderson Park barely mentioned Lisa—sometimes simply referring to her as Travis's girlfriend or fiancée and not always naming her, much less exploring who she was as a person.

It is worth asking whether the mutual-aid groups, especially street medics, may have helped or hindered, or at least complicated, the situation for people experiencing homelessness and behavioral health crises, like those for Lisa and Travis. Early on in CHAZ/CHOP, street medics reported that providing physical and behavioral health care to people experiencing homelessness became their major focus. Rose, a street medic, told a reporter, "We want CHAZ to be sustainable and inclusive of everyone who lives here, even homeless."[63] Behind the scenes, though, some of the medics were questioning their ability to handle the severe behavioral health issues of many people experiencing homelessness in their midst. The street medics were unprepared to handle the escalating violence, including the shooting and killing of Lorenzo Anderson and Antonio Mays Jr. With CHAZ/CHOP being a police-free zone full of protestors, SPD and medical first responders were hindered in their work to assist people who were sick or injured in the area. Police were limited in their ability to investigate crimes, like the multiple sexual assaults, stabbings, and shootings. Were the street medic volunteers in over their heads, unprepared to work effectively with people experiencing homelessness, especially when severe behavioral health issues and/or intimate partner violence were also factors? Did they inadvertently contribute to Lisa's death despite their good intentions?

Very few people seem to have asked who is to blame for Lisa Vach's death, putting the blame solely on the shoulders of Travis Berge. Having recently become homeless and not having the same level of substance use disorder and mental illness as did Travis, Lisa should have been easier to assist in getting out of homelessness and escaping the abusive and fatal relationship with Travis. Lisa lost her job early in the pandemic, before rental assistance programs were in place to help people like her retain their housing. If Lisa could have maintained her housing, it is plausible that she would not have spiraled into depression and intimate partner violence at the hands of Travis. Her friends and family members were likely distracted by their own worries and stressors, compounded by the ongoing pandemic and political and social unrest in our country. They do not seem to have realized just how difficult Lisa's life had become.

In health care, when a patient dies under questionable circumstances or through some other serious adverse event, debriefing and root cause analyses occur as close to the event as possible.[64] There are procedures to carefully examine all of the factors involved with the adverse outcome, with plans developed and implemented to avoid a similar event in the future. Is there anything like that to deal with and learn from the messy aftermath of a murder-suicide of people experiencing homelessness?

Could digging through the layers of causation and past the eva-
nescent sensational news aspects of the stories of Lisa Vach and
Travis Berge to reach the bedrock of truths about the multiple
failures and missed opportunities for safety, social, health, and
community supports have prevented Lisa Vach's death?

Notes

1. "Travis Berge," Facebook, accessed May 20, 2022, https://www
   .facebook.com/TravsMagicalEmporium.
2. "Seattle Police Stand by and Watch Phoenix Jones Fistfight,"
   MyNorthwest.com, November 12, 2012, https://mynorthwest.com
   /32084/seattle-police-stand-by-and-watch-phoenix-jones-fistfight/;
   Amy Radil, "Seattle Police Won't Sideline Superheroes on May Day,"
   KUOW, April 26, 2013, https://www.kuow.org/stories/seattle-police
   -wont-sideline-superheroes-may-day/.
3. "Phoenix Jones out of Retirement, Checks Out CHAZ or CHOP,"
   MyNorthwest.com, June 14, 2020, https://mynorthwest.com/1945268
   /phoenix-jones-retirement-chaz-chop/; Stuart Heritage, "Who Is
   That Masked Man? The Real-Life Superhero Who Inspired a Wild
   Podcast," *Guardian*, sec. Television & radio, April 12, 2022, https://
   www.theguardian.com/tv-and-radio/2022/apr/12/the-superhero
   -complex-masked-man-real-life-inspired-podcast-phoenix-jones.
4. Joseph O'Sullivan, "Washington Legislature Approves Ban of Open
   Carry of Guns at Demonstrations, State Capitol," *Seattle Times*,
   April 20, 2021, https://www.seattletimes.com/seattle-news/politics
   /washington-legislature-approves-bill-to-ban-open-carry-of-guns-at
   -demonstrations-the-capitol/; "Breaking Down New 2022 Washington Firearm Laws," Harborview Injury Prevention & Research
   Center, April 5, 2022, https://hiprc.org/blog/breaking-down-new
   -2022-washington-firearm-laws/.
5. "Subtitle I—Criminal Code | Municipal Code | Seattle, WA | Municode
   Library," Seattle.gov, accessed May 25, 2022, https://library.municode
   .com/wa/seattle/codes/municipal_code?nodeId=TIT12ACRCO
   _SUBTITLE_ICRCO_CH12A.06OFAGPE_12A.06.025FI.
6. "Marijuana in Seattle," Seattle.gov, accessed March 15, 2024, https://
   www.seattle.gov/council/issues/past-issues/marijuana-in-seattle.

7. "Know the Risks of Meth," Substance Abuse and Mental Health Services Administration, accessed May 18, 2022, https://www.samhsa.gov/meth.

8. Mike Rosenberg, "Turmoil inside KOMO News as Conservative Owner Sinclair Mandates Talking Points," *Seattle Times*, April 3, 2018, https://www.seattletimes.com/entertainment/tv/turmoil-inside-komo-news-as-conservative-owner-sinclair-mandates-talking-points/.

9. KOMO News Staff, "'Fight for the Soul of Seattle': Program Looks at Effects of City's Permissive Posture," KOMO, updated December 14, 2020, https://komonews.com/news/local/fight-for-the-soul-of-seattle-program-looks-at-effects-of-citys-permissive-posture.

10. "The Long Wait," King County Sexual Assault Resource Center, accessed May 22, 2022, https://www.kcsarc.org/en/resource/the-long-wait/.

11. Sydney Brownstone and Ashley Hiruko, "Seattle Police Stopped Investigating New Adult Sexual Assaults This Year, Memo Shows," *Seattle Times*, June 1, 2022, https://www.seattletimes.com/seattle-news/times-watchdog/seattle-police-halted-investigating-adult-sexual-assaults-this-year-internal-memo-shows/.

12. "System Failure: Report on Prolific Offenders in Seattle's Criminal Justice System," Scribd, accessed May 21, 2022, https://www.scribd.com/document/400523100/System-Failure-Report-on-prolific-offenders-in-Seattle-s-criminal-justice-system.

13. Eric Johnson, "KOMO News Special: Seattle Is Dying," KOMO, updated March 20, 2019, https://komonews.com/news/local/komo-news-special-seattle-is-dying.

14. Emily Gillespie, "On Washington's McNeil Island, the Only Residents Are 214 Dangerous Sex Offenders," *Guardian*, sec. US news, October 3, 2018, https://www.theguardian.com/us-news/2018/oct/03/dangerous-sex-offenders-mcneil-island-commitment-center.

15. Tim Harris, "KOMO Asserts Seattle Is Dying with Misery Porn," *Real Change*, March 20, 2019, https://www.realchangenews.org/news/2019/03/20/komo-asserts-seattle-dying-misery-porn.

16. Catherine Hinrichsen, "6 Reasons Why KOMO's Take on Homelessness Is the Wrong One," Crosscut, March 20, 2019, https://crosscut.com/2019/03/6-reasons-why-komos-take-homelessness-wrong-one.

17. Lynne C. Manzo and Richard Desanto, "Uncovering Competing Senses of Place in a Context of Rapid Urban Change," in *Changing Senses of Place*, ed. Christopher M. Raymond et al. (Cambridge: Cambridge University Press, 2021), 209–20, https://doi.org/10.1017/9781108769471.019.
18. John Carlson, "Why KOMO's 'Seattle Is Dying' Special Resonated," Crosscut, March 22, 2019, https://crosscut.com/2019/03/why-komos-seattle-dying-special-resonated.
19. Matt Markovich, "Travis Berge: Suspect in Cal Anderson Murder Led Troubled, Drug-Fueled Life," KOMO, September 17, 2020, https://komonews.com/news/operation-crime-justice/travis-berge-suspect-in-cal-anderson-murder-led-troubled-drug-fueled-life.
20. Dave Wagner, "Meth, Mental Illness and Murder: How One Prolific Offender Was Given Chance after Chance," KIRO, October 12, 2020, https://www.kiro7.com/news/local/meth-mental-illness-murder-how-one-prolific-offender-was-given-chance-after-chance/OLIJ2GQJ2JHTJFXW2YUD7GCVPM/.
21. Earthworm, "Seattle CHOP (Formerly CHAZ) Day 8—Introducing Travis Berge, the Diogenes of the CHOP," YouTube video, 2020, https://www.youtube.com/watch?v=qeqs4dDbCyw.
22. Matt Markovich, "Travis Berge: Repeat Offender out of Jail but Drug Struggle Remains," KOMO, February 21, 2020, https://komonews.com/news/local/travis-berge-repeat-offender-out-of-jail-but-drug-struggle-remains.
23. Markovich, "Travis Berge," September 17, 2020.
24. Wagner, "Meth, Mental Illness and Murder."
25. Wagner, "Meth, Mental Illness and Murder."
26. Rich Smith, "CHOP Medic Intervened in a Sexual Assault in Cal Anderson," Stranger, June 19, 2020, https://www.thestranger.com/slog/2020/06/19/43938596/chop-medic-intervened-in-a-sexual-assault-in-cal-anderson.
27. Ryan Yamamoto, "Omari Salisbury and 'Red Revolution' Capture Seattle History from the Frontlines," KOMO, November 7, 2020, https://komonews.com/news/local/omari-salisbury-and-red-revolution-record-seattle-history-on-the-frontlines.
28. Kirk Johnson, "Another Fatal Shooting in Seattle's 'CHOP' Protest Zone," *New York Times*, sec. U.S., June 29, 2020, https://www

.nytimes.com/2020/06/29/us/seattle-protests-CHOP-CHAZ
-autonomous-zone.html; Gregory Scruggs and Meryl Kornfield,
"Police Enter Seattle Cop-Free Zone after Shooting Kills a
19-Year-Old, Critically Injures a Man," *Washington Post*, June 20,
2020, https://www.washingtonpost.com/nation/2020/06/20/chop
-shooting-seattle/.

29. Priscilla DeGregory, "Seattle CHOP Zone Murder Suspect Arrested a
    Year after Fatal Shooting," *New York Post* (blog), July 13, 2021,
    https://nypost.com/2021/07/13/seattle-chop-zone-murder-suspect
    -arrested-a-year-after-shooting/.

30. Mike Carter, "Mother of 19-Year-Old Killed during CHOP Sues
    Seattle, Claims Officials Invited 'Lawlessness,'" *Seattle Times*,
    April 29, 2021, https://www.seattletimes.com/seattle-news/mother-of
    -19-year-old-killed-during-chop-sues-city-claims-officials-invited
    -lawlessness/.

31. Scruggs and Kornfield, "Police Enter Seattle Cop-Free Zone."

32. Yamamoto, "Omari Salisbury and 'Red Revolution.'"

33. Katelyn Burns, "The Violent End of the Capitol Hill Organized
    Protest, Explained," Vox, July 2, 2020, https://www.vox.com/policy
    -and-politics/2020/7/2/21310109/chop-chaz-cleared-violence
    -explained.

34. Arun Gupta, "Seattle's CHOP Went Out with Both a Bang and a
    Whimper," Intercept, July 2, 2020, https://theintercept.com/2020/07
    /02/seattle-chop-zone-police/; Jim Brunner, "Fox News Runs Digitally
    Altered Images in Coverage of Seattle's Protests, Capitol Hill Autono-
    mous Zone," *Seattle Times*, June 12, 2020, https://www.seattletimes
    .com/seattle-news/politics/fox-news-runs-digitally-altered-images-in
    -coverage-of-seattles-protests-capitol-hill-autonomous-zone/.

35. Paul Roberts, "Dubbed a 'Lawless State' by Some, the CHAZ or
    CHOP, Seattle's Newest Neighborhood, Tries to Create Its Own
    Narrative," *Seattle Times*, June 13, 2020, https://www.seattletimes
    .com/seattle-news/dubbed-a-lawless-state-by-some-the-chaz-or-chop
    -seattles-newest-neighborhood-tries-to-create-its-own-narrative/.

36. Julia Musto, "Seattle Police Union Chief Says His City Is 'Closest I've
    Ever Seen' to Being 'Lawless State,'" Fox News, June 12, 2020,
    https://www.foxnews.com/media/seattle-police-union-chief-city
    -close-lawlessness.

37. Sam Dorman, "Head of Seattle Police Guild Warns 'CHAZ' Could 'Metastasize across the Country,'" Fox News, June 13, 2020, https://www.foxnews.com/media/solan-police-seattle-chaz-across-country.

38. Public Affairs, "Mayor Durkan Issues Executive Order Regarding Capitol Hill Protest Zone," SPD Blotter, July 1, 2020, https://spdblotter.seattlemulti.wpengine.com/2020/07/01/mayor-durkan-issues-emergency-order-regarding-capitol-hill-protest-zone/.

39. Gupta, "Seattle's CHOP."

40. Mike Carter et al., "How a Year of Protests Changed Seattle," *Seattle Times*, December 29, 2020, https://www.seattletimes.com/seattle-news/how-a-year-of-protests-changed-seattle/.

41. Julianne Holt-Lunstad, "The Double Pandemic of Social Isolation and COVID-19: Cross-Sector Policy Must Address Both," Health Affairs Forefront, June 22, 2020, https://www.healthaffairs.org/do/10.1377/forefront.20200609.53823/full/.

42. "New Analysis Shows 8% Increase in U.S. Domestic Violence Incidents Following Pandemic Stay-at-Home Orders," *Council on Criminal Justice* (blog), February 24, 2021, https://counciloncj.org/new-analysis-shows-8-increase-in-u-s-domestic-violence-incidents-following-pandemic-stay-at-home-orders/.

43. Peter Sterling and Michael L. Platt, "Why Deaths of Despair Are Increasing in the US and Not Other Industrial Nations—Insights from Neuroscience and Anthropology," *JAMA Psychiatry* 79, no. 4 (2022): 368–74, https://doi.org/10.1001/jamapsychiatry.2021.4209.

44. Alexa Peters, "CHAZ Is Becoming a Refuge for Homeless People as Well as Protestors in Black Lives Matter Movement," Converge, accessed June 8, 2022, https://www.whereweconverge.com/post/chaz-is-becoming-a-refuge-for-homeless-people-as-well-as-protestors-in-black-lives-matter-movement.

45. "Black Lives Matter Seattle–King County," Facebook, July 20, 2020, https://www.facebook.com/blmseattle/.

46. "Black Lives Matter Seattle–King County," Facebook.

47. Sydney Brownstone and Scott Greenstone, "Will Defunding Seattle's Navigation Team Stop the Removal of Homeless Camps?," *Seattle Times*, August 6, 2020, https://www.seattletimes.com/seattle-news/homeless/will-defunding-seattles-navigation-team-stop-the-clearings-of-homeless-camps/.

48. Carter et al., "How a Year of Protests."

49. Carmen Best, *Black in Blue: Lessons on Leadership, Breaking Barriers, and Racial Reconciliation* (New York: HarperCollins Leadership, 2021); Casey Martin, "Carmen Best, Seattle's Police Chief, Resigns after City Council Cuts Department Funds," NPR, sec. Law, August 12, 2020, https://www.npr.org/2020/08/12/901605449/carmen-best-seattles-police-chief-resigns-after-city-council-cuts-department-fun.

50. Carolyn Bick, "BREAKING: Texts Show Fmr. SPD Chief Best Involved in Plan to Abandon East Precinct," South Seattle Emerald, June 3, 2022, https://southseattleemerald.com/2022/06/03/breaking-texts-show-fmr-spd-chief-best-involved-in-plan-to-abandon-east-precinct/.

51. Amanda Ong, "CALM Launches Medic Hotline to Provide Community Health Navigation," South Seattle Emerald, December 14, 2021, https://southseattleemerald.com/2021/12/14/calm-launches-medic-hotline-to-provide-community-health-navigation/.

52. Rich Smith, "Mutual Aid Group Occupies Cal Anderson Shelterhouse to Serve Homeless," Stranger, August 13, 2020, https://www.thestranger.com/slog/2020/08/13/44280419/mutual-aid-group-occupies-cal-anderson-shelterhouse-to-serve-homeless.

53. Daniel Beekman and Sydney Brownstone, "Seattle Plans to Clear Homeless Encampment from Cal Anderson Park on Capitol Hill," *Seattle Times*, December 15, 2020, https://www.seattletimes.com/seattle-news/homeless/seattle-plans-to-clear-homeless-encampment-from-cal-anderson-park-on-capitol-hill/.

54. Converge, "The Morning Update Show | August 13, 2020," YouTube video, 2020, https://www.youtube.com/watch?v=nPI0TqeKP7s; "Homelessness Activists Occupy Cal Anderson Shelterhouse—UPDATE: Swept," *Capitol Hill Seattle* (blog), August 14, 2020, https://www.capitolhillseattle.com/2020/08/homelessness-activists-occupy-cal-anderson-shelterhouse/.

55. Sydney Brownstone, "Body Cam Footage Captures Seattle Officers Directing Homeless Person to Cal Anderson Park for Services," *Seattle Times*, January 18, 2021, https://www.seattletimes.com/seattle-news/homeless/body-cam-footage-captures-seattle-officers-directing-homeless-person-to-cal-anderson-park-for-services/.

56. "House Keys Not Sweeps—a Campaign for Dignity and Respect," *WRAP* (blog), August 31, 2020, https://wraphome.org/2020/08/31/house-keys-not-sweeps-a-campaign-for-dignity-and-respect/.

57. Ari Hoffman, "Homicide Suspect in Seattle Slaying Was Arrested and Released More Than 34 Times," Post Millennial, September 17, 2020, https://thepostmillennial.com/homicide-suspect-in-seattle-slaying -was-arrested-and-released-more-than-34-times.

58. Markovich, "Travis Berge," September 17, 2020.

59. Public Affairs, "Homicide Investigation in Cal Anderson Park, Person of Interest Found Deceased after Barricading Himself in Building," SPD Blotter, September 17, 2020, https://spdblotter.seattlemulti .wpengine.com/2020/09/17/homicide-investigation-in-cal-anderson -park-person-of-interest-found-deceased-after-barricading-himself -in-building/.

60. Wagner, "Meth, Mental Illness and Murder."

61. Wagner, "Meth, Mental Illness and Murder."

62. Markovich, "Travis Berge," September 17, 2020.

63. Peters, "CHAZ Is Becoming a Refuge."

64. "Root Cause Analysis," AHRQ Patient Safety Network, accessed May 29, 2022, https://psnet.ahrq.gov/primer/root-cause-analysis.

CHAPTER 3

Compromised

. . . .

> *I am coming to see the middle path as a walk with*
> *wisdom where conversations of complexity can be*
> *found, that the middle path is the path of*
> *movement.*

—TERRY TEMPEST WILLIAMS, *LEAP*

IN THE DAYS THAT FOLLOWED the murder-suicide of Lisa Vach and Travis Berge, the thick wildfire smoke smothering Seattle and much of western North America continued. The smoke was so dense and widespread that it created its own weather patterns and caused the Seattle area to have the worst air quality in the world.[1] Finally, beginning on Saturday, September 19, 2020, two days after Lisa was killed, a steady rainstorm moved into the Seattle area and cleared the air.

At the time of the violent deaths, the thirty or so people living in the Cal Anderson tent encampment were on edge. Although Cal Anderson Park had been closed since June 30 for repairs, people continued to use the park for smaller protests, exercise, dog walking, homeless encampments, and mutual-aid services.[2] Homeless residents lived through an increasing number of encampment clearances, forcibly removed by police officers, the residents' belongings either confiscated or thrown away, only to return to the area and to the people in the community they knew. The Shelterhouse was cleaned and secured by Seattle Parks and Recreation; the public restrooms were boarded up. The deaths drew attention to the residents' encampment and likely lessened their trust in outreach and mutual-aid workers and in each other.

People, especially those who had known Lisa Vach and Travis Berge, tried to make sense of what had happened. Sunny, a friend of Lisa's who lived in the Cal Anderson encampment, said of Lisa, "She was a warrior. She always did what she could to help people."[3] Sunny added that Lisa had found community at the park, "she just liked to have fun," she did not like too many rules, and "she absolutely was here for Black Lives Matter." Sunny linked the dwindling resources caused by city crews barricading the park's bathrooms and Shelterhouse with an increase in Travis's erratic behavior. "I think we failed both of them. They were hurt. They were sick. They needed help," Sunny said. Sirena Ross, Lisa's former coworker, told reporters that Lisa "was a fighter with a strong sense of social justice who once confronted another employee over his abuse of a homeless woman."[4] William Parham, a thirty-five-year-old Black Seattle resident who was a BLM protestor and security guard at CHAZ/CHOP, told reporters that he was grieving for Travis Berge, saying, "He was a tragic character because of the drug addiction and mental health crisis that was going on."[5] "The city failed Travis," he added, "but they also failed a woman who is dead today because that person was allowed to be on the streets."[6]

KOMO NEWS REPORTER MATT MARKOVICH, who followed Travis Berge for the last two years of Travis's life, interviewed Travis in the weeks before his death. Travis showed Markovich "a bag of meth he said was worth more than $100," as well as a roll of $20 bills.[7] Travis, once again, exposed his genitals. Travis said he was seeking appointments with a psychiatrist but was having difficulty finding one. He said that "he had refused offers of housing because he preferred staying on the streets," claiming that the streets were safer.[8]

It is likely that both Lisa and Travis qualified at some point for emergency housing established in response to the COVID-19 pandemic. It is probable that both of them were offered shelter or housing by the city's Navigation Team or other outreach workers. It appears that Travis had permanent supportive housing through DESC at the Morrison when he was released from jail in late February 2020 but had left by the time he began living outside at Cal Anderson Park during CHAZ/CHOP.

THE NAVIGATION TEAM, dubbed the Nav Team, was begun in 2017 by the then Seattle mayor Ed Murray, after having declared, along with King County executive Dow Constantine, a state of emergency for homelessness for Seattle and King County on November 2, 2015.[9] At the same time, the city established a Navigation Center run by DESC in the Chinatown International District, adjacent to Pioneer Square. The Navigation Center is a low-barrier, harm reduction shelter, open 24/7, where people are given a bed that is theirs even if they come and go. This is different from regular emergency shelters, where people lose their bed if they leave the shelter. The Navigation Team was headed by specially trained Seattle police officers, accompanied by case managers and outreach nurses funded by Health Care for the Homeless Public Health—Seattle & King County. The team visited people living outside and in unsanctioned encampments and attempted to move people to the Navigation Center and then into shelters or permanent housing. The outreach team often resorted to carrying out encampment clearances, citing public health and fire safety hazards. They then encountered legal and ethical issues in doing these sweeps.[10] Critics saw the Navigation Team and their encampment sweeps as another example of the criminalization of poverty and homelessness.[11]

In its early years, the Navigation Center staff had access to designated funds to relocate homeless people to other areas of the country, ostensibly to reunite with family members.[12] It is possible that DESC or other staff members at the Navigation Center offered to relocate Travis Berge back to his family in Reno, Nevada, and that he refused. Such relocation is a modern-day version of the warning out, moving on aspect of the English Poor Laws, aimed to be punitive, criminalizing poverty and homelessness.[13] Like encampment clearances, the practice disrupts any connections people have made to health care, including behavioral health care, and any other positive support systems they may have established. Proponents of this practice either did not realize or did not want to acknowledge that people experiencing chronic homelessness oftentimes come from resource-strapped and chaotic families struggling with their own housing insecurities. Sending them back to their families rarely works, and people end up living in homelessness once again, and sometimes in worse situations.[14]

In 2019, King County council member Reagan Dunn proposed $1 million funding by the county to send homeless people to other parts of the country. He said that Seattle had "'become a dead-end street for the nation's homeless population.'"[15] Surveys included with the Seattle–King County annual PIT counts indicate that most homeless people first became homeless while living in King County or at least in Washington State.[16] This fact does not always sway public opinion that "Freeattle," Seattle's overly permissive and generous stance toward and services for homelessness, is a magnet for homeless people moving to Seattle—people like Travis Berge.[17] More common is what happened to Lisa, in terms of her moving to Seattle and being marginally housed with a string of temporary jobs for years, before a combination of the COVID-19 pandemic, a behavioral health crisis, losing her job, and then losing affordable housing contributed to her becoming newly homeless. From Lisa's Facebook posts at the beginning of the COVID-19 pandemic, we know that she was following public health advice on social distancing and the wearing of masks. Travis most likely ignored the public health recommendations, and his probable lack of compliance could have negatively affected his access to services and housing.

WITHIN THE FIRST FEW WEEKS of the documented community spread of the novel coronavirus, King County and the city of Seattle worked with health, housing, and social service providers across the region to create additional, safer shelter spaces and "a range of temporary housing options for people who are unable to recover in their own homes, or who do not have a home."[18] These actions included providing ninety-five additional spaces for people experiencing unsheltered homelessness; adding de-intensifying shelters for people already sheltered in large, congregant shelters; creating the I & Q sites; creating assessment and recovery centers for nonemergency COVID cases; and establishing a temporary enhanced shelter for people requiring sobering services at the recently opened Recovery Café in an industrial area south of Pioneer Square in Seattle.

Community centers, large indoor spaces at the Seattle Center (where the iconic Space Needle is located), and even the King

County International Airport–Boeing Field were sites for de-intensified emergency shelters. Besides motels and modular units, the old Nurse's Home, Harborview Hall, at Harborview Medical Center was the site of a busy I & Q center. Since Seattle–King County was the first area in the United States to identify the community spread of COVID-19, and because of the co-ordinated efforts to reduce the spread of the coronavirus among people experiencing homelessness, other municipalities looked to King County experts for guidance as they began to be affected.[19]

In the announcement of COVID-19 homelessness actions on March 25, 2020, King County executive Dow Constantine pointed out that the overall goal was to slow the community spread of the virus and ensure that hospital beds were going to the most severely ill with COVID-19. He added, "We are committed to the proposition that no one will be left behind. Not the old, not the sick, not those living in homelessness. We are all in this together, and we have to get each other through it."[20] The then Seattle mayor Jenny Durkan added that they were calling for state and federal assistance to staff and run the programs. She said, "We know that individuals experiencing homelessness are some of the most at risk for exposure."[21]

Early in the COVID-19 pandemic, public health experts emphasized that people experiencing homelessness not only were at higher risk of exposure to the novel coronavirus but also were at greater risk for severe illness and death from the infection. People experiencing homelessness have higher rates of chronic diseases, including diabetes and cardiovascular diseases; higher rates of behavioral health issues, including depression and substance use disorders; and poorer access to health care and basic hygiene facilities—all leading to a higher risk of infection, illness, and mortality from COVID-19.[22] Approximately 40% of all HCH patients nationwide are older adults, and older people are at a much higher risk of medical complications and death from COVID-19.[23]

HCH BEGAN AS A national demonstration program of the Robert Wood Johnson Foundation and the Pew Memorial Trust in 1985, was replicated and expanded in the 1987 McKinney Act, and, as of the most recently available data (2019), serves over 1 million people experiencing homelessness each year through 295 federally funded health centers.[24] HCH is part of the more extensive national community health center program, a program that benefits from bipartisan support. The Healthcare for the Homeless Network (HCHN) locally, administered through Public Health–Seattle & King County, was one of the original national demonstration programs begun in the mid-1980s. Currently, HCHN subcontracts with nine community-based partner organizations to provide comprehensive health care, including behavioral health services, to people experiencing homelessness at over sixty locations throughout King County.[25] In addition, HCHN operates mobile medical units to provide accessible services. These mobile medical units were used to provide COVID testing and then, once available, COVID vaccinations throughout Seattle and King County, targeting high-risk BIPOC and homeless populations with more barriers to access to care according to guidelines of the King County unified equitable vaccine delivery plan.[26]

The King County I & Q units were for people exposed to or positive for COVID who either were homeless or lacked sufficient housing. These units were developed rapidly at the start of the COVID-19 pandemic in the Seattle area; were located in hotels, motels, and other facilities in downtown Seattle and south and north King County; and were staffed 24/7 by nurses, counselors, and other support personnel using a harm reduction approach. Besides meals and a room with a bathroom to themselves, patients at the I & Q units were given opiate replacement medications if they were dependent, prescribed specific amounts of alcohol daily if they had alcohol dependence, and provided with cigarettes if they smoked. Prescribing alcohol to alcohol-dependent patients is lifesaving since alcohol withdrawal can be fatal. With a lack of adequate harm reduction approaches for people addicted to stimulants like meth, staff at the King County I & Q units sent such patients to hospitals, mainly Harborview Medical Center, for managed withdrawal while they recovered from COVID-19.

Many homeless people testing positive for COVID-19 or who had been in close contact with someone infected with COVID-19 were reluctant to go to the I & Q units because of the rules to stay inside their rooms until they were cleared medically to leave. Rumors circulated that once a person went to an I & Q unit, they would not be allowed to leave. Hedda McClendon, director of the King County Department of Community and Human Services COVID Emergency group, said, "For a lot of people living unsheltered, they have not had the best experience in the homeless shelters," which translated into hesitancy to access the I & Q units.[27]

THERE IS NO DOCUMENTATION of either Travis or Lisa going for any shelter, housing, or COVID-19 services—if they had and if they had been given separate rooms, could the I & Q public health nurses and support staff have screened Lisa for domestic violence and connected her with safe housing after discharge, assuming, that is, that she would accept such offers? We know that Travis had a DESC case manager and that he had permanent supportive housing through DESC at the Morrison after he was released from King County Jail at the end of February. This was before Governor Jay Inslee announced his Stay Home, Stay Healthy lockdown order on March 23.[28] Available evidence shows that Travis and Lisa were in the Morrison at the same time in early March when Lisa posted the photograph of the seagull on the windowsill of the Morrison. The permanent supportive housing units at the Morrison are for single, chronically homeless, high-need adults and do not accommodate couples. This could explain why Lisa and Travis ended up living together in the Cal Anderson encampment. A common barrier for people transitioning from encampments to other shelter or housing is that they could not live with their "chosen family" members or take their pets or too many belongings with them. In terms of belongings, it is important to note that hoarding is a common coping behavior for people experiencing housing instability and homelessness.[29] After Lisa's death, some of her friends said she had told them that she had housing options about to come through.[30] With rainy weather and a cold winter approaching, Lisa likely felt more urgency to find housing—perhaps to find safe housing away from Travis.

FROM WHAT WE KNOW of Lisa Vach and how sensitive she was to people around her, she likely suffered from the stigma attached to being homeless, which probably contributed to her mental health challenges. At the beginning of the COVID-19 pandemic in the Seattle area in late February and early March 2020, portions of the general public feared the presence of homeless people on the streets, in parks, or in other public spaces. This view of homeless people both as vectors of a deadly disease and as signs of social chaos has built off of a long-standing fear of homeless people in our country. Dating back to the economic depression starting in 1873 and continuing through the Great Depression with the presence of Hoovervilles, the rising and visible population of homeless people led to the "tramp scare." Also called the "tramp evil," newspapers, including those in Seattle, claimed not only that tramps were diseased and dirty but also that their presence showed "the struggles between the propertied and the unpropertied over the uses of public space, fears about the growth of a propertyless proletariat, and anxieties about the loss of traditional social controls in American cities."[31]

Homeless advocates and people in charge of public health messaging in Seattle and King County worked hard to counter this fear by emphasizing that homeless people were more at risk of contracting and dying of COVID-19 than they were of spreading the infection in the wider community.[32] It is worth remembering how little was known about COVID-19 in the early months of the pandemic, including how contagious it was indoors versus outdoors and what effective prevention measures could be implemented in hospitals and communities. In the United States, which lacks a robust, nonpartisan national public health agency, and with the then president Trump spreading confusing and non-evidence-based information about COVID-19, the general public experienced confusion, fear, anger, and deepening sociopolitical divisions.[33] As Leana Wen, MD, former Baltimore health commissioner, put it, "Of all factors that caused the calamity of COVID-19 in the United States, the biggest culprit was the deliberate misinformation and active disinformation that came from the White House."[34]

All of this fueled an already growing distrust of medical, science, and government officials among a significant subset of the American public.[35] Within Seattle and high-income suburbs like Bellevue, Kirkland, and Redmond (the headquarters of Microsoft), which have higher education levels than among the general public, there is high trust in science. This, combined with one of the country's best health departments, Public Health–Seattle & King County, led to high rates of community compliance with public health mandates like the wearing of masks, social distancing, and, early on in the pandemic for people who had homes, a stay-at-home order.[36] Seattle and King County leaders worked closely with public health officials to craft public health messaging and coordinate the timing of the messaging, managing trade-offs along the way. Closing public schools was a difficult decision, and "everyone also knew that, if the city shut down, domestic-violence incidents would rise."[37] Suburban and rural areas of King County and surrounding counties with more politically conservative populations saw pushback against evidence-based public health measures, echoing divisions found across the United States.[38]

IN ONE OF THE MORE developed public debriefs on the life and death of Travis Berge, *Seattle Times* columnist Danny Westneat wrote, "Probably everyone would agree, especially now, that about the last place Travis Berge should have been living was in a makeshift fort in a Seattle city park."[39] He acknowledged the fact that many people were blaming "the system" for the murder-suicide and writes, "So it's worth asking: Did Seattle's infamous liberal compassion enable this tragedy?" He adds, "A chorus on one side is saying Berge should have been locked up. Had he been in jail instead of at Cal Anderson, two people wouldn't be dead." But he pointed out that in 2019, when Berge was arrested for breaking windows downtown, he served three months for malicious mischief, but a Seattle municipal judge, noting Berge's parole violation for a previous sentence, kept Berge in jail for 240 days. This sentence removed Travis from the streets and community but did nothing to rehabilitate him in terms of his behavioral health issues. Westneat quoted the then city attorney Pete Holmes as saying, "This tragic alleged domestic violence incident signals the urgent need for more behavioral health treatment resources, more housing access, and additional resources to combat addiction."

A judge had ordered Berge to attend mandatory outpatient drug treatment, the Community Center for Alternative Programs, Enhanced, in exchange for not going to jail. Travis showed up at the drug treatment center on his first day not wearing a shirt, and when he was refused entry because of this, he broke a window, returning him to jail.[40] While in jail, Travis was interviewed by a KOMO News reporter. He said, "I'm just trying to turn around my life and never try to come back to jail, never try to commit another crime."[41] But he consistently refused to participate in substance abuse treatment offered to him while in jail and immediately returned to using meth daily once he was released. Seattle Probation Department supervisor Carol Bell told the judge in early July 2019, "He does have under-addressed substance abuse issues and those are really interfering with the ability to do an adequate mental health evaluation."[42] But when Travis Berge was jailed in 2019–20 for 240 days and was away from meth, did he receive a mental health evaluation?

Washington State has long had one of our nation's highest incidences of mental illness, combined with having poor access to mental health treatment.[43] Obtaining a mental health evaluation for Travis Berge while in jail, as it is for anyone else in or out of jail or prison, was challenging and plagued with significant delays. In 2015, a successful class action lawsuit known as *Trueblood* was brought against the Washington State Department of Social and Health Services (DSHS) because of delays in competency evaluations for people with mental disabilities.[44] DSHS has the obligation under state law to provide people with mental health evaluations and restoration services whether they are charged with serious crimes or misdemeanors. The US District Court ruled that DSHS violated the constitutional rights of people with mental disabilities. A settlement agreement in a 2018 court case finding DSHS in contempt of the *Trueblood* ruling has led to efforts to improve the mental health workforce, emphasizing arrest diversion and better community-level support for people with mental illness.[45]

DANNY WESTNEAT, IN HIS debrief of the very public and tragic life of Travis Berge, wondered whether involuntary inpatient drug treatment could have worked for him. Also known as secure detox, the Washington State Legislature passed involuntary drug treatment legislation in 2016. Ricky's Law is designed for people like Travis who pose a significant threat to themselves or others or are gravely disabled owing to substance use disorder.[46] Typically, emergency department staff call a county designated crisis responder to determine whether the person should be sent to a Secure Withdrawal Management and Stabilization facility for up to five days. A public defender represents the patient to defend their rights, and the case goes to an Involuntary Treatment Act Court to decide on more extended involuntary treatment. Unfortunately, many patients are refused treatment by the private involuntary treatment facilities if they are violent or have other medical conditions, which would have disqualified Travis. In addition, unlike for involuntary inpatient psychiatric treatment, hospitals do not have to hold patients under Ricky's Law until an inpatient drug treatment bed is available, so many patients are discharged back onto the streets or wherever they were living.

Ricky's Law is seldom used, not only because of the problems with private drug treatment facilities cherry-picking compliant patients and hospitals discharging patients prematurely but also because involuntary drug treatment rarely works. Most physicians and other health care providers, especially in the Seattle area, follow the evidence-based practice of voluntary harm reduction substance use disorder treatment options. Harm reduction is the public health approach aimed at reducing harm to the substance user and others in their lives and community.[47] In many ways, harm reduction is a pragmatic compromise between meeting patients' autonomous preferences, their addictions, and the needs of public health and society.[48] Harm reduction approaches for substance use disorders recognize addiction as a disease, often with a coexisting mental illness.[49]

Our nation's first publicly funded needle exchange program, a form of harm reduction, was started in nearby Tacoma, Washington, in 1988 in an attempt to counter the HIV/AIDS crisis.[50] Public Health–Seattle & King County has long had a robust needle exchange and other harm reduction programs, including the provision of naloxone for reversing opioid overdoses, medication-assisted opioid treatment, and the provision of glass pipes to avoid infectious disease transmission among substance users.[51] As UW substance use disorder researcher Caleb Banta-Green puts it, "Harm reduction is health care," especially for homeless people with substance use disorders, and "I feel we need to bubble wrap people and keep them alive until they can get more stable housing and treatment."[52]

"SO WHAT'S NEXT?" asked a hand-painted sign on a large piece of plywood in red lettering on a pink background in front of the East Precinct Police Station at CHAZ/CHOP on the morning of

June 24, 2020. "Life after CHOP" was written in the bottom right-hand corner, and someone had added "Say her name" at the top. "Say her name" had become a familiar phrase, which in Seattle referred not only to Breonna Taylor, the twenty-six-year-old Black woman shot and killed in her Kentucky home by white police officers, but more specifically to Charleena Lyles. Lyles was a petite thirty-year-old pregnant Black woman living in permanent supportive housing in North Seattle when she was shot and killed by white Seattle police officers in 2017. The two police officers involved in killing Lyles in front of her young children were still working with the SPD in the summer of 2020, never having been charged with any wrongdoing. Protests and demands during CHAZ/CHOP helped push for justice for Charleena Lyles and her children.

At various times throughout the month-long existence of CHAZ/CHOP, different groups listed a series of demands, many of which changed over time. One of the groups, the King County Equity Now Coalition, called for redistributing $180 million from the SPD budget and "shift[ing] resources into Black-led, community organizations to ensure that COVID-19 does not exacerbate the widening racial resource/wealth gap."[53] Another demand was to end contracts between SPD and Seattle Public Schools owing to the documented "school to prison pipeline," especially for BIPOC youth and youth with disabilities.[54] The groups also called for amnesty for protestors, wanting all charges dropped against them.[55] Council member Kshama Sawant called for the East Police Precinct to be turned "into a community center for restorative justice."[56] In talks with protestors, the then mayor Jenny Durkan considered turning over the East Precinct to the BLMSKC group.[57]

CHAZ/CHOP built on Seattle's long tradition of radicalism, from massive labor movements beginning in the early 1900s to experimental communities.[58] The alternative community that sprung up, albeit briefly, within CHAZ/CHOP was viewed differently by journalists across the sociopolitical spectrum. Some journalists referred to the area and the movement as an "anarchist summer camp."[59] Another journalist described it like this: "Part street fair, part commune, the so-called CHOP became an experiment in maintaining order with no police in sight."[60] The communal living aspect of CHAZ/CHOP probably appealed to Lisa Vach since, according to her friend Shade Falcon Remelin, Lisa's happiest years were while living in co-op housing in Pomona, California, when she was in her twenties. After her death, people who knew Lisa from the Cal Anderson encampment said she was "known as a regular around the ongoing efforts to establish a mutual-aid center and camp in the park."[61]

In early August 2020, the Seattle City Council voted to defund the Navigation Team.[62] On September 30, the then mayor Jenny Durkan suspended all operations of the Navigation Team.[63] It is unclear what, if any, outreach the Navigation Team or other official outreach teams were even doing with people like Lisa and Travis living in Cal Anderson Park after CHAZ/CHOP ended on July 1. Outreach teams including SPD officers, like the Navigation Team, would not have been welcome within CHAZ/CHOP or afterward, especially by anti-police mutual-aid activists such as the Stop the Sweeps group, which grew out of the mutual-aid group Lisa was involved with after CHAZ/CHOP.

A significant missed opportunity for intervening to stop the murder-suicide of Lisa Vach and Travis Berge occurred in the days leading up to this tragedy. People who knew Lisa and Travis during that time recounted knowledge of their escalating fights: "she and Berge became known as a dangerous combination living in a mix of addiction and mental crisis amid the activism and camping."[64] They added that a mutual-aid volunteer tried to intervene between Lisa and Travis the day before their deaths, and the volunteer was injured enough that he had to go to the hospital.[65] Most likely, the volunteer was injured by Travis, perhaps due to one of Travis's delusions about mutual combat. This assault was never reported to the police, and it is unlikely that the police would have been called in anyway, due to the distrust of the SPD by the mutual-aid group.

AT NOON ON WEDNESDAY, September 23, 2020, a rainy, cool day in Seattle, on the steps of City Hall at the corner of Fourth Avenue and James Street, with a view of the Morrison Hotel down the hill toward Puget Sound, Women in Black held a vigil for homeless people who had died in the previous days and weeks. Women in Black is a homeless remembrance and advocacy project begun in 2000 by WHEEL. WHEEL started in 1993 as a housing and advocacy group that is self-managed by currently and formerly homeless women. Working with faith communities, community volunteers, and donors, they built and dedicated a bronze statue, "The Tree of Life," in Victor Steinbrueck Park near Pike Place Market in 2012. Designed by the artist Clark Wiegman and considered the first and still only public homeless remembrance project in the United States, the Tree of Life has cutouts of missing bronze leaves. The bronze leaves of remembrance, etched with the names and birth and death dates of homeless people who died outside in Seattle, are epoxied to Seattle sidewalks after receiving permits from the city. The Women in Black receive names of the dead from the King County Medical Examiner's Office and the HCHN. Allene Steinberg, a member of Women in Black, says of the project, "We stand because everyone has a right to have a ceremony when they leave this planet. This may be the only ceremony they have. I see the leaves as headstones."[66] She added, "We have to treat people with dignity in death in order to learn how to treat people when they are alive."[67]

Michelle Marchand, one of the founders of both WHEEL and Women in Black, wrote a piece on the National Memorial Day for Homeless People, started by the National Coalition and held across the country on December 21, the winter solstice. Referring to the origins of what became Women in Black's homeless remembrance project, she recounted, "Every time a small news brief runs in the local papers about the missing, dead, injured, or beaten homeless people, it talks of 'transients,' of 'histories of prostitution and drug use.' Every time, this reductive description hurts homeless people and their family members."[68]

On that rainy September day in 2020, the women, mostly dressed in black and wearing raincoats, held handmade signs with the names of the dead: Andrew Busch, Lisa Vach, and Travis Berge. The lives and deaths of Lisa Vach and Travis Berge were, by then, widely known. Less well-known to the general public was Andrew Joseph Busch, a thirty-five-year-old white man from Sammamish, a wealthy East Side suburb of Seattle in King County, who died on September 1. He burned to death in a tent encampment at Seventh Avenue and Seneca Street, in Freeway Park, adjacent to the Convention Center and built atop Interstate 5 in downtown Seattle. Busch's longtime friend and former roommate in the U District of Seattle, Dec'lan Amadeus Colburn, posted a eulogy for his friend on the Women in Black memorial page, recounting what a gifted guitar player Andrew was but how he became addicted to opioids. The last time Dec'lan talked with Andrew, Andrew was in an inpatient drug rehab center in Portland, Oregon, a drug treatment center from which he left early. Dec'lan adds, "Like millions before him, opioids altered the trajectory of his life. Like countless gifted people before him, it robbed the world of his. I loved him like a brother."[69]

Many of Lisa's friends stood vigil for her at the September Women in Black event on the steps of City Hall. One young woman showed a large photograph of a smiling Lisa, a photograph sent to the Women in Black group by Lisa's sister. Several of Lisa's friends objected to having a memorial service for both Lisa and Travis at the same time and place, pointing out that Travis had physically abused and then murdered her. Speaking about this controversy, Anitra Freeman, a woman who was formerly homeless and works with Women in Black, told me, "We stand vigil for anybody who dies by violence or outside, and suicide is a death by violence. We decided that we stand for everyone no matter what."[70]

Lisa's Leaves of Remembrance page states, "Lisa was described by friends as kind, funny, and an artist. She was murdered in Cal Anderson Park on September 16, 2020, at 38."[71] Sirena Ross, Lisa's former coworker, said of Lisa, "She was a real person. She wasn't broken."

Lisa's older sister from Southern California came to Seattle after Lisa's death and, along with Lisa's friend Shade Falcon Remelin, took care of her few belongings left in her old truck parked on a Seattle street. Shade rescued Lisa's hand-painted Loteria set and has featured it on his Facebook page in her memory. Travis Berge does not have a leaf of remembrance; Anitra Freeman told me that this is because no one has requested one. Perhaps his family did not want to have such a reminder of his life and death in Seattle.

Someone who is not included in the leaves of remembrance is Charleena Lyles. Although Lyles had been homeless for ten years, she was living in permanent supportive housing at the time of her death. The leaves of remembrance are for people who died while living in homelessness outside, not people who died in shelters, transitional or permanent supportive housing, or hospitals. In many ways, Charleena Lyles was a homelessness success story, at least until her killing by two SPD officers.

Notes

1. Jeff Masters, "Reviewing the Horrid Global 2020 Wildfire Season," Yale Climate Connections, January 4, 2021, http://yaleclimate connections.org/2021/01/reviewing-the-horrid-global-2020-wildfire -season/.
2. Elise Takahama, "Woman Killed in Cal Anderson Park, Man Found Dead after Refusing to Leave City Building, Police Say," *Seattle Times*, September 16, 2020, https://www.seattletimes.com/seattle-news /seattle-police-investigating-death-in-cal-anderson-park/.
3. Takahama, "Woman Killed in Cal Anderson Park."
4. jseattle, "Remember Lisa Vach," *Capitol Hill Seattle* (blog), September 23, 2020, https://www.capitolhillseattle.com/2020/09/remember -lisa-vach/.
5. KOMO News Staff, "Murder Suspect in Cal Anderson Park Slaying ID'd as Well Known Habitual Offender," KOMO, September 17, 2020, https://komonews.com/news/local/police-detectives-investigating -death-at-cal-anderson-park; James Ross Gardner, "Seattle's Capitol Hill Occupied Protest Has Always Been in Flux," *New Yorker*, June 26, 2020, https://www.newyorker.com/news/dispatch/seattles -capitol-hill-occupied-protest-has-always-been-in-flux.
6. KOMO News Staff, "Murder Suspect in Cal Anderson Park."
7. Matt Markovich, "Travis Berge: Suspect in Cal Anderson Murder Led Troubled, Drug-Fueled Life," KOMO, September 17, 2020, https:// komonews.com/news/operation-crime-justice/travis-berge-suspect -in-cal-anderson-murder-led-troubled-drug-fueled-life.
8. Markovich, "Travis Berge."
9. "Executive, Seattle Mayor Declare Emergencies, Announce New Investments to Respond to Homelessness," King County, November 2, 2015, https://kingcounty.gov/elected/executive/constantine/news /release/2015/November/02-homeless-emergency.aspx.

10. Jay Willis, "Sweeps Trample the Rights and Lives of the City's Homeless," *Seattle Times*, May 24, 2016, https://www.seattletimes .com/opinion/sweeps-trample-the-rights-and-lives-of-the-citys -homeless/.
11. Willis, "Sweeps Trample the Rights."
12. Vernal Coleman, "A New Way to Help Seattle's Homeless: Navigation Center Set to Open Wednesday," *Seattle Times*, July 10, 2017, https:// www.seattletimes.com/seattle-news/northwest/navigation-center-for -seattle-homeless-to-open-next-week/.
13. Josephine Ensign, *Skid Road: On the Frontier of Health and Homelessness in an American City* (Baltimore: Johns Hopkins University Press, 2021).
14. Mike Baker, "Homeless Residents Got One-Way Tickets Out of Town. Many Returned to the Streets," *New York Times*, sec. U.S., September 14, 2019, https://www.nytimes.com/2019/09/14/us/homeless -busing-seattle-san-francisco.html.
15. Sydney Brownstone, "King County Council Will More Than Triple the Funding to Reunite Homeless People with Their Families. It's Not Clear How Well It Will Work," *Seattle Times*, November 23, 2019, https://www.seattletimes.com/seattle-news/homeless/county-votes -to-more-than-triple-the-funding-available-to-reunite-homeless -people-with-their-families-its-not-clear-how-well-it-will-work/.
16. "Point-In-Time Count," KCRHA, accessed March 14, 2024, https:// kcrha.org/data-overview/king-county-point-in-time-count/.
17. Lisa Edge, "Despite the Data, the 'Freeattle' Myth Persists," *Real Change*, December 27, 2017, http://www.realchangenews.org/news /2017/12/27/despite-data-freeattle-myth-persists.
18. "King County and Seattle Expand COVID-19 Emergency Shelter and Housing Response," King County, March 25, 2020, https:// kingcounty.gov/elected/executive/constantine/news/release/2020 /March/25-kingcounty-seattle-covid-19-shelter.aspx.
19. "Coronavirus Disease 2019 (COVID-19) Update—What Clinicians Need to Know to Prepare for COVID-19 in the United States," Clinician Outreach and Communication Activity, webinar, March 5, 2020, https://emergency.cdc.gov/coca/calls/2020/callinfo_030520.asp.
20. "King County and Seattle Expand," King County.
21. "King County and Seattle Expand," King County.

22. "Coronavirus and Influenza Resources," National Health Care for the Homeless Council, accessed June 30, 2022, https://nhchc.org/clinical -practice/diseases-and-conditions/influenza/.

23. "Coronavirus and Influenza Resources," National Health Care for the Homeless Council.

24. Josephine Ensign, *Health Care for the Homeless: A Vision of Health for All* (Nashville: National Health Care for the Homeless Council, August 30, 2016).

25. "Healthcare for the Homeless Network (HCHN)," King County, accessed July 8, 2022, https://kingcounty.gov/depts/health/locations /homeless-health/healthcare-for-the-homeless.aspx.

26. "Summary of COVID-19 Vaccination among Residents," King County, accessed July 8, 2022, https://kingcounty.gov/depts/health/covid-19 /data/vaccination.aspx.

27. Erica C. Barnett, "As COVID Cases at Shelters Rise, Many Are Reluctant to Enter County Quarantine Sites," South Seattle Emerald, September 22, 2021, https://southseattleemerald.com/2021/09/22/as -covid-cases-at-shelters-rise-many-are-reluctant-to-enter-county -quarantine-sites/.

28. Benjamin Cassidy, "Seattle's Coronavirus Timeline, from Toilet Paper to Mask Laws," Seattle Met, August 4, 2020, https://www.seattlemet .com/health-and-wellness/2020/08/seattle-s-coronavirus-timeline -from-toilet-paper-to-mask-laws.

29. Astrea Greig, David Tolin, and Jack Tsai, "Prevalence of Hoarding Behavior among Formerly Homeless Persons Living in Supported Housing," *Journal of Nervous and Mental Disease* 208, no. 10 (October 2020): 822–27, https://doi.org/10.1097/NMD.00000000 00001205; Leah Sottile, "Homeless and Hoarding," *Atlantic*, January 7, 2015, https://www.theatlantic.com/health/archive/2015/01/homeless -and-hoarding/384036/.

30. "Lisa Vach RIP," Reddit post, R/SeattleWA, September 20, 2020, www.reddit.com/r/SeattleWA/comments/iwixf9/lisa_vach_rip/.

31. Todd DePastino, *Citizen Hobo: How a Century of Homelessness Shaped America* (Chicago: University of Chicago Press, 2003).

32. "King County and Seattle Expand," King County.

33. Charles Pillar, "The Inside Story of How Trump's COVID-19 Coordina- tor Undermined the World's Top Health Agency," *Science*, October 14,

2020, https://www.science.org/content/article/inside-story-how
-trumps-covid-19-coordinator-undermined-cdc.

34. Leana Wen, *Lifelines: A Doctor's Journey in the Fight for Public Health* (New York: Metropolitan Books, 2021), 271.

35. Cary Funk et al., "Americans Reflect on Nation's COVID-19 Response," *Pew Research Center Science & Society* (blog), July 7, 2022, https://www.pewresearch.org/science/2022/07/07/americans-reflect
-on-nations-covid-19-response/.

36. Charles Duhigg, "Seattle's Leaders Let Scientists Take the Lead. New York's Did Not," *New Yorker*, April 26, 2020, https://www.newyorker
.com/magazine/2020/05/04/seattles-leaders-let-scientists-take-the
-lead-new-yorks-did-not.

37. Duhigg, "Seattle's Leaders."

38. Danny Westneat, "The Political Vaccine Divide in Washington State Is Widening—and COVID Rushes In," *Seattle Times*, May 2, 2021, https://www.seattletimes.com/seattle-news/politics/the-political
-vaccine-divide-in-washington-state-is-widening-and-covid-rushes
-in/.

39. Danny Westneat, "Too Much Jail Time, or Not Enough? All the Ways Seattle Tried to Deal with Travis Berge," *Seattle Times*, September 18, 2020, https://www.seattletimes.com/seattle-news/law-justice/too
-much-jail-time-or-not-enough-all-the-ways-seattle-tried-to-deal
-with-travis-berge/.

40. Westneat, "Too Much Jail Time."

41. Matt Markovich, "Repeat Offender Travis Berge Remains in Jail," KOMO News, July 12, 2019, https://komonews.com/news/local/repeat
-offender-travis-berge-sentenced-to-more-time-in-jail.

42. Markovich, "Repeat Offender Travis Berge."

43. "Ranking the States 2023," Mental Health America, accessed March 15, 2024, https://mhanational.org/issues/2023/ranking
-states.

44. "A.B. by and through Trueblood v. DSHS," Disability Rights Washington, accessed March 15, 2024, https://homepagedisabilityrightswashi
ngton.wpcomstaging.com/cases/trueblood/.

45. Sherry Lerch and Jacob Mihalak, *Stakeholder Input to the Trueblood Task Force: Key Issues and Themes* (Technical Assistance Collaborative, May 25, 2018), 35.

46. "The Hope and Hurdles of Involuntary Drug Treatment," *Seattle Times*, March 11, 2022, https://www.seattletimes.com/opinion/the-hope-and-hurdles-of-involuntary-drug-treatment/.

47. "Principles of Harm Reduction," National Harm Reduction Coalition, accessed July 7, 2022, https://harmreduction.org/about-us/principles-of-harm-reduction/.

48. "Harm Reduction," Substance Abuse and Mental Health Services Administration, accessed July 7, 2022, https://www.samhsa.gov/find-help/harm-reduction.

49. "Substance Use and Co-occurring Mental Disorders," National Institute of Mental Health, accessed July 9, 2022, https://www.nimh.nih.gov/health/topics/substance-use-and-mental-health.

50. S. G. Sherman and D. Purchase, "Point Defiance: A Case Study of the United States' First Public Needle Exchange in Tacoma, Washington," *International Journal on Drug Policy* 12, no. 1 (April 1, 2001): 45–57, https://doi.org/10.1016/s0955-3959(00)00074-8.

51. Sheryl Gay Stolberg, "Uproar over 'Crack Pipes' Puts Biden Drug Strategy at Risk," *New York Times*, sec. U.S., February 21, 2022, https://www.nytimes.com/2022/02/21/us/politics/biden-harm-reduction-crack-pipes.html.

52. Caleb Banta-Green and Noah Fey, "Methamphetamine and Opiate Trends and Harm Reduction Based Interventions in Permanent Supportive Housing" (Housing First Partners Conference, Building Community Through Housing First—Health, Wellness and Inclusion, Seattle, WA, April 11, 2022).

53. Becca Savransky, "How CHAZ Became CHOP: Seattle's Police-Free Zone Explained," Seattle Post-Intelligencer, updated June 22, 2020, https://www.seattlepi.com/seattlenews/article/What-is-CHOP-the-zone-in-Seattle-formed-by-15341281.php.

54. Roxanna Gomez, "The School-to-Prison Pipeline: What It Is, How It Functions, and How We Can Work to Dismantle It," ACLU of Washington, September 22, 2023, https://www.aclu-wa.org/story/school-prison-pipeline-what-it-how-it-functions-and-how-we-can-work-dismantle-it.

55. Savransky, "How CHAZ Became CHOP."

56. Savransky, "How CHAZ Became CHOP."

57. Daniel Beekman and Lewis Kamb, "As Police Were Abandoning East Precinct, Seattle Officials Drafted Plan to Give Station to a Black Lives Matter Group," *Seattle Times*, January 30, 2022, https://www

.seattletimes.com/seattle-news/politics/as-police-were-abandoning -spd-east-precinct-seattle-officials-drafted-plan-to-give-station-near -chop-to-a-black-lives-matter-group/.

58. Hallie Golden, "Seattle's Activist-Occupied Zone Is Just the Latest in a Long History of Movements and Protests," *Guardian*, sec. US news, June 21, 2020, https://www.theguardian.com/us-news/2020/jun/21 /seattle-activist-occupied-zone-chop-long-history-movements-protests.

59. Lia Eustachewich, "How the Seattle CHOP Zone Went from Socialist Summer Camp to Deadly Disaster," *New York Post* (blog), July 1, 2020, https://nypost.com/2020/07/01/how-seattle-chop-went-from -socialist-summer-camp-to-deadly-disaster/.

60. Rachel Abrams, "Police Clear Seattle's Protest 'Autonomous Zone,'" *New York Times*, sec. U.S., July 1, 2020, https://www.nytimes.com /2020/07/01/us/seattle-protest-zone-CHOP-CHAZ-unrest.html.

61. jseattle, "Remember Lisa Vach."

62. Sydney Brownstone and Scott Greenstone, "Will Defunding Seattle's Navigation Team Stop the Removal of Homeless Camps?," *Seattle Times*, August 6, 2020, https://www.seattletimes.com/seattle-news /homeless/will-defunding-seattles-navigation-team-stop-the -clearings-of-homeless-camps/.

63. Erica C. Barnett, "Durkan Suspends Navigation Team," South Seattle Emerald, October 1, 2020, https://southseattleemerald.com/2020/10 /01/durkan-suspends-navigation-team/.

64. jseattle, "Remember Lisa Vach."

65. jseattle, "Remember Lisa Vach."

66. Ashley Archibald, "Another Year, Too Many Gone: Women in Black Recognizes Those Who Died on Seattle's Streets," *Real Change*, October 20, 2021, https://www.realchangenews.org/news/2021/10/20 /another-year-too-many-gone-women-black-recognizes-those-who -died-seattle-s-streets.

67. Bettina Hansen, "Women in Black: They Stand Vigil, Speak the Names of Seattle Area's Homeless Who've Died," *Seattle Times*, June 28, 2017, https://www.seattletimes.com/seattle-news/women-in -black-they-stand-vigil-speak-the-names-of-seattle-areas-homeless -whove-died/.

68. Michelle Marchand, "The Longest Night: National Memorial Day for Homeless People," *Real Change*, December 13, 2001, https://www .realchangenews.org/sites/default/files/20011213.pdf.

69. "Andrew Busch 1985–2020," Leaves of Remembrance, October 11, 2021, https://fallenleaves.org/andrew-busch-1985-2020/.
70. Anitra Freeman, Skid Road Oral History, interview by Josephine Ensign, October 25, 2022.
71. "Lisa Vach 1982–2020," Leaves of Remembrance, October 10, 2021, https://fallenleaves.org/?s=Lisa+Vach&id=6720&post_type=post.

CHAPTER 4

Lifelines

• • • • • • • • • • • • • • • • •

*Bearing witness, then, may be the most effective
way we know of carrying the weight of the past in
order to arrive at generative resolutions.*

—TIYA MILES, *ALL THAT SHE CARRIED: THE JOURNEY OF
ASHLEY'S SACK, A BLACK FAMILY KEEPSAKE*

"SAY HER NAME! CHARLEENA LYLES! Say her name! Charleena
Lyles!" Hundreds of people, including many of Charleena's family
members, chanted this refrain at an early-evening rally in front
of the three-story brick and clapboard Brettler Family Place 3
Apartments in Sand Point, North Seattle. The rally, on a warm
June 20, 2017, was just days after two white SPD officers from
the North Precinct shot and killed Charleena inside her home
in the presence of three of her children, including her youngest
son, a one-year-old, who clung to her body. Charleena was almost four months pregnant with another son at the time.
Photographs of Charleena, a brown-eyed woman with chiseled
cheeks and a wide smile, were held high on signs and taped to
chairs on the concrete patio and grassy lawn outside what had
been her home. A sweeping access ramp led to the entrance of

the apartment building since Brettler Family Place 3 is for families with members with disabilities and special needs. Charleena's then four-year-old daughter with Down syndrome had difficulty walking.

Charleena, named for her father Charles Lyles Jr., stood five feet three inches and weighed one hundred pounds when she was killed. A King County Coroner's report found that Charleena had been shot seven times in the chest, arm, and abdomen by the police officers; four of those shots came from the back. She had no drugs or alcohol in her system.[1] According to police, Charleena had been holding a four-inch kitchen paring knife. Although the two police officers claimed they feared for their lives, they admitted that Charleena had not cut or even touched them. Both police officers were over six feet tall, and one weighed 225 pounds.[2] They carried batons and pepper spray that they did not use. One officer was supposed to carry a taser, but he had left it in his locker at the precinct. The other officer had taken extra training to become a certified crisis intervention specialist.[3] In Charleena's coat pocket after her death, police found Seattle Public Library cards and King County Metro bus transfer slips.[4]

Charleena Lyles loved libraries. In her ten years of homelessness in Seattle and King County—beginning in 2005, when her mother died suddenly and she, at age seventeen, was pregnant with her first child—Charleena likely spent a lot of time in public libraries. It is not hyperbole to say that public libraries save lives, especially for people experiencing homelessness. Libraries give sanctuary and shelter, both emotionally and physically. Libraries offer quiet, peacefulness, community, heat, and, hopefully, air conditioning when it's hot and smoky outside. Libraries have public restrooms, which are surprisingly scarce in Seattle. Harried parents like Charleena can find respite in libraries, with their bright, colorful children's book sections, free access to the internet and computers, and children's story hours. In libraries, children, teens, adults, and older adults, no matter their race, ethnicity, gender, sexual identity, differing abilities, or socioeconomic and housing situations, can all find stories of people who deal with challenges like the ones they face and who find ways to not only survive but also endure, resist, and thrive.

Viewed as a whole and not just by her death or what occurred in the months before her death, Charleena Lyles's all-too-brief life was a success. Whether labeling it resilience, resistance, endurance, or survival, she overcame significant obstacles, including childhood trauma, poverty, domestic violence, racism, and homelessness as a teen and young adult. According to family members and other people who knew her, Charleena, or Leena as they called her, was an outspoken and fierce defender of her children. Her relatives described Charleena as energetic, as someone who loved dancing, dressing up, and writing poetry.[5] Shanee Isabell, a cousin who grew up with Charleena, said, "I truly admired her as a mother and I just admired her drive. She was very courageous and dependable, and she was very loyal."[6] Monika Williams, Charleena's older half-sister, described her as strong and independent, adding, "I don't care what she was going through or what anybody was trying to bring on her, she would hit it with a smile."[7]

Alice Olmstead, co-owner of the Poverty Bay Coffee Company in Federal Way south of Seattle, recalled that almost ten years before, when Charleena was a young mother with two children, Charleena had an internship with their company through a Federal Way job training program for homeless and unstably housed people.[8] Charleena worked as a barista, cook, and cashier. Olmstead described Charleena as "really sweet," a fast learner and "a great team player, she got along with everyone."[9] Charleena's father said, "Her whole life was her kids," adding,

"They're trying to portray her as someone who wanted police to kill her—which is a bold-face lie. She called them for help. They ended up coming and killing her."[10] Laurie Davis, Charleena's aunt, reflected on the disproportionate police killings of BIPOC people and said that she hoped Charleena's death could "be the one that's going to make a difference."[11] She added, "Charleena told me that she would make an impact on this world. And she's doing that now."[12]

AT THE TIME of her death, Charleena was living with her four children in permanent, supportive, Section 8 housing in one of the most scenic parts of Seattle, her children going to some of the best Seattle Public Schools, her daughter with Down syndrome likely receiving some of the best medical and developmental care at the nearby Seattle Children's Hospital. Sand Point is considered an area of high opportunity in terms of children living in poverty being able to move out of poverty by the time they are adults, having higher educational attainment and less involvement with the criminal justice system.[13] These data are part of the pilot study "Creating Moves to Opportunity in Seattle–King County," where local housing authorities work with families qualifying for the federal Housing Choice Voucher Program, still typically referred to as Section 8 housing, to support their moves to higher-opportunity areas.[14] In Charleena's case, Kent, where most of her extended family members were living, is a low-opportunity area, whereas Sand Point is a high-opportunity area. High-opportunity areas are not necessarily higher-income areas but typically have a combination of better-quality public schools, amenities like good public libraries, more two-parent households, and community cohesion, which all contribute to better life trajectories for children. There are criticisms of this research and data-driven policymaking, pointing out that they perpetuate the "white proximity model." "This implicit assumption portrays majority white places as high opportunity areas and further stigmatizes low-income communities of color while hiding the structural forces that perpetuate racial inequality."[15]

The area of Seattle where Charleena lived with her children, Sand Point, is a rare flat area in an otherwise hilly city. Sand Point is named for the Indigenous Sand People (ww-stahl-bahbsh), who called this place s-qw-sub, or fog, since that is a characteristic of the area at certain times of the year.[16] A peninsula on Lake Washington, an almost twenty-two-mile-long glacial ribbon lake, Sand Point was the site of the World War II–era Naval Air Station, Seattle. After the war, the area was converted to the 350-acre Warren G. Magnuson Park on the shores of Lake Washington, with sports fields, playgrounds, a swim area and boat dock, wetlands, community gardens, an off-leash dog park, and, on clear days, a magnificent view of snow-covered Mount Rainier to the southeast across the lake. The old naval base was converted to offices for local nonprofits and UW researchers, to low-income housing, and to housing for people escaping domestic violence and exiting homelessness. The low-income and supportive housing developments were controversial when they began in the mid-1990s because of the surrounding majority white and affluent neighborhoods of Windermere to the south and View Ridge to the west. It remains one of the rare affordable housing sites on the "Gold Coast" along the shores of Lake Washington.

BORN ON APRIL 24, 1987, in Seattle, the only child of Sadaria Teresa Sorrells and Charles Elden Lyles, Charleena grew up south of Seattle in King County with half-siblings and a large extended family, some of whom struggled with substance use disorders. Charles Lyles had a 1990 felony conviction in California related to crack cocaine, spent time in prison when Charleena was a young child, and failed to make child support payments to Charleena's mother. These facts disqualified him from being the personal representative of Charleena's estate after her death, an estate composed of donations people made to help support her burial and care of her children.[17] Charleena's mother suddenly died when Charleena was seventeen. According to her father, Charleena was devastated by the death, drifted around to live with various relatives, became homeless, and soon became a homeless mother. Her first stable home was the Sand Point apartment. Her father said of this, "She was so happy to get her own home."[18]

A closer look into Charleena's life leading up to her death reveals fracturing in the otherwise rosy picture of what appeared to be an improved and positive life trajectory for her and her children. After her death, relatives related Charleena's worsening mental status to the fact that she did not feel safe where she was living, not only due to the repeated physical and emotional abuse by the fathers of her children but also because she reported drug use, violence, and chaos among her neighbors in the housing units.[19] She told family members that she asked to be moved to another location or put in a domestic violence safe house, but such a move would jeopardize her permanent supportive housing status. "Leena had asked to move for domestic violence reasons," but nothing was ever done about it, according to Katrina Johnson, one of Charleena's Seattle cousins.[20] Even though she was dissatisfied with her housing, she also worried about being evicted and ending up homeless again with her children. This fear of recurrent homelessness is a powerful one for many formerly homeless people. In a recent nationally representative

at higher risk of professional boundary blurring.[23] If frontline staff members have unresolved traumas of their own, through their work they can attempt to resolve their traumas unconsciously through trauma mastery, returning to the site of trauma to try to "do it right this time."[24] Frequently, frontline staff members are paid so inadequately and have such poor access to comprehensive health care that they are precariously housed. In combination, this results in high rates of professional burnout and staff turnover, complicating the stability and recovery of their clients experiencing homelessness and housing insecurity.

CHARLEENA WAS WORRIED that Child Protective Services (CPS) would take custody of her children.[25] There were reports to CPS of neglect of all four of her children, but it is unclear who made these reports. It likely was mandatory reporters such as teachers, nurses, social workers, or police officers. For at least the year before her death, Charleena had been trying to convince her CPS caseworker that it was her abusive ex-boyfriend and not she who was the problem. In the summer of 2016, at the urging of police officers called to her home for repeated domestic violence incidents, Charleena obtained a no-contact and protection order against Franklin Camphor, the father of her youngest two children and the primary source of her ongoing abuse. In Charleena's court petition for the protection order, she revealed that Camphor had physically abused her for the past four of the eight years they had been together, beginning with her pregnancy with her youngest daughter.[26] She recounted that Camphor physically assaulted her when she was pregnant and soon after the birth of their son.[27] Camphor violated the no-contact order on July 30, 2016, and was arrested and jailed for ninety days.[28]

Charleena was attending weekly CPS-mandated family therapy sessions with her children. Of note, there is ongoing documentation of discriminatory child welfare practices in the United States, especially for Black mothers who live in poverty and homelessness.[29] As Alicia Gill, then director of research and program evaluation at YMCA of the USA, wrote of these issues, highlighted explicitly by the life and death of Charleena Lyles, "I am also disturbed by the racist, sexist, and ableist victim-blaming that Black women with mental illness should not have children, or that her children should have long been taken away. These kinds of comments have real historical contexts and are pain points for many Black women, who for so long had no legal control over our bodies."[30]

Charleena's family members talked of how distressing the ongoing domestic violence incidents, combined with fear of eviction, fear of becoming homeless again, and fear of having her children taken away by CPS, were for Charleena, and they pointed to all of this as precipitating her mental health crisis.[31] By December 2016, Solid Ground staff noted that Charleena was exhibiting decompensating behavior; by May 2017, they noted paranoid behavior.[32] Ashley Fontaine, with the National Alliance on Mental Illness in Seattle, highlighted the roles of poverty and racism as contributors to Charleena Lyles's struggles: "Poverty absolutely plays a role in developing mental illness." She added, "I think historical factors play a role. Racism is trauma." She also pointed out the difficulties African Americans have in finding culturally relevant mental health services.[33]

Fontaine is referring here to historical trauma, a type of intergenerational trauma experienced by groups of people who have historically been socially excluded and targets of systematic violence.[34] In the United States, this applies primarily, but not exclusively, to African Americans and Indigenous Americans, as well as Jews and Muslims. It also applies to immigrants and refugees fleeing discrimination and violence in their countries of origin. However, researchers point out the difference between historical trauma and the historical trauma response, which can vary significantly between individuals, families, and communities. They also highlight the often overlooked resiliency strategies, including the positive, strengths-based identities and cultural practices of many people and communities faced with adversities.[35]

THE REPUTEDLY EXCELLENT schools in Northeast Seattle that Charleena's children attended were sources of additional problems for Charleena and other BIPOC parents of children in the Sand Point housing units. In late May 2017, the school principal at Sand Point Elementary School called the police to complain that Charleena had verbally threatened her over the phone and in person. The principal had seen Charleena with her children—including the two older children, who were supposed to be in school—at a bus stop near the school and called CPS to report this incident. Charleena said she was taking her children to an appointment with CPS and was angry at the school principal for her actions, which she viewed as inappropriate and further jeopardizing her custody of her children.[36]

Both Sand Point Elementary School and the nearby View Ridge Elementary School are majority white schools in terms of staff members, teachers, and students. These schools are where many of the BIPOC children living in Sand Point low-income and shelter housing units are assigned. Not long after Charleena's death, the sole Black teacher at View Ridge Elementary School raised the issue of a Black second grader with autism and PTSD being repeatedly locked in an outdoor "cage" as punishment for his behavior.[37] Other students, teachers, and staff members walked by and saw him there throughout his school days. He lived with his mother in a domestic violence shelter at Sand Point housing. After an investigation by the Seattle Public Schools and a lawsuit by the child's mother against the school system, the school principal resigned. Three years later, the mother of this child complained that her son still was not receiving the education he deserved.[38] In response to this and other cases, the community-based advocacy group Families of Color Seattle pointed out the compounding difficulties of school children who are both BIPOC and living with a disability. In an opinion piece, they wrote, "This is an egregious example of the school-to-prison pipeline that criminalizes racialized disability."[39]

ON JUNE 5, 2017, police responded to a domestic violence call at Charleena's Sand Point apartment. By the time police officers arrived, the perpetrator had left the premises. Police officers reported that Charleena was sitting on the couch in her apartment holding a pair of twelve-inch metal scissors.[40] Police officers stated that Charleena made bizarre comments, such as that she was going to "morph into a wolf," that she wanted to clone her daughter, and that the officers were "devils and members of the KKK." Additional officers arrived, successfully de-escalating the situation and getting Charleena to drop the scissors. But instead of taking her for a psychiatric evaluation at a Crisis Solutions Center or an emergency department such as the one at Harborview Medical Center, where she was already a patient, the officers arrested her, charged her with harassment and obstruction of a public officer, and booked her into King County Jail, where she did not receive any mental health evaluation or treatment.[41] On June 9, when she complained of abdominal pain while jailed, she was evaluated at Harborview Medical Center's emergency department, where the health care provider described her as a "nontoxic individual," and an ultrasound documented her fourteen-week fetus.[42] Evidently, Charleena did not receive a thorough mental health evaluation while at Harborview, and the information about her recent decompensation and psychotic episodes was not related to the medical staff at the hospital.

Lyles had been in mental health counseling at least since moving to the Sand Point apartment in November 2015 and likely before then, although perhaps more sporadically. Charleena had diagnoses of PTSD, anxiety disorder, adjustment disorder, and depression.[43] She had been prescribed an antidepressant, but in the months leading up to her death she was not taking this medication, perhaps due to her fear of the medicine potentially causing congenital disabilities.[44] The fact that she had a child with Down syndrome who required constant supervision and care could have weighed into Charleena's decision not to take antidepressants.

Charleena's PTSD was most likely caused primarily by the repeated physical abuse and intimate partner violence she experienced. Intimate partner violence and sexual assault are among the most potent precipitating traumatic events associated with the development of PTSD symptoms, which include avoidance, numbing, hypervigilance, flashbacks, negative thoughts, and self-harming behaviors like drug use.[45] She had been seeing a therapist at Sound Mental Health and had previously undergone drug treatment for meth use through Valley Cities behavioral health.[46] It is unclear whether Charleena received evidence-based trauma-informed psychotherapy, the recommended treatment for PTSD.[47] A psychological autopsy of Charleena Lyles by Dr. Mark Whitehall, an expert witness in a wrongful death and negligence suit against the city by several of Charleena's family members, concluded that Charleena's mental health status had decompensated in the weeks and months before her killing and that she demonstrated emerging psychosis. He concluded that "she was in a psychotic state and did not have the capacity to assault [the officers] when she encountered police on June 18, 2017."[48]

During her last stay in King County Jail, on June 13, 2017, Charleena Lyles appeared in Mental Health Court. Her public defender, Ashwin Kumar, told the judge that he objected to how the police responded, saying, "She calls for help and she gets arrested. We think that's a big problem." The judge, noting Charleena's mental health and drug treatment histories and her recent interactions with police, recognized that her recent behavior seemed "like a crisis or break" and added, "But the fact that she's engaged in mental health treatment and this still happened causes me extreme concern."[49] The judge ordered that Charleena be released from jail the following day with contingencies. These contingencies included that she (1) not possess any weapons, (2) check in with the court's Day Reporting Program every Tuesday and Thursday, and (3) submit to random drug and alcohol testing.[50] Her next Mental Health Court appearance was scheduled for June 27. Four days after her release from jail, police officers shot and killed Charleena in her Sand Point apartment.

IN THE YEAR leading up to her death, Charleena Lyles had been under supervision by the Mental Health Court. Begun in 1999, the King County District Court Regional Mental Health Court is a therapeutic court "which aims to reduce recidivism and improve community safety by facilitating treatment for individuals with a mental health disorder involved in the criminal justice system." A recent outcome study of the impact of the King

County Mental Health Court indicates that it is effective in significantly reducing reoffending rates and psychiatric hospitalization and that participants have fewer emergency department visits and shorter incarceration times.[51] In retrospect, Charleena Lyles likely would have been better served by not being jailed for the June 5 incident, not being seen in Mental Health Court during that specific time, but instead taken to Harborview Medical Center for a seventy-two-hour psychiatric hold and evaluation since she was showing signs of decompensation and psychosis.[52] She might have received the inpatient psychiatric evaluation and treatment that could have stabilized her, thus avoiding her fatal interaction with the police.

An essential aspect of Charleena Lyles's life and death is the negative stereotyping, bias, and fear among the general public of people experiencing homelessness and people with apparent mental illness, especially for Black people and other people of color. Studies have found that people equate persons "appearing homeless" and persons "appearing to be mentally ill" with a higher propensity for violence.[53] Unbalanced and sensational media coverage often fuels these unfounded and hurtful biases and fears.[54] This fear, bias, and negative stereotyping likely contributed to the police killing of Lyles.

WHEN CHARLEENA WAS HOMELESS with her children, she probably stayed at one of the family shelters run by agencies such as Mary's Place, Catholic Community Services, or the YWCA. Through the HUD longitudinal Family Options Study, we know that emergency shelter is extremely expensive and is bad for families, especially for children's mental health, education, and development.[55] In addition, through the local Family Homelessness Systems Initiative, the older model of transitional housing with the goal of "housing readiness" services has been found to be ineffective.[56] The evidence-based goal now is to implement rapid rehousing, a subset of Housing First, for families experiencing homelessness, including domestic violence survivors. Also effective is family homeless prevention through legal and short-term financial support. In the Family Homelessness Systems Initiative, which included changes to the family homelessness system in King County beginning in 2012, families with four or more children, like Charleena's family, had more difficulty finding and maintaining permanent housing.[57]

Besides being oftentimes crowded, chaotic, and noisy, family emergency shelters increase stress on the parents, who are mainly mothers. Parenting can be challenging under the most ideal of circumstances. But parenting while homeless in a setting where mothers are constantly under surveillance by shelter staff, dubbed "parenting in public," is highly stressful, can contribute to mental health problems for mothers, and can lead to further family fragmentation.[58] This situation is a form of sanctuary trauma, where otherwise well-meaning people providing emergency shelter services can unintentionally retraumatize the people they are attempting to help.[59] This type of experience in homeless family shelters likely complicated Charleena's fears of her children being taken from her and worsened her mental health status.

Upon Charleena's death, her four children became wards of Washington State. When appropriate and with sufficient support services, kinship care is preferable to foster care for children since it maintains familial, sibling, and cultural bonds.[60] Francis Butts, the paternal grandmother to Charleena's two older children, "J" and "Q," took care of them after Charleena's death. The younger two children, "Za" and "Zy," by then both special needs children, including the daughter with Down syndrome, lived with one of Charleena's half-sisters. Katrina Johnson, a cousin of Charleena, told a reporter the month after Charleena's death, "There's been a division, two different sides of the family, about what should happen with the children. It's been hell, really."[61]

By November 2020, the Washington State Department of Children, Youth, and Families moved to have Charleena's oldest daughter, J, then age twelve, appointed by the court to be guardian ad litem. J decided that she and her three younger siblings would live with her paternal grandmother south of Seattle, even though this grandmother was not directly related to the younger two children.[62] Katrina Johnson, who became a de facto spokesperson for Charleena Lyles's family, advocated for all four children to be placed with a family member who had the children's best interests in mind. "Someone to take care and love those babies, and not because they see a payday in their future."[63] As of June 2022, Charleena's paternal aunt, Merry Kilpatrick, who lives in California, is raising Charleena's four children. This placement is likely important psychologically and developmentally, so that the children are raised together and away from Seattle to help give them some distance, at least physically, from reminders of their mother's violent death. As Charleena had and still has an extensive family network in Seattle, her family buried her on July 10, 2017, at Hillcrest Burial Park in Kent, Washington.[64]

CHARLEENA'S KILLING BY white SPD officers created an outcry, not only in Seattle but nationally and internationally.[65] From the rallies held soon after her death; through a Town Hall meeting of Seattle City Council with Charleena's family members and the general public at the UW's Kane Hall on June 27, 2017; to the summer 2020 CHAZ/CHOP protests, during which protestors and speakers frequently invoked her name—along with the numerous painted murals of Charleena's name and face on buildings throughout Seattle—people have not forgotten her name or her life or her death.[66]

"The name Charleena Lyles has become synonymous with a score of systemic issues, from mental health services to public housing to police training to racism."[67] Charleena was caught not so much in a safety net but in a confusing, tangled web of overlapping, disjointed, and too often broken systems and programs: Mercy Housing, Solid Ground, Catholic Community Services, YWCA, Mary's Place, King County Jail, Mental Health Court, Harborview Medical Center, Seattle Children's Hospital, Neighborcare Community Health Center's Housing and Homelessness Outreach Team, Valley Cities behavioral health, Sound Mental Health, Seattle Public Schools. A probable oasis for Charleena and her children in the midst of all these well-intentioned agencies and systems was the Seattle Public Libraries, as well as the support of her extended family. It is no wonder, then, that Charleena died with library cards and bus transfers in her coat pocket.

MICHELLE MERRIWEATHER, PRESIDENT and CEO of the Urban League of Metropolitan Seattle, said of Charleena Lyles during a panel on racism and homelessness in the summer of 2020, "Her death upended the city, complicating the police department's efforts to fulfill federally mandated reforms and seeding doubts that the SPD had made the progress it claimed."[68] The story of Charleena Lyles's killing by police officers contributed to the passage of the statewide Initiative 940, "Police Training and Accountability in Cases of Deadly Force Measure," in 2018.[69] This initiative reversed a thirty-two-year-old Washington State law, the most restrictive in the nation, that required proof of "evil intent" or "malice" by police officers in deadly encounters with people. The burden of proof was changed from malice to what a reasonable officer would do in the same circumstance and that the officer believed that deadly force was necessary. The initiative, the first of its kind in the nation, requires de-escalation and mental health training for all police officers, requires officers to administer first aid to victims, and requires independent investigations into the use of deadly force. Amendments in 2019 added antibias training for police officers. However, it is unclear whether this training includes homelessness and mental illness as specific too-common biases, along with biases toward race and ethnicity.

Unfortunately, when Charleena Lyles's case finally made it to a King County Coroner's inquest with a jury in the summer of 2022, it was investigated according to the old, pre–Initiative 940 law in effect when she was killed. Although a revised inquest process allowed for more involvement from Charleena's family and required the physical presence of the police officers, the jury found in favor of the two police officers who shot and killed Charleena.[70] In the aftermath of the inquest, Katrina Johnson said, "I'm just not sure it served any purpose but to traumatize my family." She added, "I just think a lot of families are going to get their hopes up, like we did, only to be let down, like we are."[71] Johnson, because of her advocacy work as a police reformer after her cousin's death, has been appointed to a commission overseeing the state police academy.

More encouraging was the outcome of the lawsuit for wrongful death brought against the City of Seattle and the two police officers who killed Charleena Lyles by lawyers representing Charleena Lyles's four children. Having been delayed owing to court battles and pushback from a powerful SPD police union, the lawyers for Charleena Lyles's family negotiated a $3.5 million settlement with the city before the case went to trial. At the lawyers' press conference on November 30, 2021, during which Charleena Lyles's two teenage children were present via Zoom, accompanied by their great aunt Merry Kilpatrick, Ed Moore, one of the lawyers, said of the police officers who killed Charleena, "There's three and a half million reasons why they were wrong—that's what our settlement really tells us."[72] Another lawyer, Karen Koehler, said of the settlement, "It's an acknowledgment for the family, especially for the children. It's a restoration of dignity. Those children need to know that their mother should not have died. She did nothing that should have led to her death. She should have received compassion. She should have received resources. She should have received assistance. She should not have received seven bullets in their presence." Charleena's eldest son said that while they appreciated the money from the settlement, "no amount of money will bring my mom back."

On the independent Black media group Converge's Morning Show after the settlement announcement, Omari Salisbury played footage of his prior interview with his mother, the activist and cofounder of Mothers for Police Accountability, Rev. Harriet Walden. Reverend Walden said that, even though she did not know Charleena personally, she felt as if Charleena could have been one of her daughters. She continued, "Ninety-seven pounds and the police couldn't figure out how not to kill her."[73] Salisbury added, "How do we respond to people in our community that are in crisis? Do we see their humanity the same? Do we see somebody who might be living in low-rent housing in a North Seattle apartment building the same as someone in an affluent neighborhood who might be having a mental health break?" Salisbury said he saw hope because many different people are working on solutions for "responding to the people most vulnerable in our community" and having better outcomes for community members and police officers. He pointed out that the story of Charleena Lyles hit home for so many people. "They saw a family member in Charleena Lyles. Seattle uplifted her name."

Notes

1. Marlin Appelwick, "Washington State Courts—Opinion No. 79480-9-1," December 30, 2019, https://www.courts.wa.gov/opinions/index.cfm?fa=opinions.showOpinion&filename=788191MAJ.
2. Appelwick, "Washington State Courts."
3. Gene Johnson and Phuong Le, "Seattle Police Shooting May Show Limits of Crisis Training," *Spokesman-Review*, June 21, 2017, https://www.spokesman.com/stories/2017/jun/21/seattle-police-shooting-may-show-limits-of-crisis-/.
4. "Charleena Lyles," Say Their Names Memorial, accessed July 3, 2022, https://www.saytheirnamesmemorials.com/charleena-lyles; Carla Bell, "Police, Power, Policy, and Privilege vs. The People: We're All Charleena Lyles," *Essence* (blog), updated November 18, 2020, https://www.essence.com/news/police-power-policy-and-privilege-vs-the-people-were-all-charleena-lyles/.
5. Sam Levin, "Seattle Insists It's a Model for Progressive Policing—so Why Was Charleena Lyles Killed?," sec. US news, *Guardian*, July 17, 2017, https://www.theguardian.com/us-news/2017/jul/17/seattle-police-model-charleena-lyles-killed.
6. Levin, "Seattle Insists It's a Model."
7. Associated Press and Phuong Le, "Family Members: Seattle Mom Killed by Police Adored Her Kids," *Vacaville Reporter*, June 24, 2017, https://www.thereporter.com/general-news/20170624/family-members-seattle-mom-killed-by-police-adored-her-kids.
8. Olivia Sullivan, "Poverty Bay Cafe Is Federal Way's Living Room—and Back Open for Business," *Federal Way Mirror*, June 23, 2021, https://www.federalwaymirror.com/news/poverty-bay-cafe-is-federal-ways-living-room-and-back-open-for-business/.
9. Daniel Beekman and Paige Cornwell, "Charleena Lyles Loved Her Children, Dancing and Fourth of July, Says Brother of Woman Killed

by Seattle Police," *Seattle Times*, June 19, 2017, https://www
.seattletimes.com/seattle-news/charleena-lyles-loved-her-children
-dancing-and-fourth-of-july-says-brother-of-woman-slain-by-seattle
-police/.

10. Associated Press and Le, "Family Members."
11. Sara Bernard, "'Murder Is Murder': Despite Reforms, Mourners Fear
Justice Will Be Elusive for Charleena Lyles," *Seattle Weekly*, June 21,
2017, https://www.seattleweekly.com/news/murder-is-murder
-despite-reforms-mourners-fear-justice-will-be-elusive-for-charleena
-lyles/.
12. Bernard, "'Murder Is Murder.'"
13. Emily Badger and Quoctrung Bui, "Detailed Maps Show How
Neighborhoods Shape Children for Life," *New York Times*, sec. The
Upshot, October 1, 2018, https://www.nytimes.com/2018/10/01
/upshot/maps-neighborhoods-shape-child-poverty.html.
14. "Creating Moves to Opportunity in Seattle–King County," Abdul Latif
Jameel Poverty Action Lab (J-PAL), accessed July 25, 2021, https://
www.povertyactionlab.org/evaluation/creating-moves-opportunity
-seattle-king-county.
15. Edward G. Goetz, "'Opportunity Areas' Shouldn't Just Be Places with
a Lot of White People," *Shelterforce* (blog), January 4, 2021, https://
shelterforce.org/2021/01/04/opportunity-areas-shouldnt-just-be
-places-with-a-lot-of-white-people/.
16. Coll Thrush, *Native Seattle: Histories from the Crossing-Over Place*,
2nd ed., Weyerhaeuser Environmental Books (Seattle: University of
Washington Press, 2017).
17. Sara Jean Green, "Father of Charleena Lyles Out as Representative of
Daughter's Estate in Probate Case," *Seattle Times*, November 2, 2017,
https://www.seattletimes.com/seattle-news/law-justice/father-of
-charleena-lyles-out-as-representative-of-daughters-estate-in
-probate-case/.
18. Associated Press and Le, "Family Members."
19. Tiana Smith, "Charleena Lyles (1987–2017)," BlackPast, March 11,
2018, https://www.blackpast.org/african-american-history/lyles
-charleena-1987-2017/.
20. Bell, "Police, Power, Policy."
21. Jack Tsai et al., "Is Homelessness a Traumatic Event? Results from
the 2019–2020 National Health and Resilience in Veterans Study,"

Depression and Anxiety 37, no. 11 (2020): 1137–45, https://doi.org/10
.1002/da.23098.

22. Lilly Fowler, "Who Was Charleena Lyles? Family, Court Records Paint Picture," Crosscut, July 8, 2017, https://crosscut.com/2017/07/charleena-lyles-funeral-seattle-family-speaks.

23. Laura van Dernoot Lipsky, *Trauma Stewardship: An Everyday Guide to Caring for Self While Caring for Others* (Oakland, CA: Berrett-Koehler, 2009); Jeannette Waegemakers Schiff and Annette M. Lane, "PTSD Symptoms, Vicarious Traumatization, and Burnout in Front Line Workers in the Homeless Sector," *Community Mental Health Journal* 55, no. 3 (April 1, 2019): 454–62, https://doi.org/10.1007/s10597-018-00364-7.

24. Lipsky, *Trauma Stewardship*.

25. Matthew Haag, "Fatal Police Shooting of Seattle Woman Raises Mental Health Questions," *New York Times*, sec. U.S., June 20, 2017, https://www.nytimes.com/2017/06/20/us/seattle-police-shooting-charleena-lyles.html.

26. Fowler, "Who Was Charleena Lyles?"

27. Appelwick, "Washington State Courts."

28. Steve Miletich, "Charleena Lyles Had Long Turned to Seattle Police for Help before Fatal Confrontation," *Seattle Times*, August 27, 2017, https://www.seattletimes.com/seattle-news/law-justice/charleena-lyles-had-long-turned-to-seattle-police-for-help-before-fatal-confrontation/.

29. Erin Cloud, Rebecca Oyama, and Lauren Teichner, "Family Defense in the Age of Black Lives Matter," *CUNY Law Review Footnote Forum* 20 (March 3, 2017): 27.

30. Alicia Gill, "Charleena Lyles: Ableism, Racism, and Gendered Violence," *YWCA USA* (blog), June 22, 2017, https://www.ywca.org/blog/2017/06/22/charleena-lyles-ableism-racism-and-gendered-violence/.

31. Fowler, "Who Was Charleena Lyles?"

32. Appelwick, "Washington State Courts."

33. Fowler, "Who Was Charleena Lyles?"

34. Stefanie L. Gillson and David A. Ross, "From Generation to Generation: Rethinking 'Soul Wounds' and Historical Trauma," *Biological Psychiatry* 86, no. 7 (2019): e19–20, https://doi.org/10.1016/j.biopsych.2019.07.033.

35. Aaron R. Denham, "Rethinking Historical Trauma: Narratives of Resilience," *Transcultural Psychiatry* 45, no. 3 (2008): 391–414, https://doi.org/10.1177/1363461508094673; Gillson and Ross, "From Generation to Generation"; Nena Močnik et al., *Engaging with Historical Traumas: Experiential Learning and Pedagogies of Resilience* (Milton Park: Taylor & Francis Group, 2021); Josephine Ensign, *Soul Stories: Voices from the Margins,* Perspectives in Medical Humanities (San Francisco: University of California Medical Humanities Press, 2018).
36. Miletich, "Charleena Lyles."
37. Ann Dornfeld, "Locked in 'the Cage.' Report Finds Disturbing Discipline Measures at Seattle School," KUOW, December 5, 2020, https://www.kuow.org/stories/locked-in-the-cage-report-finds -disturbing-discipline-measures-at-seattle-school.
38. Deborah Horne, "Mother Says Seattle Schools Failing Her Special Needs Son 3 Years after He Was Placed in Cage," KIRO 7 News Seattle, July 11, 2022, https://news.yahoo.com/mother-says-seattle -schools-failing-031133651.html.
39. Families of Color Seattle, "No More Black and Brown Children in Cages: The Reality of Racism and Ableism in SPS Today," South Seattle Emerald, December 11, 2020, https://southseattleemerald .com/2020/12/11/55545/.
40. Miletich, "Charleena Lyles."
41. Appelwick, "Washington State Courts."
42. Appelwick, "Washington State Courts."
43. Appelwick, "Washington State Courts."
44. Bell, "Police, Power, Policy."
45. "PTSD and *DSM-5*," National Center for PTSD, accessed July 27, 2022, https://www.ptsd.va.gov/professional/treat/essentials/dsm5 _ptsd.asp.
46. Fowler, "Who Was Charleena Lyles?"
47. "PTSD and *DSM-5*," National Center for PTSD.
48. Appelwick, "Washington State Courts."
49. Fowler, "Who Was Charleena Lyles?"
50. Appelwick, "Washington State Courts."
51. "Welcome to the King County District Court Regional Mental Health Court," King County, accessed July 17, 2022, https://kingcounty.gov /courts/district-court/regional-mental-health-court.aspx.

52. Appelwick, "Washington State Courts."

53. Jo C. Phelan and Bruce G. Link, "Fear of People with Mental Ill-nesses: The Role of Personal and Impersonal Contact and Exposure to Threat or Harm," *Journal of Health and Social Behavior* 45, no. 1 (March 2004): 68–80, https://doi.org/10.1177/002214650404500105; Marcus Harrison Green, "How I Survived the Collision of Racism and the Stigma of Mental Illness," South Seattle Emerald, October 2, 2020, https://southseattleemerald.com/2020/10/02/how-i-survived -the-collision-of-racism-and-the-stigma-of-mental-illness/; Fiona Cuthill, *Homelessness, Social Exclusion and Health: Global Perspectives, Local Solutions*, Policy and Practice in Health and Social Care (Edinburgh: Dunedin Academic Press, 2019).

54. "Housing, Equity, and Health in U.S. News, 2020–2021: Findings and Recommendations," Berkeley Media Studies Group, July 6, 2022, https://www.bmsg.org/resources/publications/housing-equity-and -health-in-u-s-news-2020-2021-findings-and-recommendations/; Deborah Padgett, "Opinion: Outrage and Fear about Homelessness Never Seem to Lead to the Obvious Choice," CNN, April 11, 2022, https://www.cnn.com/2022/04/11/opinions/homelessness-solutions -mental-health-new-york-city-padgett/index.html.

55. Daniel Gubits et al., "What Interventions Work Best for Families Who Experience Homelessness? Impact Estimates from the Family Options Study," *Journal of Policy Analysis and Management* 37, no. 4 (September 2018): 835–66, https://doi.org/10.1002/pam.22071; Daniel Gubits et al., *Family Options Study: 3-Year Impacts of Housing and Services Interventions for Homeless Families* (Washing-ton, DC: Office of Policy Development and Research, US Department of Housing and Urban Development, October 2016), https://www .huduser.gov/portal/sites/default/files/pdf/family-options-study-full -report.pdf.

56. Debra J. Rog et al., "Evaluation of the Family Homelessness Systems Initiative: Examining the Effects of Systems Reform on 18-Month Housing Stability and Related Outcomes" (prepared for the Bill and Melinda Gates Foundation, February 2021).

57. Rog et al., "Evaluation."

58. Donna Haig Friedman, *Parenting in Public: Family Shelter and Public Assistance* (New York: Columbia University Press, 2000); Denise M. Zabkiewicz, Michelle Patterson, and Alexandra Wright, "A

Cross-Sectional Examination of the Mental Health of Homeless Mothers: Does the Relationship between Mothering and Mental Health Vary by Duration of Homelessness?," *BMJ Open* 4, no. 12 (2014): e006174–e006174, https://doi.org/10.1136/bmjopen-2014 -006174.

59. "What Is Sanctuary Trauma?," Steve Rose PhD, December 3, 2014, https://steverosephd.com/sanctuary-trauma-and-the-sacred/.

60. Rob Geen, *Kinship Care: Making the Most of a Valuable Resource* (Washington, DC: Urban Institute Press, 2003).

61. Bell, "Police, Power, Policy."

62. Bell, "Police, Power, Policy."

63. Bell, "Police, Power, Policy."

64. KUOW staff, "Judge Dismisses Claims against Two Seattle Police Officers in Charleena Lyles Case," KUOW, January 9, 2019, https:// www.kuow.org/stories/king-county-judge-dismisses-charleena-lyles -lawsuit-against-two-police-officers.

65. Haag, "Fatal Police Shooting"; "Police Officers Shoot and Kill Pregnant Black Woman after She Reports Burglary," *Independent*, June 19, 2017, https://www.independent.co.uk/news/world/americas /charleena-lyles-seattle-shooting-pregnant-black-mother-of-four -brettler-family-place-a7797971.html.

66. Teddi Beam-Conroy, "'Speaking Power to Power': Women of Color Take Lead at Charleena Lyles' Town Hall," South Seattle Emerald, July 3, 2017, https://southseattleemerald.com/2017/07/03/speaking -power-to-power-women-of-color-take-lead-at-charleena-lyles-town -hall/.

67. David Kroman, "'Charleena Lyles'—Still Saying Her Name a Year after Fatal Shooting," Crosscut, June 18, 2018, https://crosscut.com /2018/06/charleena-lyles-still-saying-her-name-year-after-fatal -shooting.

68. Kroman, "'Charleena Lyles.'"

69. Steve Miletich, "Initiative 940, Modifying Law Regulating Police Use of Deadly Force, Passes with Strong Support," *Seattle Times*, November 6, 2018, https://www.seattletimes.com/seattle-news/politics /initiative-940-modifying-law-regulating-police-use-of-deadly-force -holds-strong-lead-in-tuesdays-returns/.

70. Vee Hua, "Summary of Inquest Hearings into the SPD Shooting of Charleena Lyles," South Seattle Emerald, updated July 7, 2022,

https://southseattleemerald.com/2022/06/30/summary-of-inquest
-hearings-into-the-spd-shooting-of-charleena-lyles/.

71. Mike Carter, "Transparency vs. Trauma: Are Inquests into King
County Killings by Police Worthwhile?," *Seattle Times*, August 21,
2022, https://www.seattletimes.com/seattle-news/law-justice/public
-disclosure-vs-family-trauma-are-inquests-into-king-county-killings
-by-police-worthwhile/.

72. KING 5 Seattle, "LIVE: Family of Charleena Lyles Discusses Wrongful Death Settlement," YouTube video, 2021, https://www.youtube
.com/watch?v=dDcC_R268PQ.

73. Converge, "Morning Update Show | Wednesday, December 1, 2021,"
YouTube video, 2021, https://www.youtube.com/watch?v
=XwLXGn4WxdY.

study of post-traumatic stress disorder (PTSD) in veterans, many of whom had seen active combat, homelessness was the most prevalent lifetime "worst" traumatic event of those who had experienced homelessness.[21] Researchers concluded that homelessness itself should be considered a precipitating event or situation from which PTSD symptoms can arise.

Charleena complained about her Sand Point apartment being too far from her extended family support network in Kent, outside of Seattle in South King County. Although these two areas are only eighteen miles apart, Charleena traveled by public transit, which would take close to two hours, an arduous trip with small children, one of whom had Down syndrome. Charleena told relatives that she was afraid she would be evicted from her housing owing to the frequent domestic violence incidents and property damage from her ex-boyfriends. As typically happens with permanent supportive housing for people exiting homelessness, her apartment complex was managed by one nonprofit agency, in this case, Mercy Housing, and the supportive services were provided by another nonprofit, Solid Ground. Leading up to Charleena's death, Solid Ground was experiencing leadership difficulties. The agency had been undergoing staff turnover in case managers, and the two mental health specialists were spread out over multiple Solid Ground housing units across the city.[22]

These difficulties are not unique to Solid Ground. Frontline workers in homelessness and supportive housing programs are overworked, are underpaid, and deal with cumulative vicarious or secondary trauma from hearing and witnessing the stories of clients with whom they work. In addition, many people are drawn to this type of work because of their own lived experience of homelessness and other traumas, a fact that can contribute to them having higher levels of empathy but also can place them

Leaf of remembrance for Lisa Vach (1982–2000), June 2022.
Source: Photo by author.

Cal Anderson Park encampment, December 2020.
Source: Photo by Peter Kahn.

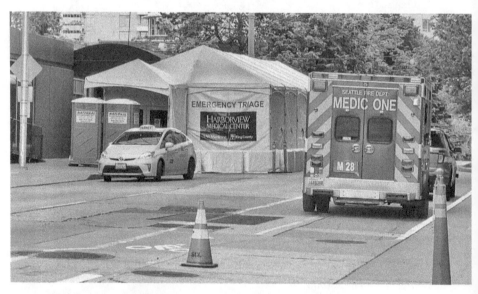

Harborview Medical Center, COVID-19 triage, May 2020.
Source: Photo by author.

Charleena Lyle's image, Pioneer Square, May 2020.
Source: Photo by author.

City Hall Park, June 2022.
Source: Photo by author.

Tree of Life, Victor Steinbrueck Park, November 2022.
Source: Photo by author.

Tent City 3 at the University of Washington, February 2023.
Source: Photo by author.

Vehicle resident, Bryant neighborhood, November 2022.
Source: Photo by author.

Doorway Café pop-up event, University Heights Center,
February 2018.
Source: Photo by author.

Leaves of remembrance rededication, University District,
April 2023.
Source: Photo by author.

CHAPTER 5

Contesting Spaces

. . . .

> *Compassion becomes real when we recognize our
> shared humanity.*
>
> —PEMA CHODRON, *THE PLACES THAT SCARE YOU:
> A GUIDE TO FEARLESSNESS IN DIFFICULT TIMES*

FRIDAY, AUGUST 13, 2021, dawned oppressive in Seattle, after the area's hottest overnight temperature on record, with yet more thick, gray smoke from wildfires raging nearby in British Columbia, spreading what local newscasters and spokespersons from the American Lung Association called a "toxic stew" of unhealthy-for-all haze.[1] Bright yellow "Police Line Do Not Cross" tape cordoned off the perimeter of the small, flatiron-shaped City Hall Park in Pioneer Square. Several Seattle police officers and REACH outreach workers through the coordinating group JustCARE stood inside the tape in the park, and the mutual-aid protestors from Stop the Sweeps Seattle yelled "Fuck the Sweeps!" and anti-police slogans from the sidewalks outside the police tape. Outreach workers attempted to explain to the angry protestors what they were doing, but the atmosphere was not conducive to a constructive conversation.[2]

A group of SPD bicycle patrol unit officers circled the park, keeping the mutual-aid protestors and onlookers away from the now grassless, compacted dirt park mostly emptied of tents and people's belongings. That morning, amid the choking smoke, baking heat, and presence of police officers, social workers, and angry protestors, only three bewildered-looking homeless people remained in the park. The REACH workers offered these people shelter and assisted them in moving out before city park workers cleaned the area and barricaded the entire park with six-foot-tall temporary chain-link fencing. Bright red signs affixed to the fence stated, "Park Temporarily Closed."

"This is not a sweep. This is not a removal. This is not a clearing. This is the opposite: taking the time needed to make meaningful offers of shelter and support to people based on their actual needs and situations, while respecting individual self-determination," declared a written statement from JustCARE. JustCARE is an alliance of organizations with city and county funding working on community-based solutions to address the increase in people living unsheltered in Seattle due to the COVID-19 pandemic. Their statement was issued the day before the city closed City Hall Park, the site of a large homeless encampment of numerous tents and tarps sheltering up to seventy people. Over the previous six weeks, outreach workers through JustCARE had connected sixty-five people living in City Hall Park with housing, including in tiny house villages, hotels, and enhanced 24/7 shelters. The three people who remained living in the park the morning of its closure included a woman with severe mental health issues, a man who had repeatedly refused all help from outreach team members, and a young man who had shown up at the camp overnight and who did not realize what was going on.[3]

Notices from the city attached to light poles in the park and on the Seattle Parks and Recreation website read, "City Hall Park is closed effective Friday, August 13 at 9:00 A.M. until 8:00 A.M. Tuesday, October 12, as per emergency action SMC 3.02.050 to address significant public health and safety issues at the site."[4] The public health concerns included overcrowding and lack of adequate sanitation, especially in light of the then Delta variant surge in COVID-19 infections, hospitalizations, and deaths in Seattle and King County, as in many parts of the United States. Safety concerns included frequent fights, fires, overdoses, harassment of people who work in the King County Courthouse, and high-profile violent crimes in the area, including attempted rapes, stabbings, robberies, and beatings. The cleanup of the park had begun earlier in the week, with Seattle Parks officials teaming up with city sanitation workers to remind people of the impending closure and to cart away the detritus of people's existence lived in the shadow of the fourteen-story King County Courthouse. City officials said that the police presence at the City Hall Park cleanup was due to the likelihood of protestors blocking the cleanup. Leading up to the final encampment sweep at Cal Anderson Park in mid-December 2020, Stop the Sweeps protestors barricaded off the encampment using metal fencing, furniture, and wooden pallets, threw rocks at police officers, and intentionally set an unoccupied tent on fire.[5] Police responded with flash-bang devices and rubber bullets, showing up in full riot gear as they had during CHAZ/CHOP.[6] City officials did not want a repeat of such events.

Along with the homeless encampment in Cal Anderson Park, where Lisa Vach and Travis Berge lived and died, the City Hall

Park encampment grew to be one of the largest, most highly visible, and most controversial in the city. People removed from other encampments around the city by sweeps or who had been staying in the now permanently closed two-hundred-person shelter at DESC across the street from the King County Courthouse frequently made their way to City Hall Park. Volunteers with Stop the Sweeps Seattle visited the park regularly. They brought food and basic supplies to the encampment residents, as they had done for Lisa and Travis and other homeless people at the Cal Anderson Park encampment in the summer and fall of 2020. Various faith-based groups offered similar feeding programs in the park, with subtle or not-so-subtle proselytizing and without the socialist activism of Stop the Sweeps. JustCARE leaders pointed out that the increase in people living unsheltered in Seattle and King County was, and continues to be, due to "de-intensification of shelters and jails, closure of publicly accessible spaces, economic stress, and retreat of the behavioral health service world to remote access." All of these factors came together on that August day in that particular and otherwise nondescript parcel of land in the heart of Seattle's original settler-colonial section.

LONG A CONTESTED and controversial space, City Hall Park bears remnants of its layers of stories, whose murmurs are discernible today for those who listen. This particular land was first the heavily cedar- and fir-forested ancestral land of the Coast Salish Duwamish People, before being deforested by the early white settlers, especially by sawmill owner Henry Yesler, whose sawmill lay on Elliott Bay at the terminus of what is now Yesler Way. During the brief Battle of Seattle in January 1856, when Indians from neighboring tribes attacked the settlers because Indigenous land was being taken from them, a map of the settlement of Seattle drawn by Captain Thomas Stowell Phelps of the USS *Decatur* marked this area "Hills and Woods Thronged with Indians."[7] The land had a stream running through it, providing fresh water to the settlers and Native people and emptying into a large lagoon on the bay, a swampy area eventually filled in with sawdust from Yesler's Mill. Cannonballs from the USS *Decatur* involved in the Battle of Seattle were unearthed near City Hall Park during the construction of Interstate 5, which ran through and divided Seattle beginning in the late 1950s. In the corner of the park today lies a commemorative plaque with a cannonball from the 1856 battle for control of the area.

The land where City Hall Park is located was fought over in other, rather bizarre ways. Three early white homesteaders, David Swinson Maynard, Arthur Armstrong Denny, and Carsen Dobbins Boren, disagreed on the platting of the first dirt streets in Seattle. Whereas the teetotalling Methodist Arthur Denny and Carsen Boren, King County's first sheriff, laid out roads on their land to be parallel with the waterfront, the more scientific and whisky-loving Doc Maynard insisted on a street grid running with the cardinal points of the compass. Yesler's Mill Street, renamed Yesler Way, and roughly the site of a long-established Indian trail from Elliott Bay to Lake Washington, became the dividing line between those opposing street grids. Where the grids clashed, to the north of Yesler Way, which was controlled by Denny and Boren, strange triangular parcels of land, like neatly fracturing fault lines, emerged, including the land that became City Hall Park. It is called City Hall Park because it was the site of the second city-owned City Hall, jail, and police station, housed in a wonky building nicknamed the Katzenjammer Castle for its resemblance to a building designed by an architect with a hangover and for a popular comic strip of the time. The building had been the former King County Court-house, King County sheriff's office, and county jail.

City Hall Park opened in 1913 as a grassy park of 1.3 acres with some bushes and small trees. As proposed by the Seattle City Council, its first name was Oratory Park, but progressives opposed the name, thinking that it was an effort by government officials to limit free speech to just the park. During that time, people with the radical, socialist labor union Industrial Workers of the World (IWW), or "Wobblies," gave frequent open-air speeches and recruited new members in the nearby Skid Road area of Seattle south of Yesler Way.[8] Their speeches competed with Christian proselytizers, including members of the Salvation Army, who called on people to repent of their sins, quit drinking alcohol, and stop using opium or morphine, as well as for girls and women to stop being involved in prostitution. The Salvation Army still operates a day center on the northern edge of the park, and they still emphasize sobriety.[9] Yesler Way was the original dividing line, called a dead-line, in Seattle, with most saloons, brothels, and cheap lodging hotels purposefully located south of the street in what is now Pioneer Square. More respectable businesses and homes were located north of the dead-line.[10]

When City Hall moved into the 400 Yesler Building on the park's eastern edge and the King County Courthouse was built north of the park, the area was called Court House Square, with the land owned by King County. In 1890, the county sold the park to the city. There is a long history in Seattle of land and building swaps and shares between city and county governments, with City Hall Park being one such space.

IN ECHOES OF GROUPS today with opposing views on what should constitute help or aid or advocacy for people experiencing poverty and homelessness, mutual-aid groups that thrived during the Great Depression in Seattle emphasized the need for solidarity among the working class, the impoverished, and those experiencing homelessness. They eschewed reliance on either government aid or charity from faith-based and other nongovernmental aid organizations, calling them "handouts." Mutual-aid groups had their roots in Marxist socialist ideology and were anti-capitalist, pro-union proponents of working-class rights and anti-poverty work. Although there was always pushback against their work and the work of the influential Communist Party from more pro-business and politically conservative people in Seattle, the area and the state were leftist enough for US postmaster general James A. Farley to refer, in a speech in 1936, to "the forty-seven states in the Union and the soviet of Washington."[11]

Currently, there is an active Seattle branch of the IWW. Socialist Alternative member Kshama Sawant has been on the Seattle City Council since 2014 but is not seeking reelection in November 2023. Sawant was a vocal proponent of passage of the $15-per-hour minimum wage, increasing tenant rights, and securing funding for non-incarceration alternatives for youth involved with the criminal justice system. An ardent advocate of taxing Amazon, Sawant was involved in the passage in 2020 of the Jumpstart Seattle payroll tax for big businesses, a tax they now pay for their Seattle-based employees making more than $150,000 a year. Initially, 62% of the Jumpstart tax revenue was earmarked for new affordable housing, but some of the money has been diverted into ongoing pandemic relief efforts.[12]

During the Great Depression, the park was used for frequent rallies of the unemployed, as well as for hunger marches. For close to a week starting on April 4, 1939, after Governor Clarence Martin announced his austerity program and people lost welfare and food benefits, activists erected a large white tent on the park lawn with a sign that read "Governor Martin's Starvation Camp 2."[13] Inside were benches and tables, and the activists planned to erect a second tent for free food distribution. Seattle mayor Arthur B. Langlie ordered the tent removed, so protestors moved it a few feet onto the King County Courthouse property. King County commissioners reportedly were more sympathetic to the protestors because they had just received a 45% state cut to the county's welfare department and were forced to drop 13,214 people from the relief rolls.[14]

The semiflat area of City Hall Park has been a battleground and has witnessed political, social, and even violent conflicts. It became the WWII drill grounds for the Seattle Air Defense Wing Fighter Command troops. In 1993, city officials closed the park for relandscaping and activation to rid the park of its reputation as "Muscatel Meadows" for the open consumption of cheap fortified wine by park frequenters.[15] The shrubbery and lower limbs of trees were removed, and more lighting was added. Activation is a thinly veiled message of inviting the presence of desirable people doing nice, civil, and legal activities and excluding all others.[16] "Activation" is an urban planning term for attempts to revitalize public spaces.

Different city laws over the years have attempted to curtail the sale of fortified wine, like Wild Irish Rose, Night Train, and Thunderbird (the latter two are no longer made), and malt liquor in "alcohol impact areas" like Pioneer Square, and they have had mixed results in curbing public intoxication.[17] Since 1990, a series of so-called civility laws have been enacted in Seattle, including the drug traffic loitering law and the Stay Out of Drug Area (SODA) orders, modeled after the existing Stay Out of Areas of Prostitution (SOAP) orders. People under a SODA or SOAP order are excluded from specified areas of the city.[18] Despite complaints that these laws disproportionately affect BIPOC people, they remain in effect in Seattle.[19]

Exclusion laws like these affect not only people living unsheltered, as in the City Hall Park encampment, but also people staying in traditional overnight shelters that close during the day, leaving people to rely on public spaces like parks and libraries, or riding public transit. In 1997, Seattle enacted a parks exclusion ordinance. Before the passage of this ordinance, people could be removed from public parks only if police had probable cause of a criminal offense. Minor violations like littering, urinating, possessing an open container of alcohol, or being present in a park after posted hours resulted in citations. The new law allowed police officers and uniformed park rangers to immediately remove people from city parks and officially ban them from some or all city parks for up to a year.[20]

As sociologist Katherine Beckett and geographer Steve Herbert state, these laws resulted in larger areas of urban space "delimited as zones of exclusion from which the undesirable are banned."[21] They term this "banishment" in a nod to the banishing of paupers from parishes and localities under the English Poor Laws adapted by the thirteen colonies and then in the expanding US states and territories, including what became Washington State. Banishment keeps people from accessing essential health and social support services and disproportionately affects BIPOC populations. The year after the implementation of the parks exclusion law, an ACLU report showed that 45% of people who were issued parks exclusion orders were persons of color, and 42% were homeless.[22] Many people issued parks exclusion notices from city parks were excluded from City Hall Park and Victor Steinbrueck Park adjacent to Pike Place Market, a longtime gathering place for Indigenous people and called "Native

Park" even then by Native American residents. Officials justified the parks exclusion ordinance by saying that people were banned from parks but not arrested, thus keeping more people with low-level, nonviolent offenses out of the criminal justice system.

HEALTH, SOCIAL, AND LEGAL services utilized by single adults experiencing chronic homelessness are concentrated downtown around City Hall Park. When people are banned from the park, either they risk being arrested if they return there, or they have to avoid the area and have breaks in needed services. The park is surrounded by a myriad of agencies providing services for the large number of single homeless adults with chronic physical and behavioral health issues. Besides the King County Courthouse and the adjacent City of Seattle Courthouse with its Mental Health Court and Drug Court, DESC's Morrison Hotel is across Third Avenue to the west of the park, the Salvation Army's day center and shelter is across Fourth Avenue to the east, and the 234-room low-income housing in the historic Frye Hotel is across Yesler Way. Nearby are the Lazarus Center, Chief Seattle Club's day shelter and new permanent supportive housing, and Harborview Medical Center's Pioneer Square Clinic. City Hall and the King County Jail are just blocks away to the park's northeast. The Pioneer Square light-rail station is across the street next to the Morrison.

Adjacent to the underground station entrance is an even smaller triangular-shaped scrap of land, set aside originally for a public library. The land was too small for this purpose, so the city built Prefontaine Place there in 1925, named in honor of Father Prefontaine, who served as the priest for Seattle's first Catholic church. Large stone benches are situated in a U shape around what was originally a large, round fountain, lined with blue tiles and now waterless. It currently functions as a trash receptacle and unofficial public urinal, the area long the site of open-air drug dealing.

In interviews with people affected by the parks exclusion ordinance, Beckett and Herbert noted that many people spoke about how being excluded, no matter the length of time or location of their exclusion, negatively affected their self-esteem and feeling of belonging. Several of their Black and Native American interviewees pointed out how this ordinance compounds the racism, especially from Seattle police officers, they had already experienced.

THE CITY HALL PARK encampment began as a small and largely peaceful one in the early days of the pandemic in the spring of 2020. But as the pandemic dragged on and encampment sweeps increased throughout the city, the encampment at City Hall Park grew in size and conditions deteriorated. Outreach teams from many homeless serving agencies, nonprofits like DESC, and city-contracted agencies frequently visit parks and other encampment sites to build relationships with encampment residents and to try to link them with shelter options and other needed services. In the wake of the CHAZ/CHOP protests in the summer of 2020, the Seattle City Council not only terminated the city's Navigation Team but also voted to cut almost 20% of the SPD's budget in 2021. With budget constraints caused by the economic fallout of the ongoing COVID-19 pandemic, city council members made significant budget cuts to the Department of Transportation and the Department of Parks and Recreation. Cuts to the latter contributed to increased maintenance problems in city parks, including City Hall Park. Uniformed park rangers, tasked with helping to "enhance the safety and quality of life in Seattle's downtown parks" and who issue Parks Trespass Warnings and Exclusions, had positions and hours cut.[23] The City Council made increased investments in low-income housing, city-funded shelter options, BIPOC-community-led development projects, and COVID-19 response efforts. In addition, they created and funded the Homelessness Outreach and Provider Ecosystem (HOPE) Team.

Just three blocks from City Hall Park is the sixty-two-story Seattle Municipal Tower, where the HOPE Team coordinates efforts by collaborating with agencies' outreach teams like REACH, shelter providers, and city departments like Parks and Recreation to connect people living unsheltered in encampments and in vehicles to services and shelter. The HOPE Team does not do outreach and does not conduct homeless encampment clearances, but rather matches unsheltered people whom other agencies' outreach team members screen with shelter bed options. The team has access to set-aside shelter resources, representing 30% of all city-funded shelter beds. Outreach workers engage with and screen people living in encampments and vehicles for their identified needs and preferences for shelter. People are prioritized for shelter based on identified vulnerability characteristics, similar to the Vulnerability Index used by DESC staff, and people living in "high-priority areas" slated by the city for encampment removal are given priority for shelter beds leading up to the sweep.

This priority for shelter was implemented during the clearance of the homeless encampment in City Hall Park, before the park was closed and fenced off. Before she left office at the beginning of 2022, the then mayor Jenny Durkan proposed moving the HOPE Team to the Seattle Parks and Recreation department.[24] The city retained control over the HOPE Team even as the newly formed King County Regional Homelessness

Authority came into existence. People from the Seattle Human Services Department point to the US Ninth Circuit *Martin v. Boise* ruling and maintain that if the city gave up the HOPE Team, the city would be at risk of violating such rules over encampment removals in the absence of adequate shelter options for people.[25]

How well the HOPE Team works in practice is unclear, and the answer depends on who is asked, for what time period, and which encampment is under consideration. Stop the Sweeps Seattle activists often complain on social media that these outreach and housing efforts are viewed by many unsheltered people as coercive, ineffective, and violent, and they say that people are "slated for displacement by the State."[26] In a 2022 report by the HOPE Team, 1,072 people were referred through them to shelters in 2021, and of those, 512 people showed up and stayed at least one night at the shelter within forty-eight hours of the referral.[27] Cutting through competing groups' rhetoric, people living in encampments or vehicles oftentimes form community, behavioral health, and social service connections that are strained if not broken when they move into the various housing options.

IN THE FALL OF 2020, with the surge of COVID-19 cases causing continued disruptions and deaths locally, public sentiment began to sour on the city's tolerance of visible homelessness, especially for tent encampments in public parks, on public sidewalks, and even on school property. A large sixty-plus-person encampment grew on the shores of Bitter Lake in North Seattle adjacent to Broadview Thomson K–8 School. Residents and parents of schoolchildren, especially once some in-person teaching and team sports resumed in the fall of 2021, complained of the continued presence of this encampment. Mayor Durkan refused to provide city assistance, saying that the encampment was on school property, so it was the responsibility of Seattle Public Schools.[28] The School Board, in a well-intentioned if misguided decision, contracted with the newly formed and unvetted non-profit Anything Helps, run by Mike Mathias. He used his previous experience of homelessness as a way to gain the $20,000 contract. The contracted services did not go smoothly. In late 2021, the city finally stepped in with outreach workers and the HOPE Team to find alternative shelter for most of the residents, and the encampment was cleared in early December.[29]

An additional volunteer community group, We Heart Seattle, emerged during the early months of the pandemic. We Heart Seattle began in the summer of 2020 as a one-woman enterprise called I Heart Seattle by Andrea Suarez, a resident of a Belltown condominium in downtown Seattle. Andrea Suarez, a woman with a bachelor's degree in food science, calls herself a case manager, even though she is not, despite being publicly criticized for doing so. The We Heart Seattle website describes their organization as "an action-based movement to making Seattle beautiful and safe for all."[30] They regularly fundraise and organize volunteer groups to go into homeless encampments and remove the trash. They claim that "cleaning up our public spaces is inevitably intertwined with homelessness, drug addiction, crime, gridlocked politics and questionable policy." In media interviews, Suarez is openly disdainful of the "homelessness industrial complex" and appears to misrepresent herself on purpose, claiming to be more effective than real case managers.[31] She calls herself "the energizer bunny of volunteerism in Seattle" and claims that her group does not enable people with "free housing," adding, "Let's get back to work. I believe that housing is earned." She also stated that "mutual aid got mad at me."[32]

Suarez was referring to a series of encounters both in person and on social media between her group of volunteers and volunteers with Stop the Sweeps Seattle.[33] De facto leaders of Stop the Sweeps accused Suarez and her group of destroying people's belongings at encampments, deeming the belongings trash, and of coercing people into an abstinence-only, $250-per-month inpatient treatment facility near Portland, Oregon, operated by the board president of We Heart Seattle. There is an interesting similarity between people like Suarez claiming to be a case manager despite not having any training and mutual-aid workers who eschew formal training for social work or health care work and attempt to take on those roles. The public conflict between We Heart Seattle and Stop the Sweeps Seattle highlights the fact that people use the issue of homelessness to further their ideological causes across the socioeconomic spectrum and, in effect, enact their own versions of social control over people marginalized by poverty and homelessness.

After the August 2021 clearing of the City Hall Park encampment, Karen Salinas, director of REACH, spoke about the disagreement between their outreach workers and activists with Stop the Sweeps Seattle. She pointed out that REACH has worked with several different mutual-aid groups, adding, "But that also takes a lot of alignment and recognizing, you know, what do we bring to the table as service providers? What do they bring to the table as community members? And how do we do this together? Because if we're constantly at odds, the people who miss out are our clients."[34]

EMERGING IN 2020 IN SEATTLE, a group composed of mainly business people, led by Tim Burgess, a moderate Democrat and briefly mayor of Seattle in 2017, called their effort to codify a city mandate for conducting mandatory homeless encampment clearances "Compassion Seattle," in what became the City of Seattle Charter Amendment 29.[35] The group attempted to secure enough registered voter signatures to bring to a citywide vote a change in the Seattle City Charter requiring the city to provide more permanent, supportive housing and simultaneously to clear parks and other public spaces of homeless encampments by criminalizing them. Compassion Seattle received enough registered voter signatures to be placed on the November 2021 ballot, but a judge ruled that the Charter amendment went beyond the power given to cities by state law, and it was struck from the ballot.[36]

A countermeasure to Compassion Seattle arose, the House Our Neighbors coalition, spearheaded by the long-standing anti-poverty newspaper and advocacy group *Real Change*.[37] The coalition includes people with the lived experience of homelessness and advocates for social housing in Seattle. Social housing is characterized by being publicly owned, permanently affordable. It includes cross-class communities of different income groups and has democratically controlled renter leadership.[38] Social Housing Initiative 135 was up for a special City of Seattle vote in February 2023. It passed in the election.[39]

The news coverage about Compassion Seattle, combined with the increase in visible homelessness not only in Seattle but throughout King County, led to more widespread backlash and an increase in the criminalization of homelessness. In February 2021, the city of Mercer Island, the highest-income zip code not only in King County but also in Washington State, as well as one of the highest in the country, enacted legislation to ban camping in public parks.[40] The Auburn City Council passed more punitive anti-homelessness legislation, allowing the charging of criminal trespassing for people camping overnight on any city property.[41] People now face a $1,000 fine and/or ninety days in jail if they fail to follow through with individualized plans to move them into housing or at least out of the jurisdiction. Council members who voted in favor of this criminal penalty characterize the new law as "compassionate accountability."[42] Similar laws are being enacted throughout the United States. In the summer of 2021, Tennessee passed legislation making it a felony for a person to sleep or camp on public property.[43]

As the National Homelessness Law Center documents, criminalization worsens homelessness and racial inequities by weighing down already impoverished people with hefty fines, jail sentences, and criminal records.[44] Criminalization diverts money away from supportive housing and basic health, including mental health and substance use disorder treatment, which are more cost-effective at preventing and addressing homelessness.[45] Communities that criminalize homelessness have higher rates of violence against people living, or even appearing to be, homeless.[46]

Hostile architecture, a close cousin to the activation of public spaces, has increased. From raised and sharp-looking metal dividers in the middle of benches in the Pioneer Square light-rail station to metal spikes and jagged boulders under bridges, urban design to dissuade people experiencing homelessness from using public spaces abounds. In Seattle, in areas where vehicle residents have parked during the pandemic, large, concrete barriers have been placed illegally by community members and business owners.[47] Just as inclusive design, such as ramps onto sidewalks, helps many people and signals a friendly, welcoming stance, hostile architecture is ugly and off-putting to everyone, even on a subliminal level.[48] Some cities and more rural areas have gone to absurd extremes and cut down trees in parks and near community health clinics to dissuade people experiencing homelessness from using the park or adjacent area for any legal or illegal activities, including camping or urinating in the absence of public restrooms.[49] The presence of shade-giving trees to offset the heat retention of buildings and pavement in cities is an important part of improving air quality and heat mitigation in our rapidly worsening environment.[50] So the loss of tree canopy for political purposes seems wrongheaded and ends up hurting everyone living and working in that area.

"ENOUGH IS ENOUGH!" chanted King County employees, union workers, and their supporters at a rally as they marched around the outside perimeter of the King County Courthouse around lunchtime on Friday, August 6, 2021.[51] Organized by employees, mostly women, the protestors wore teal-colored T-shirts, the color for rape and sexual assault, highlighting continued sexual harassment and assaults they endured doing their work at the courthouse. The logo on the front of their T-shirts read, "Aware of my surroundings. Still not safe." A woman held a sign saying, "Public place safety is a right, not an option. RAPE. COVID. RACISM. ASSAULT. These are not okay. I can't believe that this still needs to be said."[52]

The march took protestors past City Hall Park, with its still large homeless encampment. Speakers at the rally made clear that they were not placing the blame for safety concerns on the unhoused and historically excluded community members.[53] The rally occurred because of increased assaults and harassment of courthouse employees and even jurors on the streets outside the courthouse. Then, less than a week before the march, a female courthouse employee had been sexually assaulted by a thirty-five-year-old homeless man, Clint Jory, in a women's bathroom.[54] Jory had just been released from King County Jail, having served twenty-one months for sexually motivated assaults on women. Senior deputy prosecuting attorney Amy Freedheim, who had worked at the King County Courthouse for thirty years, said there had been longtime public and worker's safety concerns at the courthouse. She said that after the recent attempted rape of one of her colleagues, employees had been sent an e-mail by administrators reminding them to be aware of their surroundings and for women to wear longer skirts. She added, "We are done with being told to be aware of our surroundings. We are done with the city saying it's a county problem, the county saying it's a city problem."[55] Mayor Harrell attended the rally.

"WHILE POVERTY IS not good to look at, we all see it. We shouldn't have to look at the human suffering of people."[56] Bruce Harrell made this oddly revealing statement during his successful 2021 campaign for the city of Seattle mayor. Harrell, who identifies as Black and Asian American, a former Seattle City Council member who was briefly acting mayor of Seattle in 2017, stated during his campaign that the homelessness crisis was his number one priority and that "inaction and finger-pointing is not only frustrating—it is inhumane."[57] He called on Seattle to once again become a "compassionate and can do" city.[58] He publicly supported Compassion Seattle.

When he began his tenure as mayor in January 2022, Harrell hired Tim Burgess, one of the main crafters of Compassion Seattle, as director of strategic initiatives. Critics have pointed out that Mayor Harrell has enacted much of the strategy included in the Compassion Seattle initiative, escalating the scale and frequency of encampment sweeps and using a newly enacted obstruction designation loophole to bypass the mandatory seventy-two-hour notification of clearances to encampment residents.[59]

The obstruction designation can be invoked for any tent encampment or vehicle residency units deemed to obstruct a sidewalk or other public space.[60]

Many of the mayoral candidates, including Bruce Harrell,
mentioned the need to address homelessness through a county-
wide, coordinated response, something that has been talked
about for decades and was finally underway with the establishment of the King County RHA. Marc Dones, who identifies as
Black and queer and has lived experiences with homelessness
and mental illness, started in April of 2021 as the first chief executive officer of the RHA. Coming to Seattle from Boston and
New York City, Dones clashed with pro-business Mayor Harrell
on homelessness strategies, especially around encampments.[61]
The RHA works to "resolve encampments in a person-centered
way" instead of doing traditional encampment clearances.[62]
Leaked information indicates that Mayor Harrell thinks that the
RHA is "working against" his efforts to address homelessness,
adding that no one "has the right to sleep on a sidewalk."[63] Marc
Dones resigned his leadership position with the RHA in
May 2023.[64]

ON A WARM, cloudless, and blessedly smokeless July morning in
2022, a bright red plastic and metal shopping cart, partially
filled with metal drink cans, stood on a bicycle path beside two
electric rental bikes under the shade of mature oak and maple
trees in front of tall metal temporary fencing at City Hall Park.
A large red sign affixed to the fence in front of the cart still proclaimed "Park Temporarily Closed," with the Seattle Parks and
Recreation and the City of Seattle's official logo, a profile of Chief
Seattle, in the lower right-hand corner. Originally slated to be
closed for just two months starting in mid-August 2021, the park

remained closed and remained a hotly contested piece of land in downtown Seattle. The City of Seattle planned for a transfer of City Hall Park to King County in exchange for small parcels of land scattered throughout the city. Considering the value of the land given its location, people are concerned that the city or the county will sell it to developers to construct a high-rise building for market-rate condos or office space. There are legal stipulations that the land remain a park. King County officials planned to activate the park, place King County sheriffs there, and make it less likely to be the site of another homeless encampment or an attractor of crime. In October 2022, King County executive Dow Constantine and Seattle mayor Bruce Harrell announced a joint decision that the city of Seattle would maintain ownership of City Hall Park.[65]

In a nod to the land's original stewards, Derrick Belgarde, the executive director of the Chief Seattle Club near City Hall Park, along with Lisa Dixon Howard, the executive director of the Alliance for Pioneer Square, and Rebecca Bear, president of the Seattle Parks Foundation, call on city leaders to have City Hall Park "be a place to learn, reflect and commemorate the history of Seattle's Indigenous people, while also celebrating our collective future as a vibrant and diverse city." They describe the current closure of the park and standoff between the city, county, and community members over the park's future as "another Battle of Seattle."[66] Pointing out that Pioneer Square has the city's highest percentage of people experiencing homelessness and has a large concentration of low-income and BIPOC residents, they add, "Our crisis of homelessness and criminal activity will not be solved by fencing off the park, or by cutting down the trees to 'promote safety' or other one-off solutions that do not address the systemic challenges and contextual obstacles we can only address by working together."[67]

Notes

1. "August 13, 2021—KIRO 7 News at 5 P.M.," KIRO 7 News Seattle, August 14, 2021, https://www.kiro7.com/news/past-newscast/august-13-2021-kiro-7-news-5-pm/25831f12-98e8-4e84-ae54-bac3c1bc2dcb/.

2. Hannah Krieg, "JustCARE's 'Not a Sweep' Approach Ends with 30 Cops in City Hall Park," *Real Change*, August 25, 2021, https://www.realchangenews.org/news/2021/08/25/justcare-s-not-sweep-approach-ends-30-cops-city-hall-park.

3. Krieg, "JustCARE's 'Not a Sweep' Approach."

4. "City Hall Park—Parks," Seattle.Gov, accessed August 23, 2022, https://www.seattle.gov/parks/find/parks/city-hall-park.

5. Casey Martin, "How the Cal Anderson Sweep Went Down—and Why It's So Contentious," KUOW, December 21, 2020, https://www.kuow.org/stories/how-the-cal-anderson-sweep-went-down-and-why-it-s-so-contentious; Casey Martin, Megan Farmer, and Dyer Oxley, "Under Threat of Sweep, Seattle Protesters Defend Houseless Encampment at Cal Anderson Park," KUOW, December 16, 2020, https://www.kuow.org/stories/seattle-protesters-defend-houseless-encampment-at-cal-anderson-park.

6. jseattle, "SPD Sweeps Cal Anderson to Clear Homeless Encampments and Protesters from Park—UPDATE," *Capitol Hill Seattle* (blog), December 18, 2020, https://www.capitolhillseattle.com/2020/12/spd-sweeps-cal-anderson-to-clear-homeless-encampments-and-protesters-from-park/.

7. David B. Williams, "Thomas Phelps's 1856 Map of Seattle Is Published in the *Town Crier* on December 15, 1917," HistoryLink.org, March 24, 2015, https://historylink.org/File/11045.

8. Colin M. Anderson, "The Industrial Workers of the World in the Seattle General Strike," Civil Rights and Labor History Consortium / University of Washington, accessed August 25, 2022, https://depts.washington.edu/labhist/strike/anderson.shtml.

9. Ally Butler, "Homeless to Hopeful in King County," Salvation Army, Northwest Division, April 11, 2019, https://northwest.salvationarmy.org/northwest_division/news/homeless-to-hopeful-in-king-county/.

10. Josephine Ensign, *Skid Road: On the Frontier of Health and Homelessness in an American City* (Baltimore: Johns Hopkins University Press, 2021).

11. "Communism in Washington State History and Memory Project," Civil Rights and Labor History Consortium / University of Washington, accessed December 25, 2019, https://depts.washington.edu/labhist/cpproject/.

12. Rick Morgan, "Less Than Half of Seattle's JumpStart Tax Revenue Will Go toward Housing," *Puget Sound Business Journal*, July 12, 2022, https://www.bizjournals.com/seattle/news/2022/07/12/payroll-tax-update-spending-housing-general-fund.html.

13. Paul Dorpat, "Seattle's 'Starvation Camp,' ca. 1939," *Seattle Times*, February 18, 2012, https://www.seattletimes.com/life/lifestyle/seattles-starvation-camp-ca-1939/.

14. Jean Sherrard, "Seattle Now & Then: Governor Martin's Starvation Camp," Seattle Now & Then, February 18, 2012, https://pauldorpat.com/2012/02/18/seattle-now-then-governor-martins-starvation-camp/.

15. Jean Sherrard, "Seattle Now & Then: The Public Safety Building," Seattle Now & Then, May 1, 2011, https://pauldorpat.com/2011/05/01/seattle-now-then-the-public-safety-building/.

16. B. Cannon Ivers, *Staging Urban Landscapes: The Activation and Curation of Flexible Public Spaces* (Basel: Birkhäuser, 2018), https://doi.org/10.1515/9783035610468.

17. Philip Dawdy, "What Booze Ban?," *Seattle Weekly*, October 9, 2006, https://www.seattleweekly.com/news/what-booze-ban/.

18. Katherine Beckett and Steve Herbert, *Banished: The New Social Control in Urban America*, Studies in Crime and Public Policy (New York: Oxford University Press, 2009), https://doi.org/10.1093/acprof:oso/9780195395174.001.0001.

19. *Centering Impacted Voices: Community Task Force Report on the Criminal Legal System* (Seattle Office for Civil Rights, September 2021).

20. "Rules & Regulations—Parks," Seattle.gov, accessed September 1, 2022, https://www.seattle.gov/parks/about-us/rules-and-regulations#codeofconduct.

21. Beckett and Herbert, *Banished*, 8.

22. Beckett and Herbert, *Banished*, 48.

23. "Park Rangers—Parks," Seattle.gov, accessed September 1, 2022, https://www.seattle.gov/parks/about-us/special-initiatives-and-programs/park-rangers.

24. Erica C. Barnett, "Most City Shelter 'Referrals' Don't Lead to Shelter, Police Preemptively Barricade Encampment against Protests, City Says It Can't Risk Handing HOPE Team to County," PubliCola, March 18, 2022, https://publicola.com/2022/03/18/most-city -shelter-referrals-dont-lead-to-shelter-police-preemptively-barricade -encampment-against-protests-city-says-it-cant-risk-handing-hope -team-to-county/.

25. Barnett, "Most City Shelter 'Referrals.'"

26. "Stop the Sweeps Seattle (@stopthesweepsseattle)," Instagram, accessed March 10, 2022, https://www.instagram.com/p /Ca1XWxmrX-L/.

27. Barnett, "Most City Shelter 'Referrals.'"

28. Kara Kostanich, "Durkan Says Seattle Public Schools Need to Clear Homeless Camp near School," KOMO, June 1, 2021, https:// komonews.com/news/local/mayor-durkan-says-seattle-public -schools-need-to-clear-homeless-encampment-near-school.

29. Scott Greenstone, "Bitter Lake Encampment Could Empty Out This Month as Homeless Hotels Begin to Fill," *Seattle Times*, November 2, 2021, https://www.seattletimes.com/seattle-news/homeless/bitter-lake -encampment-could-empty-out-this-month-as-homeless-hotels-begin -to-fill/; Erica Barnett, "As Longtime Encampment at Bitter Lake Closes, Allegations against Nonprofit Founder Raise Questions about Oversight," PubliCola, December 8, 2021, https://publicola.com/2021 /12/08/as-longtime-encampment-at-bitter-lake-closes-allegations -against-nonprofit-founder-raise-questions-about-oversight/.

30. "We Heart Seattle," We Heart Seattle, accessed November 29, 2021, https://weheartseattle.org.

31. "We Heart Seattle Founder Andrea Suarez Is Cleaning Up," KATU, June 29, 2022, https://katu.com/amnw/am-northwest-lifestyle -health/we-heart-seattle-founder-andrea-suarez-is-cleaning-up.

32. "We Heart Seattle Founder," KATU.

33. Ashley Archibald, "Volunteer Group That Removes Trash from Home-less Encampments Draws Criticism," South Seattle Emerald, March 23, 2021, https://southseattleemerald.com/2021/03/23/volunteer-group -that-removes-trash-from-homeless-encampments-draws-criticism/.

34. Krieg, "JustCARE's 'Not a Sweep' Approach."

35. Daniel Beekman and Scott Greenstone, "Proposal to Address Homelessness in Seattle City Charter Met with Intrigue, Skepticism,"

Seattle Times, April 13, 2021, https://www.seattletimes.com/seattle
-news/politics/seattle-begins-to-digest-proposal-that-would-change
-city-charter-to-address-homelessness/.

36. Natalie Bicknell Argerious, "Appeal Denied: Compassion Seattle's
    Charter Amendment Is Dead," Urbanist, September 3, 2021, https://
    www.theurbanist.org/2021/09/03/appeal-denied-compassion
    -seattles-charter-amendment-is-dead/.

37. Tiffani McCoy and Jacob Schear, "Opinion: Don't Be Fooled by
    'Compassion' Seattle," South Seattle Emerald, July 11, 2021, https://
    southseattleemerald.com/2021/07/11/opinion-dont-be-fooled-by
    -compassion-seattle/.

38. See https://www.houseourneighbors.org.

39. Donna Gordon Blankinship, "Seattle's Social Housing Measure Is
    Likely to Pass," Crosscut, February 17, 2023, https://crosscut.com
    /politics/2023/02/seattles-social-housing-measure-likely-pass.

40. Paige Cornwell, "Mercer Island Restricts Camping on Public Property
    in Near-Unanimous Vote," *Seattle Times*, February 16, 2021, https://
    www.seattletimes.com/seattle-news/eastside/in-near-unanimous
    -vote-mercer-island-restricts-camping-on-public-property/.

41. Sydney Brownstone, "Auburn City Council Votes to Create Criminal
    Penalty for Camping on City Property," *Seattle Times*, April 19, 2021,
    https://www.seattletimes.com/seattle-news/homeless/auburn-city
    -council-creates-criminal-penalty-for-camping-on-city-property/.

42. Brownstone, "Auburn City Council Votes."

43. Associated Press, "Tennessee Is About to Become the 1st State to
    Make Camping on Public Land a Felony," NPR, sec. National, May 26,
    2022, https://www.npr.org/2022/05/26/1101434831/public-camping
    -felony-tennessee-homeless-seek-refuge.

44. Karianna Barr, "Housing Not Handcuffs 2019," *National Homeless-
    ness Law Center* (blog), December 10, 2019, https://homelesslaw.org
    /housing-not-handcuffs-2019/.

45. Joseph W. Mead and Sara Rankin, "Why Turning Homelessness into
    a Crime Is Cruel and Costly," Conversation, June 20, 2018, http://
    theconversation.com/why-turning-homelessness-into-a-crime-is
    -cruel-and-costly-97290.

46. "No Safe Street: A Survey of Violence Committed against Homeless
    People," National Coalition for the Homeless, accessed January 18,
    2022, https://nationalhomeless.org/no-safe-street/.

47. Amanda Zhou, "Illegally Placed Concrete Blocks Have Taken over Public Parking in Seattle. Why Are They There?," *Seattle Times*, July 30, 2022, https://www.seattletimes.com/seattle-news/homeless /illegally-placed-concrete-blocks-have-taken-over-public-parking-in -seattle-why-are-they-there/; Erica C. Barnett, "'Eco Blocks' Are Concrete Signs of Seattle's Failure to Address RV Homelessness," PubliCola, July 1, 2021, http://publicola.com/2021/07/01/eco-blocks -are-concrete-signs-of-seattles-failure-to-address-rv-homelessness/.

48. Noreena Hertz, *The Lonely Century: How to Restore Human Connection in a World That's Pulling Apart* (New York: Currency, 2021).

49. Juan Carlos Castillo, "Lakewood Cut Down Town Square Trees to Deter Homeless," Asbury Park Press, updated August 30, 2022, https://www.app.com/story/news/local/jackson-lakewood/lakewood /2022/08/29/lakewood-nj-town-square-trees-cut-deter-homeless /65420495007/.

50. "Using Trees and Vegetation to Reduce Heat Islands," US Environmental Protection Agency, accessed September 1, 2022, https://www .epa.gov/heatislands/using-trees-and-vegetation-reduce-heat-islands.

51. Lewis Kamb, "After Latest Attack, King County Courthouse Employees Rally for 'Violence-Free' Workplace," *Seattle Times*, August 6, 2021, https://www.seattletimes.com/seattle-news/law-justice/after -latest-attack-king-county-courthouse-employees-rally-for-violence -free-workplace/.

52. Hannah Krieg, "March to 'Protect Public Spaces' Meets Anti-sweep Protest at City Hall Camp," August 18, 2021, https://www .realchangenews.org/news/2021/08/18/march-protect-public-spaces -meets-anti-sweep-protest-city-hall-camp.

53. Krieg, "March to 'Protect Public Spaces.'"

54. Sara Green, "King County Prosecutors Rush-File Attempted Rape Charge in Sexual Attack in Courthouse Restroom," *Seattle Times*, July 30, 2021, https://www.seattletimes.com/seattle-news/law-justice /king-county-prosecutors-rush-file-attempted-rape-charge-in-sexual -attack-in-courthouse-restroom/.

55. "Video: Dozens March for Safety at King County Courthouse," KIRO 7 News Seattle, August 7, 2021, https://www.kiro7.com/news/local /video-dozens-march-safety-king-county-courthouse/af6910fb-ccbd -48da-aaaf-a0b715ed7f18/.

56. "Seattle's Next Mayor: One-on-One with the Candidates," Crosscut, accessed June 4, 2022, https://crosscut.com/event/seattles-next -mayor-one-one-candidates.

57. "Video Voters' Guide: 2021 General Election," King County, accessed September 1, 2022, https://kingcounty.gov/depts/KCTV/VVG.aspx.

58. Bruce Harrell, "From the Desk of Bruce Harrell," campaign mailer, October 10, 2021.

59. Erica Barnett, "New Details Emerge about Harrell Administration's Encampment Removal Plans," PubliCola, July 5, 2022, https:// publicola.com/2022/07/05/new-details-emerge-about-harrell -administrations-encampment-removal-plans/.

60. Guy Oron, "Seattle Conducted More Than 900 Sweeps of Homeless People in 2022," South Seattle Emerald, April 3, 2023, https:// southseattleemerald.com/2023/04/03/seattle-conducted-more-than -900-sweeps-of-homeless-people-in-2022/.

61. Sarah Taylor, "Seattle Mayor Does Damage Control after Leaked Criticism of Homelessness Agency, City Council," *Seattle Times*, August 31, 2022, https://www.seattletimes.com/seattle-news/politics /seattle-mayor-does-damage-control-after-leaked-criticism-of -homeless-agency-city-council/.

62. martensesq, "FAQ: Our Role in Encampment Removals," KCRHA, August 25, 2022, https://kcrha.org/faq-our-role-in-encampment -removals/.

63. Taylor, "Seattle Mayor Does Damage Control."

64. Greg Kim, "Regional Homelessness Authority's Ex-CEO Now Working for Seattle," *Seattle Times*, July 25, 2023, https://www .seattletimes.com/seattle-news/regional-homelessness-authority-and -former-ceo-move-on-after-breakup/.

65. David Gutman, "Why the Deal to Give Seattle's Troubled City Hall Park to King County Fell Apart," *Seattle Times*, October 14, 2022, https://www.seattletimes.com/seattle-news/politics/troubled-city -hall-park-will-remain-seattles-ending-plan-to-transfer-to-county/.

66. Derrick Belgarde, Lisa Dixon Howard, and Rebecca Bear, "Nix the Deal to Trade Seattle's City Hall Park to the County," *Seattle Times*, December 10, 2021, https://www.seattletimes.com/opinion/nix-the -deal-to-trade-seattles-city-hall-park-to-the-county/.

67. Belgarde, Howard, and Bear, "Nix the Deal."

CHAPTER 6

Displaced

· · · · · · · · · · · · · · · · ·

Homelessness is a shaky feeling. Like a leaf clinging to a branch in winter, trembling before it falls.

—SASHA LAPOINTE, *RED PAINT: THE ANCESTRAL AUTOBIOGRAPHY OF A COAST SALISH PUNK*

Because these times and those times and all times are connected through land and bodies and water.

—TONI JENSEN, *CARRY: A MEMOIR OF SURVIVAL ON STOLEN LAND*

ON MONDAY, AUGUST 30, 2010, a sunny, mild, and pleasant day in Victor Steinbrueck Park next to Pike Place Market, three men sat on a wooden bench, talking and laughing together. Two of the men wore black cloth headbands; one had a large eagle feather attached to his headband, the feather hanging down beside his deeply etched face. With dark chin-length hair, a salt-and-pepper mustache and goatee, and a slight build, the third man wore a baseball hat with a picture of an eagle and the words "Native Pride" written across the front. Behind the men stood two totem poles and what would become the "Tree of Life."

The man wearing the baseball hat was fifty-year-old John T. Williams. The "T" stood variously for Timothy or Trouble, the latter being his acquired street name from decades of homelessness in Seattle. The moniker of Trouble was not because he was

violent. John was known to friends and family members as being gentle and even peace loving.[1] The two men with John that
day were his older brother Rick and his younger brother Eric,
neither of whom had seen John in fifteen years. Their mother
sent them to Seattle from Canada, telling them, "Go get John.
He needs us now."[2] The brothers searched all over Seattle and
had finally found John two days prior at Victor Steinbrueck Park.
The park, dubbed Native Park by locals, including Native people,
had been a longtime hangout and meeting place for Native
Americans, Native Alaskans, and First Nations Canadians, especially for Indigenous people experiencing homelessness and
housing instability. Richard, a Native American interviewed for
a study on the effects of Seattle's parks exclusion ordinance,
stated, "All the natives like Victor Steinbrueck Park, you know,
it's how we find each other."[3] He mentioned access to public restrooms, the beautiful view across Puget Sound, and shared meals
with friends as reasons he frequented the park. Built on top of
the market's parking lot, the park was treeless, with gently slop-
ing berms of grass, concrete and wooden bench seating, the two
totem poles, and what would become the "Tree of Life," all over-
looking Seattle's waterfront on Elliott Bay and the snow-topped
Olympic mountain range in the distance.

Native Park was popular for people like John because of its
location and the people it attracted. Next to the park, Pike Place
Market, one of our country's oldest public farmers markets, was
a popular tourist destination with its fish tossing, food, and craft-
bearing stalls. The market had the public restrooms mentioned
by Richard. A variety of social, health, and supportive housing
services were located in the market area, especially for low-
income elders and people living with disabilities. Although
John, at age fifty, was not yet eligible for elder services (reserved
for those fifty-five years old and older), he likely was a guest at

the Pike Place Food Bank to help supplement the food he accessed through his 1811 Eastlake permanent supportive housing. He was a frequent guest at the Chief Seattle Club in Pioneer Square near City Hall Park. John was by then considered an elder at the Chief Seattle Club, which during his time provided day shelter, health care, meals for Seattle's urban Native community, and culturally relevant activities, including spiritual practices and traditional crafts like beading and wood carving.[4] It continues to offer these services, plus permanent supportive housing and an array of other services. Whereas initially the Chief Seattle Club was run by its Catholic founders, it is now native led and operated.

John and his brothers were First Nations Ditidaht from the Nitinaht region on the west coast of Vancouver Island, British Columbia, northwest of Seattle. They were seventh-generation wood carvers, mostly of smaller tourist trade Northwest Coast–style totem poles. Their grandfather Sam Williams, a fisherman and wood carver, had moved from his ancestral home on Vancouver Island to Seattle in 1900 at the tail end of the Alaska-Yukon-Klondike Gold Rush. He lived in a makeshift shack on the tidal flats of the Duwamish River, in an encampment known as Indian Village, along with displaced Native people and migrants attracted to the then burgeoning city, dubbed the "Gateway to Alaska."[5] During that time, amid the bustling Seattle waterfront docks with steamers sailing to Alaska, Ye Olde Curiosity Shop was opened by J. E. "Daddy" Standlass as a trading post for the sale of Indigenous artifacts popular among tourists and even locals who kept "curio corners" in their parlors and who bought into the pervasive myth of the vanishing Indian.[6] Daddy Standlass admired Sam Williams's carvings and began selling them in his shop. Ye Olde Curiosity Shop—filled with Native American, Native Alaskan, and Northwest Coastal Indigenous carvings; cedar bark baskets; a wine bag made of a bull's scrotum; buffalo horns; and even entire human skeletons and a mummified man called Sylvester with bullet holes—continues to sell totem poles carved by the Williams family today.

The three brothers had carved together for the past few days as they talked and laughed. In recounting events of this late August afternoon, Rick said of John, "Street life really hurt him. He sounded like a child," adding, "He's telling me he's losing his sight. You know, he's saying he's embarrassed by it and could barely hear you." Rick recounts that he reminded John that their grandfather had gone blind yet continued to carve and sell his carvings. Rick offered to teach John to carve blind. On this particular day, John had left his single-blade three-inch knife and the piece of cedar he was carving an eagle on in his room at 1811 Eastlake, a DESC permanent supportive housing unit for people with chronic alcoholism. After Rick offered to teach him to carve blind, Rick recalled that John said, "Okay, I'll go get my stuff." Rick added that John "said he'd be back in two hours." John was happy seeing and spending time with his brothers, who had finally convinced him to stay with them in a hotel in Seattle and then move back to Canada with them. That was the last time they saw John alive.

JOHN BECAME A heavy drinker, and despite his multiple attempts to get sober, he had been unable to maintain sobriety. During one of his recent conversations with his brother Rick, who had had a drinking problem in the past and was now nine years sober, John asked Rick how he did it and if he would help him stop drinking. John's decades of public drunkenness had landed him in King County Jail and in the sobering center, sometimes dubbed the "drunk tank," in Seattle numerous times. In addition, he had frequent stays at Harborview Medical Center for alcohol-related injuries, including to his legs from being hit by a car while intoxicated in a Safeway parking lot. In an episode of psychosis with paranoia years before, John, convinced that all his family members were dead, landed in Western State Hospital, where doctors started him on psychiatric medications.

After having spent decades living on the streets of Seattle and in various shelters, including at DESC's Morrison Hotel near City Hall Park, John began residing at 1811 Eastlake, a controversial yet evidence-based and well-known seventy-five-unit "wet house" DESC-run permanent supportive housing for Seattle's most costly chronic public inebriates. They are costly because of their frequent stays in King County Jail, the sobering center, Harborview Medical Center, and other public services. Opened in 2005, 1811 Eastlake is an example of the Housing First model of care. Housing First was developed in New York City by psychologist Sam J. Tsemberis in the 1990s with the Pathways to Housing Program.[7] Instead of the traditional stepwise progression of emergency shelter, transitional shelter, and permanent housing approach to "housing readiness" for people experiencing chronic homelessness, people were given a choice and placed directly from the streets into permanent housing with support services. The people served by Housing First programs were not required to be treatment compliant or to maintain sobriety in order to qualify for permanent housing. Researchers found that people placed in Housing First permanent supportive housing achieved much higher rates of housing stability and had better health outcomes than those in traditional shelter and housing services.[8]

The Housing First model of care was so successful that in 2003 it was expanded through funding by the federal Interagency Council on Homelessness.[9] Seattle was an early adopter of Housing First, with 1811 Eastlake for chronic inebriates undergoing rigorous studies that found significant improvements in housing retention, decreases in the use of publicly funded medical and legal services, and even decreases in alcohol consumption among residents like John.[10] For someone as deeply entrenched in alcoholism, mental illness, and homelessness as John was, permanent supportive housing at 1811 Eastlake was an ethical and effective choice for him, especially when there were no good alternatives at the time. Housing First in Seattle and King County, being a cost-effective, evidence-based model for addressing homelessness, has had broad political support despite criticism from some community members who point to the costs of such programs and others who see it as enabling substance use.[11]

Rev. Rick Reynolds, the former executive director of the long-running Seattle-based street ministry, food, and shelter program Operation Nightwatch, says, "The Housing First model really makes sense. And I think it takes a lot of convincing of people that aren't current in the science of it or haven't thought it through much. But even some of the people in recovery that I know sometimes feel as though the Housing First model rewards bad behavior. But I keep thinking there's a lot of folks in housing that still struggle with mental health and addiction disorders. It's a lot easier to deal with when you're inside than when you're sleeping in the jungle or in a sort of tenuous shelter situation."[12] Housing First advocates highlight the fact that safe, affordable, supportive housing is health care.

ON THE LAST August day that his two brothers saw him alive, John walked with a limp, was deaf in his left ear from an untreated ear infection years before when he slept on the streets, and was partially blind from his decades of heavy drinking. It is worth noting here that the idea that Indigenous people like John have a genetic predisposition to alcoholism, feeding into the "drunk Indian" negative stereotype, is a myth with no scientific basis.[13] Instead, high rates of alcoholism occur in many displaced, socially marginalized communities, along with higher rates of depression and suicide.[14]

Before his brothers found him at Native Park in late August, John had had five interactions with SPD officers just in the month of August. Some of the police stops were for drinking alcohol in the park. One of these interactions with police, on August 25, was for jaywalking. In the police video cam recording of this event, the officers had to raise their voices for John to hear them. The video shows that John had difficulty discerning the walk sign at the intersection where he was accused of jaywalking. The police officers did not seem to notice these clues to John's physical disabilities. At the end of the police recording of this interaction with John, the police officer states, "This ends our interaction with Mr. Williams, one of our regular mental transient Native Americans."[15] John was well known to many people in downtown Seattle, including police officers. The officers knew that he and other Indigenous people frequently carved totem poles for sale to tourists and locals. John was so accustomed to carving that he could carve and walk at the same time.

IN RECOUNTING THE STORY of the life and death of John T. Williams, it would be willfully shortsighted to talk or write about displacement and homelessness in Seattle, a city named for a Duwamish Coast Salish leader, without acknowledging Indigenous people's unique histories and the still rippling effects of settler colonialism in our city, county, state, and country. And in the case of John T. Williams, those same issues extend to our northern neighbor, Canada, and its treatment of First Nations people.

In the words of Native Americans leading the Chief Seattle Club in Pioneer Square, while only 1% of Seattle's population identifies as Indigenous, "hundreds of years of colonization, systemic racism, broken treaties, forced reservations, and more have resulted in native peoples making up a startling 15% of Seattle's homeless population," as well as 32% of people experiencing chronic homelessness.[16] They contrast these statistics with the historical context, stating, "This, of course, was not always the case. Thousands of years before white colonials and settlers arrived, people from dozens of tribes thrived in the Puget Sound region, including the Duwamish and Suquamish, whose Chief Si'ahl inspired our city's name." Significantly, the Duwamish people, on whose ancestral land much of Seattle and south King County are built, never received their own reservation as promised in the Treaty of Point Elliott of 1855. The Duwamish remain unrecognized by the US government despite having their own government and about six hundred enrolled members.[17]

The "and more" elements in Chief Seattle Club's list of reasons for such high rates of homelessness among Indigenous people in Seattle include the US government's termination of many reservations beginning in the 1950s. In addition, during this time, the US government implemented widespread forced assimilation attempts, uprooting young adult Native Americans and Native Alaskans living on reservations and sending them to large urban areas, including Seattle, ostensibly for job training but also to shed their "Indianness."

As Native writer David Treuer describes the government relocation of Native Americans in his book *The Heartbeat of Wounded Knee: Life in Native America*, "Indian agents on reservations across the country hawked the benefits of urban living with the same fervor with which land speculators enticed city dwellers to come west and homestead a century before."[18] Reflecting on the effects of forced relocation on his life, David Schildt, who was relocated with his family from the Blackfeet reservation to Los Angeles during these decades, told Treuer, "I'm a relocated Indian. I see myself as a classic example of what the government wants. The government wants you separated from your family, your home, your kids, your spiritual belief system, and they got you in the city, in white America. And now . . . you're just a number."[19]

John T. Williams and many of his family members were what is termed "Urban Indians," or, in John's case, more precisely, urban First Nations people. The Chief Seattle Club is specifically for urban Indigenous people, and John sought community and services there. As defined by the Urban Indian Health Institute, a division of the Seattle Indian Health Board, "Urban Indians are tribal people currently living off federally defined tribal lands in urban areas."[20] They point out that, according to the US Census, 71% of American Indians and Alaska Natives now live in urban areas. This high rate of urban living is likely due to a combination of the lasting effects of Indian relocation efforts by the US government and increasing urbanization across all groups of people in the United States. In addition, climate refugees fleeing increasingly uninhabitable land owing to the escalating effects of climate change, whether those effects result from drought, fires, or stronger hurricanes and typhoons, are, oftentimes, moving to urban areas.[21] These issues related to climate change disproportionately affect Indigenous communities, including Native Alaskan communities like the Yupik Village of Newtok, affected by permafrost thawing and rising sea levels, and Williams's Ditidaht tribal lands on Vancouver Island, affected by coastal erosion.[22]

In Canada, the effects of white settler colonialism on First Nations people like John and his family from Vancouver Island included the infamous story of young First Nations children being forced to move away from their families and ancestral lands and into boarding schools. Boarding school teachers and administrators punished the children for wearing traditional clothing and long hair, practicing their own spiritual beliefs, and speaking in their native languages. At these schools, the children suffered high rates of physical and sexual abuse and medical neglect.

Similar efforts to "kill the Indian" in Indigenous children and assimilate them into the majority white and Christian culture occurred in the United States, including in what became Washington State.[23] Begun in 1819 by the Civilization Fund Act and lasting until 1978, many of these federally funded boarding schools were run by the Catholic Church, and the school's administrators and teachers were charged with the moral upbringing of the Native children.

Ojibwe journalist Mary Annette Pember writes of her mother's forced stay in a boarding school in Wisconsin and her mother's lifelong resistance to the abuse she encountered, including the nun's labeling her a "dirty Indian."[24] Pember recounts the effects that this boarding school experience had, not only on her mother but also on her and her entire family. She writes, "My mother died while surviving civilization. Although she outlived a traumatic childhood immersed in its teachings, she carried the pain of those lessons for her entire life."[25] Pember remembers her mother's incessant cleaning and bleaching of laundry, frequent migraine headaches, short temper, and dissociative states as causing Pember significant anxiety as a child. This passing on of trauma illustrates the embodied reality of intergenerational and historical trauma.

Despite these abusive and traumatic experiences, Pember, her mother, and thousands of other Indigenous families and Native communities in both the United States and Canada have found ways to survive and protect their identities and cultures. John T. Williams's strong identity with his wood-carving First Nations family helped him survive difficult circumstances. Many Indigenous people call this "resistance," eschewing the problematic, overly used, and glorified term "resilience."

The punitive and deadly boarding school program in Canada likely directly impacted John T. Williams, causing more fracturing of his immediate and extended family's connections to each other, to their spiritual practices, and to their homeland. The Canadian First Nations boarding school system was much more extensive than the equivalent US system, with the last Canadian boarding school closing in 1996. Thousands of children's bodies, some as young as three years old, continue to be found in unmarked graves beside these former boarding schools in Canada.[26] The Canadian government has done more to document and acknowledge wrongdoing in authorizing and overseeing these boarding schools than has the US government.[27]

JOHN T. WILLIAMS WAS born on February 27, 1960, to his First Nations parents, Ray Williams and Ida Edward. He was one of eleven children that Ray and Ida had together before their turbulent relationship ended in 1969, after nineteen years of marriage. Ray Williams had lived in Seattle as a child and began to carve with his father at the age of three along the Duwamish River.[28] By the 1970s, he was once again living and carving in Seattle with several of his sons, including John, who elder brother Rick claims began carving at age seven and became the most gifted carver in the family.[29] In the late 1970s, when John was

entering his late teens and young adult years, his father in-
structed him to carve and sell his carvings on Broadway in Capitol Hill, while two of his brothers carved on the waterfront and at
the Seattle Center near the Space Needle. His father carved at
the old Kingdome on the southern edge of Pioneer Square.

John, who was close to his father, moved with him between
Seattle and Canada, especially Vancouver, British Columbia,
after his parent's breakup. One of John's sisters, Barb Williams,
who is also a carver, said that the only one in their family to
remember all 250 stories associated with the various figures
on their carvings was John.[30] His mother, Ida, fell out of a
second-floor window in Victoria, British Columbia, in 1984,
became quadriplegic, and lived in an assisted-living facility in
Vancouver.[31] After his father died of a heart attack in Pioneer
Square at age fifty in 1988, John lost three brothers in close suc-
cession. His brother Dave froze to death on a bus bench in Vancouver in 1991 while living homeless on the streets. His brother
Sam died of a heart attack in 1997 in a cheap hotel room in Vancouver. In 1998, his brother Nathan died from a fall near Pike
Place Market; whether the fall was intentional, accidental, or
alcohol related is unclear. After the deaths of two of his brothers
in Vancouver, John told his sister Barb that he was never setting
foot in Canada again. She added, "He never returned." Hence, it
was a significant change for John to have agreed in late August 2010 to return to Canada with his brothers to be closer to
his people's land and extended family.

JOHN NEVER MADE IT to Canada, and he never saw his brothers
again. On that August day, after telling his brothers he would
return in two hours with his carving knife and the piece of cedar on which he was carving an eagle, he returned to his room

at 1811 Eastlake to pick up these items. Later that afternoon, while walking back to Victor Steinbrueck Park to be with his brothers, John was shot four times and killed by a white SPD officer. He was inexplicably shot and killed for the crime (in the police officer's opinion) of holding a carving knife and carving a piece of wood while walking across the intersection at Howell Steet and Boren Avenue in downtown Seattle. Eyewitnesses unanimously recounted that John T. Williams was doing nothing wrong and was not threatening anyone, including the police officer who shot and killed John as he walked down the sidewalk toward the park and his brothers waiting for him to return.

Beginning at 4:12 P.M., the dashcam video from inside Officer Ian Birk's police cruiser records him stopping at a red light heading south on Boren Avenue at the intersection with Howell Street.[32] The car radio is tuned to a local sports talk show. The radio hosts banter about the Seahawks and the upcoming UW Huskies home football game. They laugh when they refer to the drunken tailgate parties on campus that occur before the games. The video shows pedestrians crossing the streets, some with backpacks and briefcases, likely leaving work early on a lovely late-summer Friday afternoon. Cries of seagulls circling the overhead sky filter through the radio noise. Then, the video shows John T. Williams, wearing his Native Pride hat, walking with a slight limp as he crosses the street in front of the cruiser. John is intent on carving his piece of wood as he walks and is not close to any other people. In addition, he is walking in the intersection with the pedestrian light still on "Walk." As John steps onto the sidewalk, Officer Birk exits his car, hand on his holster, already pulling out his gun. He yells, "Hey! Hey! Hey! Put the knife down!" three times. He does not identify himself as a police officer.

Eyewitnesses later said that John kept walking, seeming not to hear the officer behind him, and then when he stopped and started to turn around, Officer Birk fired five shots, four of them tearing through John's right side. From first yelling at John to shooting him, it took Officer Birk four seconds. Police officers who responded to the scene saw that John's carving knife was closed on the sidewalk beside his dying body. Officer Birk handcuffed John instead of providing first aid. He was pronounced dead by the firefighter paramedics who arrived soon after. Eyewitnesses agreed that John T. Williams never threatened anyone, including the police officer, with the small carving knife, which he had obviously been using to carve a piece of wood.

John's older brother Rick, waiting for John in Native Park, recalls, "Three or four minutes after John was shot, you know, it spread like wildfire. Somebody came from Boren and Howell and told me they just murdered my brother and—I set my carving down and—then after that, everything went upside down."[33]

ONCE NEWS SPREAD of the police shooting and killing of John T. Williams, street protests emerged calling for justice and an end to racist police killings. These protests were similar to those in the CHAZ/CHOP and BLM protests of the summer of 2020. Rick Williams became the de facto spokesperson for the Williams family after his brother's murder. He recalls that he got grief from some of the protestors that he was not angry enough, "saying that I should say something and my heart won't."[34]

A King County inquest into Officer Birk's killing of John T. Williams was similar to that of the officers' shooting of Charleena Lyles in that it was virtually impossible to prove criminal intent by Officer Birk. Also similar was the traumatization of family members listening to the detailed inquest proceedings and, in Mr. William's case, the testimony of eyewitnesses. However, in the case of John T. Williams, the inquest finding was that Officer Birk's killing of Mr. Williams was unjustified. Officer Birk resigned upon hearing the verdict.

John's death at the hands of an SPD officer led to an investigation by the US Department of Justice (DOJ) that found a history of racial profiling and excessive use of force by the SPD.[35] In the DOJ's investigation and lawsuit against the city of Seattle, they found that the "Police Department engaged in a systemic pattern of excessive force by its officers against people who posed little threat—and more than half of those people were minorities."[36] They also found that the excessive use of force and impact weapons was "particularly against individuals with mental illness or under the influence of alcohol or drugs."[37] This police bias and use of excessive force applied to John T. Williams and, years later, to Charleena Lyles.

Nationally recognized environmental and Indian law attorney Connie Sue Martin, who was from Seattle and knowledgeable of the case of the killing of John T. Williams, said of SPD officer Ian Birk, "Two years on the streets of Seattle. He thought it was weird that a Native American would be walking down the street with a knife and a piece of wood. It shocked me that it was not engrained in this police officer that Native Americans have been carving in Seattle since before it was Seattle. And that totem poles and in this particular family are a part of the fabric of this city."[38] In April 2011, the city of Seattle settled with the Williams family for $1.5 million, with the money going to John's mother, Ida, since John had no spouse or children.[39]

John's older brother Rick, along with other community members, channeled anger and grief into the design and carving of a thirty-four-foot cedar totem pole, the John T. Williams Memorial Pole. He invited people from the larger community to help carve or sand the memorial pole, including eyewitnesses to John's killing who were traumatized by seeing the murder and having to recount it in sworn testimony. On February 26, 2012, on what would have been John's fifty-second birthday, hundreds of people helped carry the completed thirty-five-hundred-pound cedar memorial pole from the waterfront up the hill to the Seattle Center, where it now stands, part of Seattle's public art collection. Rick says of the memorial pole, "This is going to speak louder than I ever will."[40]

Rick participated in parts of the CHAZ/CHOP BLM protests during the summer of 2020, telling the story of his brother John. Rick was still carving and living in a hotel room on Aurora Avenue by the fall of 2020, likely through Chief Seattle Club's pandemic hotel and food programs for Indigenous people, especially the elderly and disabled experiencing housing instability and homelessness. The Chief Seattle Club began putting its vulnerable members in hotel rooms at the beginning of the COVID-19 pandemic, before that model of care became more widespread in Seattle.[41]

DESIGNED, CARVED, AND PAINTED in the Northwest Coast style of the Williams family, the John T. Williams memorial pole stands at the Seattle Center near the Space Needle, where it likely will remain. In contrast, the two fifty-foot carved and painted wooden totem poles at Victor Steinbrueck Park, where John spent time with his brothers in the days before an SPD officer killed him, will be removed as a result of scheduled improvements to the park. The protective membrane between the park's soil and the garage underneath must be replaced. But these totem poles may come down permanently since they were not carved by Indigenous people and were styled in the fashion of the Tlingit, Haida, and other Indigenous people from the Northwest Coast, whose territorial land extended from Vancouver Island up to coastal Alaska—people like John and his family.[42] The Coast Salish people who lived, and continue to live, in Seattle and the Puget Sound region for thousands of years carved shorter, more streamlined welcome and story poles. These carvings adorned the entrances to their traditional cedar longhouses. Although there had long been both peaceful trading and wars between Coast Salish and Northwest Coast Indigenous people, Coast Salish people today understandably want greater recognition and representation of their traditional art and crafts on the land that has been their home for thousands of years.[43]

One of these Coast Salish welcome poles now stands at the corner of Yesler Way and Second Street near the entrance of Chief Seattle Club's recently completed building, ʔálʔal, pronounced "alal" and meaning "home" in Lushootseed Coast Salish language. ʔálʔal is an eighty-unit supportive housing building for Indigenous and some non-Indigenous chronically homeless single adults.[44] Outside, on its south-facing side, is a forty-foot matriarch statue. Inside, it has a culturally congruent medical clinic run by the Seattle Indian Health Board, integrating traditional approaches to behavioral, physical, and spiritual health.[45] It is not difficult to imagine John T. Williams thriving in this new supportive housing. Derrick Belgarde, who is Siletz and Chippewa-Cree and Chief Seattle Club's current executive director, says of ʔálʔal, "We're going to see people actually starting to work through their trauma."[46]

BELGARDE KNOWS FIRSTHAND what it means to be able to work through trauma in a safe, supportive, culturally congruent space.

In the past, Belgarde has experienced homelessness, living on the streets of downtown Seattle and battling an alcohol and methamphetamine addiction he developed starting at age thirteen. Belgarde likely crossed paths many times with John T. Williams, both on the Seattle streets and in the Chief Seattle Club. By the time Belgarde was homeless on the streets of Seattle, he was estranged from most of his family members, some of whom lived in Issaquah, an eastside suburb of Seattle. He says, "There's a lot of isolation being a Native in this country, but being in an urban area, that isolation seems compounded."[47]

Chief Seattle Club programs and staff members helped Belgarde overcome addiction and homelessness. With their support, he entered and successfully completed a seven-month inpatient drug and alcohol treatment program. "I spent seven months just reconnecting with my spirit and getting on what we call the 'red road' in our Native community. I was able to repair relationships with my wife and children. We're going strong now."[48] Belgarde knew he could not return to his previous work in construction because that type of work environment triggered alcohol and drug use, so he went back to school, where he earned his bachelor's degree and then a master's degree in public administration. He wanted to give back to his community. In early February 2015, he took a job as a program manager at the Chief Seattle Club, where he started a talking circle, a drum circle, visits to a sweat lodge, a men's group, and a women's group led by a female colleague.

For years before he began working at the Chief Seattle Club, Belgarde's oldest son was with him, including when Belgarde was still in active addiction. Belgarde relates how he then saw his son spiraling into homelessness and addiction as a young adult. Of this Belgarde says, "Seeing him, and realizing that, and when I did the treatment, I started learning about things, about trauma, about generational trauma. All that really opened my eyes. Seeing a lot of me in him; seeing how it's passed down. Things that I never worked through passed down." He adds, "A lot of what I do, I do think about him a lot. It also keeps me compassionate. I think it also helps me with not being judgmental to understand those types of things, like where he was. He didn't have a father all his life because I was an active alcoholic. I was that way—we could go back all the way to . . ." Belgarde's voice trails off as he seemingly recalls his family's history and the long history of displacement and other racist treatment of Indigenous people in the United States.[49]

Belgarde uses his lived experience, education, program planning experience, direct service experience, and position as executive director of a robust and growing Native-led organization to maintain current programs and plan and implement new ones. For the past decade, the Chief Seattle Club has had a Housing First team focused on rapid rehousing and placements in existing permanent supportive housing units, such as the 1811 Eastlake placement for John T. Williams. He says, "What we found was a lot of recidivism. Very hard just to get our community housed. Also, when you're dealing with that, and you're one percent of the general overall population in the entire region, and you're placing a person over in this building in this neighborhood, and another person in a different neighborhood, you're taking them away from their community." He adds, "We always knew we needed to have our own Native housing to keep our community together. We can actually begin strengthening and reviving our community in a good way."[50]

Learning and applying lessons from the lives and deaths of people like John T. Williams and empowering people like Derrick Belgarde, who can apply knowledge gained through the lived experience of homelessness to create innovative programs, help bring us closer to compassionate and effective solutions to our homelessness problem.

Notes

1. James Ross Gardner, "The Shooting of John T. Williams, 10 Years Later," *Seattle Met*, August 26, 2020, https://www.seattlemet.com /news-and-city-life/2020/08/the-shooting-of-john-t-williams.
2. Seattle Channel, "Community Stories: Honor Totem," YouTube video, 2014, https://www.youtube.com/watch?v=FnzoZB2E3bQ.
3. Katherine Beckett and Steve Herbert, *Banished: The New Social Control in Urban America*, Studies in Crime and Public Policy (New York: Oxford University Press, 2009), 111, https://doi.org/10.1093 /acprof:oso/9780195395174.001.0001.
4. "Our Story," Chief Seattle Club, accessed September 20, 2022, https://www.chiefseattleclub.org/our-story.
5. Coll Thrush, *Native Seattle: Histories from the Crossing-Over Place*, 2nd ed. (Seattle: University of Washington Press, 2017).
6. Thrush, *Native Seattle*; Dina Gilio-Whitaker, "'Real' Indians, the Vanishing Native Myth, and the Blood Quantum Question," ICT, updated September 12, 2018, https://indiancountrytoday.com/archive /real-indians-the-vanishing-native-myth-and-the-blood-quantum -question.
7. Deborah Padgett, *Housing First: Ending Homelessness, Transforming Systems, and Changing Lives* (Oxford: Oxford University Press, 2016).
8. Sam Tsemberis, Leyla Gulcur, and Maria Nakae, "Housing First, Consumer Choice, and Harm Reduction for Homeless Individuals with a Dual Diagnosis," *American Journal of Public Health* 94, no. 4 (2004): 651–56, https://doi.org/10.2105/AJPH.94.4.651.
9. Colleen Fitzpatrick, "'Housing First' Becoming the Standard Model for Homeless Populations," *Mental Health Weekly*, October 25, 2004, 1–4.
10. Erica C. Barnett, "After 15 Years, Seattle's Radical Experiment in No-Barrier Housing Is Still Saving Lives," Crosscut, September 25, 2019, https://crosscut.com/2019/09/after-15-years-seattles-radical -experiment-no-barrier-housing-still-saving-lives; Mary E. Larimer et al., "Health Care and Public Service Use and Costs before and after

Provision of Housing for Chronically Homeless Persons with Severe Alcohol Problems," *JAMA* 301, no. 13 (April 1, 2009): 1349–57, https://doi.org/10.1001/jama.2009.414; Susan E. Collins et al., "Project-Based Housing First for Chronically Homeless Individuals with Alcohol Problems: Within-Subjects Analyses of 2-Year Alcohol Trajectories," *American Journal of Public Health* 102, no. 3 (January 19, 2012): 511–19, https://doi.org/10.2105/AJPH.2011.300403.

11. KOMO News, "The Fight for the Soul of Seattle | A KOMO News Documentary," YouTube video, 2020, https://www.youtube.com/watch?v=WijoL3Hy_Bw; Megan Mayes, "Our Response to 'Fight for the Soul of Seattle,'" DESC, December 21, 2020, https://www.desc.org/our-response-to-fight-for-the-soul-of-seattle/.

12. Rick Reynolds, Skid Road Oral History, interview by Josephine Ensign, March 6, 2017.

13. Roxanne Dunbar-Ortiz, *"All the Real Indians Died Off": And 20 Other Myths about Native Americans* (Boston: Beacon Press, 2016); Roxanne Dunbar-Ortiz, *An Indigenous Peoples' History of the United States* (Boston: Beacon Press, 2015); Les B. Whitbeck et al., "Discrimination, Historical Loss and Enculturation: Culturally Specific Risk and Resiliency Factors for Alcohol Abuse among American Indians," *Journal of Studies on Alcohol* 65, no. 4 (2004): 409–18, https://doi.org/10.15288/jsa.2004.65.409.

14. Melissa L. Walls, Les Whitbeck, and Brian Armenta, "A Cautionary Tale: Examining the Interplay of Culturally Specific Risk and Resilience Factors in Indigenous Communities," *Clinical Psychological Science* 4, no. 4 (2016): 732–43, https://doi.org/10.1177/2167702616645795.

15. Seattle Channel, "Community Stories."

16. "Our Story," Chief Seattle Club.

17. "History of the Duwamish People," Duwamish Tribe, accessed September 21, 2022, https://www.duwamishtribe.org/history; Julia Anne Allain, "Duwamish History in Duwamish Voices: Weaving Our Family Stories since Colonization" (PhD diss., University of Victoria, 2014), https://dspace.library.uvic.ca/items/6f055a52-c6d7-4129-98b6-030453598f50.

18. David Treuer, *The Heartbeat of Wounded Knee: Life in Native America* (New York: Viking, 2022), 269.

19. Treuer, *Heartbeat of Wounded Knee*, 279.

20. "Urban Indian Health," Urban Indian Health Institute, accessed September 22, 2022, https://www.uihi.org/urban-indian-health/.
21. Madeline Ostrander, *At Home on an Unruly Planet: Finding Refuge on a Changed Earth* (New York: Henry Holt, 2022).
22. Julia Ilhardt, "'It Was Sad Having to Leave': Climate Crisis Splits Alaskan Town in Half," *Guardian*, sec. Environment, June 8, 2021, https://www.theguardian.com/environment/2021/jun/08/it-was-sad-having-to-leave-climate-crisis-splits-alaskan-town-in-half; "First Nation Adapt: Selected Projects 2020 to 2021," Government of Canada, Crown-Indigenous Relations and Northern Affairs Canada, November 17, 2021, https://www.rcaanc-cirnac.gc.ca/eng/1637164599097/1637164713750#bc.
23. Jeanie Lindsay, "Traumatized by Boarding Schools, WA Tribes Chart New Path for Native Kids," *Seattle Times*, October 10, 2022, https://www.seattletimes.com/education-lab/traumatized-by-boarding-schools-wa-tribes-chart-new-path-for-native-kids/.
24. Mary Annette Pember, "Death by Civilization," *Atlantic*, March 8, 2019, https://www.theatlantic.com/education/archive/2019/03/traumatic-legacy-indian-boarding-schools/584293/.
25. Pember, "Death by Civilization."
26. Ian Austen, "How Thousands of Indigenous Children Vanished in Canada," *New York Times*, sec. World, June 7, 2021, https://www.nytimes.com/2021/06/07/world/canada/mass-graves-residential-schools.html.
27. Pember, "Death by Civilization."
28. Neal Thompson, "The Carver's Life," *Seattle Met*, April 22, 2011, https://www.seattlemet.com/news-and-city-life/2011/04/john-williams-the-carvers-life-may-2011.
29. Gardner, "Shooting of John T. Williams."
30. Seattle Channel, "Community Stories."
31. Thompson, "Carver's Life."
32. strangervideo, "John T. Williams: Dashboard Video of SPD Shooting (AUDIO RIGHT CHANNEL ONLY)," YouTube video, 2010, https://www.youtube.com/watch?v=vcxqyp2wOzE.
33. Seattle Channel, "Community Stories."
34. Seattle Channel, "Community Stories."
35. Frank Hopper, "7 Seconds in Seattle: John T. Williams' Murder Continues to Inspire Activism and Change," ICT, updated

September 13, 2018, https://indiancountrytoday.com/archive/7
-seconds-in-seattle-john-t-williams-murder-continues-to-inspire
-activism-and-change.

36. Lynda V. Mapes, "10 Years Ago a Police Officer Shot Woodcarver
John T. Williams. The Grief Reverberates Today," *Seattle Times*,
August 30, 2020, https://www.seattletimes.com/seattle-news/10
-years-ago-a-police-officer-shot-woodcarver-john-t-williams-the
-grief-reverberates-today/.

37. Merrick Bobb, "A Long Wait for SPD Reform," *Seattle Times*, February 4, 2022, https://www.seattletimes.com/opinion/a-long-wait-for
-spd-reform/.

38. Seattle Channel, "Community Stories."

39. NPR staff, "Years after Police Shooting, Woodcarver's Brother
Remembers the Man He Lost," NPR, October 7, 2016, https://www
.npr.org/2016/10/07/496867205/years-after-police-shooting
-woodcarvers-brother-remembers-the-man-he-lost.

40. Seattle Channel, "Community Stories."

41. Derrick Belgarde, Skid Road Oral History, interview by Josephine
Ensign, April 7, 2022.

42. Luna Reyna, "Renewed Effort to Remove the Misleading Totem Poles
at Pike Place Park," Crosscut, July 1, 2022, https://crosscut.com/news
/2022/07/renewed-effort-remove-misleading-totem-poles-pike-place
-park; David Kroman, "Activists Want to Remove Seattle's Iconic
Totem Poles," *High Country News*, October 1, 2018, https://www.hcn
.org/articles/tribal-affairs-activists-want-to-remove-seattles-iconic
-totem-poles.

43. Thrush, *Native Seattle*.

44. Luna Reyna, "Chief Seattle Club Housing Project Rooted in Indigenous Culture," Crosscut, February 16, 2022, https://crosscut.com
/news/2022/02/chief-seattle-club-housing-project-rooted-indigenous
-culture.

45. Press pool, "Seattle Indian Health Board Partners with Chief Seattle
Club to Open New Clinic in Pioneer Square," ICT, accessed September 27, 2022, https://indiancountrytoday.com/the-press-pool/seattle
-indian-health-board-partners-with-chief-seattle-club-to-open-new
-clinic-in-pioneer-square.

46. Benjamin Cassidy, "A Seattle Nonprofit Builds a 'Home' to Combat
Indigenous Homelessness," *Seattle Met*, September 21, 2021, https://

www.seattlemet.com/news-and-city-life/2021/09/chief-seattle-club
-combats-indigenous-homelessness-with-affordable-housing-pioneer
-square.
47. Cassidy, "Seattle Nonprofit."
48. Belgarde, Skid Road Oral History interview.
49. Belgarde, Skid Road Oral History interview.
50. Belgarde, Skid Road Oral History interview.

CHAPTER 7

Home Base

· · · · · · · · · · · · · · · · · · ·

> *Tuna came one day, scratched at our door, begged*
> *for food, and never went away.*
> *Home is where the cat is.*
>
> —MALE RESIDENT OF TENT CITY 3

> *Home is never permanent, but I know it is where*
> *I find safety.*
>
> —FEMALE RESIDENT OF TENT CITY 3

BORN JULY 1949 INTO A WORKING-CLASS FAMILY, Anitra Le-more Freeman remembers being a young child and waking up to find her mother "naked and screaming at three o'clock in the morning throwing coffee cups at the wall because the demons were coming through."[1] Anitra's family frequently moved in the Pacific Northwest between Seattle and Portland, except for when Anitra was three to five years old, during which time they lived in Anchorage, Alaska. Her mother had what was finally diagnosed as bipolar disorder, but her mother did not receive this diagnosis until Anitra was an adult. Anitra says, "She wasn't diagnosed, so she self-medicated with alcohol."[2] Her father, a veteran of the Korean War, had scars from five bullet holes and the accompanying undiagnosed PTSD from his time in the war. He also used alcohol to cope with his PTSD. Anitra points to her parents' alcohol use as a cause of their continuous job and housing instability, saying, "Alcoholics have a hard time holding down a job."[3] For people like Anitra who experience chaotic childhoods and family homelessness, developing a sense of home as a safe, stable place is difficult but not impossible. Anitra is living proof of this.

THINK OF WORDS that describe "home" to you—nouns, verbs, whatever words come to mind. Write them down. Circle the top five that are the most important. Now, pretend you live through a series of unfortunate events: loss of a job, fire, pandemic, and insurmountable medical debt. You lose one important item or word from your list for each of these four events. Say goodbye to each one as you cross it off. You are left with only one aspect of home that you carry with you into homelessness. For many people, that remaining aspect of home is family, beloved pets, safety, or privacy. For many people who experience homelessness, they are forced to give up everything that matters to them, everything that represents home, including a sense of belonging, of community, of a place to nurture and maintain health, of dignity and self-determination. For other people experiencing homelessness, they have never had a true home, or at least have never had a safe, secure home to give up, thus making their exit from homelessness that much more difficult.

Of course, the causes of homelessness are more complex than just a series of unfortunate events and extend beyond individual vulnerabilities and experiences. These unfortunate events are based in reality, since all of them do contribute to homelessness. Not enough people know that spiraling medical debt is a

leading cause of homelessness in the United States, a factor un-
heard of among our industrialized country peers and due to our
uniquely profit-driven health care system.[4]

This "meaning of home" exercise, although incomplete and
imprecise, can help people discern the differences between a
house and a home. A home is much more than a house, or a shelter. This exercise can help people realize some degree of what
homeless people have had to give up, what they can regain with
enough community support, and what types of community supports can prevent homelessness in the first place. Listening to
people's stories of what contributed to their experience of and
exit from homelessness can help deepen our understanding of
this complex issue. Stories from people with lived experience inform us as individuals and as a society about how we can build
on individual and community strengths, as well as on lived experience knowledge, to greatly reduce homelessness, if not outright solve it.

As an adult, Anitra Freeman lost everything related to the
meaning of home, including, according to her, a sense of dignity
and self-determination. She became homeless in Seattle, but
now she is not only housed but also thriving. During what, in
hindsight, Anitra identified as a manic episode hitting her
around 1990 after she turned forty, she quit her job at Boeing in
Seattle, where she worked as a computer programmer. In her
mania, she quit her stable job in order to be an independent con-
tractor. But in 1994 she lost her consulting business because of
what she calls her "great grey fog of depression," so she couch
surfed at her younger sister's house in California for a year and
at friends' places in Seattle for eight months.[5] Then, in October 1995, as she recounts, "I ran out of couches at the end of the
longest depression of my life," adding, "I spent the last money I
had, went to the YWCA for a few nights and then I was officially

homeless." She spent several nights sleeping in a lounge area at the Seattle-Tacoma International (Sea-Tac) Airport along with a handful of other people experiencing homelessness before she ended up living on the streets of downtown Seattle and then in homeless shelters.[6]

CHILDHOOD EXPERIENCE OF homelessness is one of the biggest predictors of adult chronic homelessness, and this is apparent in Anitra's life. "My parents moved around a lot," Anitra says. "We moved sometimes in the middle of the night because, you know," alluding to the fact that her parents often could not pay the rent.[7] When times became especially tough during her childhood, she and her family couch surfed, staying with various relatives. They spent a week living in their car. Anitra links her family's housing instability and childhood brush with homelessness to her parents' and her own mental and behavioral health challenges. She says that her family's frequent moves made it difficult for any of them to establish the stable medical care necessary for diagnosis and treatment of mental illness. "It made it hard for me to ever get diagnosed. The original problems led to more problems, which led to the financial problems . . . maybe if we'd had the support of the community, that would have helped. But then we would have had to stay in one place for long enough to build the community," she says, ending with a laugh. She also links her housing instability and undiagnosed mental illness with her educational difficulties, saying, "During my childhood, I went back and forth between A+ student and 'underachiever.'"[8]

Reflecting on Anitra's difficulties growing up, she clearly endured multiple adverse childhood experiences (ACEs), or traumas. Beginning with the CDC–Kaiser Permanente ACE Study, research studies have shown a strong link between the cumulative number of ACEs and poor health and social outcomes in adulthood.[9] ACEs most often include physical, sexual, and emotional abuse; neglect; involvement in child protective services; parental behavioral health problems; parental incarceration; parental intimate partner violence; and parental death or divorce.[10] Some researchers include housing instability and homelessness in childhood and adolescence as ACEs.[11] Critics of the link between ACEs and homelessness say that it has been relied on too much by white researchers and policymakers and ignores the link between systemic racism and homelessness.[12]

Anitra was exposed to the behavioral health problems of both parents. As a child, she experienced housing instability and homelessness in the form of couch surfing and vehicle residency. In her writing, Anitra alludes to having experienced some form of abuse and neglect. Modulating the negative effects of her childhood traumas, Anitra references many positive aspects of her childhood. A lifelong reader and writer of poetry, she says, "I was born into a family of 'bookaholics' and 'workaholics'—I never stood a chance. Reading and writing were considered normal human activities."[13] Anitra credits the Christian faith of her childhood for giving her strength then as now. In reflecting on survival of her difficult childhood, Anitra says that although she never had the presence of a caring adult to help her endure, "For me, my enlightened witness was God. . . . God was there to be my witness and to strengthen me . . . to treat other people the way people ought to be treated and not the way I was being treated."[14] She adds, "I grew up with good, leftist, liberal parents who taught me that you're supposed to be directly involved with your community, in democracy and social justice. I marched with my mother for civil rights."[15] Being involved in community-building events helps bolster individual resilience. All of these factors—her Christian faith, love of reading, expressive writing, and social justice activism—served as buffers for Anitra, helping her survive a chaotic childhood, mental illness, housing instability, and homelessness as an adult.

ANITRA'S INCONSISTENT EDUCATIONAL performance as a child followed her into adulthood. When she was twenty years old, she attended a state college in Bellingham, Washington, but dropped out after a year. Following her father's path into the armed services, Anitra attended the Community College of the Air Force for computer programming, at that time based in Nebraska. She met and married her first husband when they were both in technical training for the Air Force in Mississippi. While married, they moved frequently owing to their work in the Air Force, continuing Anitra's childhood housing instability, but for different reasons. Anitra and her first husband lived in Biloxi, Mississippi; Baudette, Minnesota; Fort Fisher, North Carolina; and Offutt Air Force Base in Omaha, Nebraska. In their ten years of marriage, which ended in divorce, they had one child, a son.

During marriage counseling with her first husband, Anitra remembers asking their counselor if it was possible that she had manic depression (the name then for bipolar disorder), but the counselor told her no.[16] Anitra clarifies that she was eventually diagnosed with bipolar II, which is characterized by milder manic episodes than associated with the bipolar I that her mother had. She adds, "I wasn't manic like my mother, but what I did have was very disruptive to my life and relationships, and it would have been nice if she [the marriage counselor] recognized it." About her son, Anitra says that when she and her first husband were separated, her son "went to live with his dad and his new mom. I hadn't been diagnosed up until that point, but we all knew that I had some problems."[17]

After her divorce, Anitra was once again living on her own in the Seattle area, working hard to hold down jobs and have a stable place to live. Her patchy work history affected her living situation and mental health stability, making it difficult for her to keep health insurance long enough to establish care with a health care provider. This, in turn, kept her from receiving a diagnosis and treatment for her mental illness. She says of this time that she was "still going up and down. Up and down. I would go through extremely productive phases and disappear for a few days. Phases."[18] Her undiagnosed mental illness also negatively impacted her employment status. She speaks of going back and forth between "workaholic and drifting vaguely between jobs."[19] She adds, "As I got older and older, this erratic work history made it harder and harder to get a job. The manic highs became less and less and the depressive periods got longer and longer."[20]

BEGINNING IN 1994, Anitra lived with her sister in Southern California for over a year. She had a job there for a while and said she was doing well because she was in a manic phase. But when she went into a depression, she lost that job.[21] Anitra says that even though they did not always get along, her sister helped her seek a mental illness diagnosis by pointing out that her mood swings were similar enough to their mother's. Anitra went to a psychiatrist in California and described her life and her symptoms. "He said, 'How were you not diagnosed long before?' He gave me a sample prescription of lithium and it was like a half an hour after taking it, it was, oh, that's what they mean about reality. The fog is clearing up all around me."[22]

Anitra had Scientology friends in California who scared her about the side effects of lithium, telling her that the medication could kill her. "I said, 'Okay, I don't need to take lithium. Now that I know what's going on, I know that when I'm manic, I need to drink some milk and take a lie-down, and when I'm depressed, I need to drink some milk and go out and take a walk," she says with a laugh. She moved back to Seattle to live with a friend, Pat, and worked for him in his home office in exchange for room and board. Pat ran an order-by-mail knife and knife-sharpening business. Still off of lithium, Anitra slid into another depression. She describes spending her days in a bathrobe on Pat's couch, only getting up, showering, and dressing right before Pat came home in the evening. She says she was pretending to be fine so he would not worry about her or ask her to leave.

In October 1995, when Pat told Anitra that he had family members coming to stay with him for the holidays and that he needed his couch she had been sleeping on, "I told him that I'd found a job, I'd found an apartment. I went out the door and spent the last few bucks that I had staying up all night. I spent the night at the YWCA."[23] After eight months of sleeping on his couch, she was too embarrassed to tell Pat the truth, that she had no job and no place to stay. Anitra recounts having knives to mail off for Pat on the day that she left his house. She says she put them in a bag and carried it to a UPS store to mail them off. That night when she slept at the YWCA, she woke up to find blood all over the sheets from where the knives had slashed her hip. Likely numb from everything happening to her, a common experience for people living with severe mental illness worsened by stress, Anitra had not realized she had a cut.

While living with Pat, Anitra started going to Country Doctor Clinic on Capitol Hill, a community health center providing comprehensive primary health care, inclusive of behavioral health services, and with a sliding scale payment system. A Country Doctor physician had been treating Anitra for bronchitis, but Anitra had not told her about her diagnosis of manic depression. When Anitra saw the doctor the day after she first slept at the YWCA, the doctor checked on her bronchitis and also tended to the knife wound. On a follow-up visit a week later, a week during which Anitra stayed at the YWCA, Anitra finally told the doctor that she had manic depression and needed treatment for it. The doctor "sent me to see the psychiatrist down the hall, who immediately diagnosed me and gave me a prescription for lithium, and I didn't have the money to get the prescription filled. They could fill my antibiotics right there at the clinic, but they couldn't fill the lithium." Country Doctor Clinic, like all the other community health clinics in the Seattle area, provides free health care, including medication, to people who are homeless, but Anitra likely did not tell them that she was homeless because of the significant societal stigma attached to homelessness.

Running out of money to stay at the downtown Seattle YWCA, Anitra rode the bus to Sea-Tac Airport, this being before the Link light rail existed. Sea-Tac Airport consists of a series of large glass and steel buildings with views of snow-capped Mount Olympus to the west and Mount Rainier to the south. Anitra had heard rumors that people experiencing homelessness sometimes slept in the transit lounges of the airport. With its cold, liminal, and unsettled atmosphere; competing noise from blaring TVs, announcements, side conversations, and airplanes taking off and landing outside the glass panes; and glaring fluorescent lighting overhead, the airport is not a place conducive to relaxation or sleep. But, of course, exhausted and stranded travelers often can sleep fitfully there, as can desperate and weary people with no other place to go. Although Sea-Tac Airport seems to be a public space since it is owned and operated by the Port of Seattle, a government entity, homeless people seeking shelter there are "trespassing on private property," according to Port of Seattle police officer Michelle Bregel.[24]

Once Anitra arrived at Sea-Tac Airport, she found "two older white men with twine-wrapped boxes on old handcarts, three older black men with the same sort of 'luggage,' and two white women with newish-looking luggage, both stretched out asleep. Everyone had what I've come to call the 'pavement look' on their face."[25] She describes sleeping there with this group of people, being awakened at 4:00 A.M. by airport security workers who were asking the Black men to show their flight tickets. When the men said they did not have tickets, the security guards offered to find the men shelter bed options. She recounts that the guards only asked the Black men to leave. "They didn't ask any of the rest of us questions. So I knew that civil rights, the end to racism that my mother and I had marched for in the 60s, hadn't completely taken yet. And that was just one of the ways in which my country slowly radicalized me every single day from the time I became homeless."[26]

PERHAPS DUE TO Anitra's lifelong love of reading and expressive writing, including writing poetry, she eloquently describes the complex circumstances contributing to her homelessness in middle age and the visceral sensory details of her lived experience of homelessness and severe mental illness. After staying at the YWCA and Sea-Tac Airport, Anitra ended up living on the streets of Seattle. "One of my most vivid memories of being homeless is standing on a street corner at Third and James at three o'clock in the morning in the rain and going, 'I have no place to go.'" She recalls that when she was housed and in her car driving these same streets, she had been oblivious to the presence of homeless people. On that night, when she was homeless on the streets of downtown Seattle, she walked up to her friend's place on Beacon Hill to see whether she could sleep on his couch. He was not at home, so she slept under his back porch. When she had to urinate, she used an empty can. During her sleep that night she knocked over the can, drenching herself in urine. "That was the low point—the absolutely low point for me."[27]

Anitra describes the fear she felt as a homeless woman: "As a working woman making $48,000 a year as a computer programmer, a wife and mother with a house of my own, I might have been tense about a lot of things including the bills, but I wasn't scared. I wasn't scared as a middle-class woman walking down the sidewalk, but walking down the same sidewalk as a homeless woman at the same time of day, I was scared. It's not the same place; it's not the same world. You're surrounded by different forces; you're subject—you're susceptible—to different risks."[28] The dichotomy Anitra portrays is reminiscent of that described by George Orwell in his book *Down and Out in Paris and London*, although there, being from a man's perspective, the focus is on shame and not fear. When the main character sells his clothes for more tattered ones plus extra cash, he notices something: "Dressed in a tramp's clothes it is very difficult, at any rate for the first day, not to feel that you are genuinely degraded. You might feel the same shame, irrational but very real, your first night in prison."[29]

After Anitra became homeless, her son cut off all contact with her because of her struggles with mental illness, now combined with homelessness. She adds that a lot of women experiencing homelessness have endured similar ruptures in their relationships with their children and even permanently lose custody of and contact with their children. She knows the deep sadness and grief that this loss causes. Besides losing everything related to her meaning of home, including her dignity and self-determination, Anitra lost contact with her only child, with the accretive layers upon layers of trauma, loss, and grief that this brings. Similar issues, of course, occur for men who experience homelessness. Still, the traditional societal expectations of mothers make the stigma and pain of ruptures in relationships with children much worse for women.[30] Homeless women who lose custody of their children, especially of babies and young children, can experience chronic, unresolved grief in large part caused by stigmatization and social marginalization for going against gender role expectations. In many cases, their grief is worse and lasts longer than grief for the death of a child.[31]

DRAWING ON HER sense of humor, Anitra recounts wandering the streets of Capitol Hill, "looking in windows, daydreaming about a sign that says, 'Wanted: one manic-depressive computer programmer who will live in the office. Food provided,' and I didn't find it. I stood on a street corner, and I said, 'Okay, this is it. I'm forty-five years old. I'm manic-depressive.' . . . I knew I had bronchitis, I was physically sick; I had bad teeth; my hair's a mess. I'm overweight, and my tits hang down to my navel, and I'm homeless, and I have no place to go. I'm out of work, and I'm broke, and I've been through everything."[32] She points to this as a moment of self-acceptance and the beginning of "the biggest growth period of my life."[33]

On the day that she came to this acceptance of her situation, she walked into a subsidized apartment building she had passed on a street in Capitol Hill. She walked in and said to a front-desk worker, "I'm homeless, and I've got no place to go. . . . I'm sick. I'm manic-depressive. I need help." They sent her downtown to Angeline's, run by the YWCA and at that time the only women's shelter in Seattle. Staff members at Angeline's gave her a list of resources and pointed to their free phones near the front of the building. She recounts that she made two phone calls to service providers, left voice messages, and sat on the couch at the day shelter for the rest of the day. When the day center was closing at the end of the day, a staff member at Angeline's had another homeless woman accompany Anitra several blocks to Noel House for dinner. At Noel House, Anitra signed up for shelter, and after dinner, a van took her to an overnight mats-on-the-floor shelter in a Seattle church basement.

Anitra recalls entering the shelter for the first time. "I was doing the 'homeless shuffle.' I was one of the shuffling figures who went in, head down, and just meekly got the mat."[34] Next to her was a sixty-eight-year-old woman with severe arthritis. Of watching this woman slowly getting down onto the mat and then up again, obviously in pain, Anitra says, "And that cut into me. Even through the fog, I thought: to have that life, to have that happening to that sixty-eight-year-old woman sleeping on that little rubber mat, that concrete floor."[35] She adds, "I didn't think we let that happen."[36]

WHEN ANITRA ENTERED the shelter in Seattle for the first time, she could have become yet another single adult with a serious, untreated mental illness falling into homelessness, doing the "homeless shuffle" on the path to becoming another chronically homeless statistic within the large and oftentimes impersonal Seattle–King County homelessness system, or what critics call the homelessness industrial complex.

As a homeless single mother without custody of her son, Anitra was ineligible for programs and benefits afforded to homeless mothers or fathers with dependent children. She had not been homeless this time for long, and the rapid rehousing and Housing First efforts that would be rolled out in subsequent years had not yet been developed and implemented. Even if these efforts had been in existence, if HUD had fully developed its official definition of chronic homelessness, and even given her as-yet-untreated severe mental illness, Anitra likely would not have been deemed a chronically homeless adult and therefore would not have been prioritized for housing. The fact that she was a single woman did increase her vulnerability. Her bipolar disorder had been diagnosed by the time she entered the Seattle shelter system, and she was carrying a prescription for lithium that she was unable to afford to fill. As an Air Force veteran, it is unclear what, if any, health care and other benefits she may have been eligible to receive. Then, as now, the rate of homelessness among veterans, especially for women, is extremely high. Veterans Affairs had not yet started its programs to address homelessness among veterans, an emphasis on housing and health care access that has had a positive impact on reducing veteran homelessness across the United States.[37]

At the same time, Anitra had individual assets and strengths she could draw on to help her overcome the difficulties she found herself in. She had education, self-insight, a healthy sense of humor, friends, and compassion for others and for herself. And she was open to offers of help. As she puts it, "I was easy. I was ready for help. Medication was still scary, but the alternative was scarier."[38]

On her first night of shelter through Noel House, she met Debbie Shaw, a mental health outreach worker through DESC. As Anitra describes it, "Instead of waiting in an office for people to find their way in, these workers went out to places where homeless people were, including streets and underpasses, found people in need of help, built up a relationship with them, and got them into services and housing."[39] Anitra recalls that she was ready to talk to Debbie Shaw that first night. Debbie brought Anitra's filled lithium prescription to her the next day. Soon after starting back on lithium, Anitra participated in a Halloween craft activity led by a Noel House volunteer. "I cut out a rectangle of dark brown paper and put it onto a rectangle of orange paper, and I wrote a two line poem which was the first poem I'd written in six months: 'Now all threatening shadows open into warmth and light.'"[40]

Soon after the fog of her depression was lifting with the help of lithium, a continuous counseling relationship with Debbie Shaw from DESC, and safe shelter, Anitra says, "when I perked up a little bit more, and I realized I could not stand one more day of coming into Noel House and having my food served to me by these people and being given little plastic forks and spoons to eat with that I couldn't hurt myself with."[41] After about a week, she noticed a sign on the wall of Noel House announcing a self-managed shelter. "The next day I went down the street to the offices of SHARE (Seattle Housing and Resource Effort) and screened into CCS, the shelter hosted in the cafeteria of the Catholic Community Services Center. I was given a bus ticket and was told I could arrive any time from 9 P.M. to 10 P.M."[42] At this point, Anitra began to reclaim her dignity and sense of self-determination.

IN LATE OCTOBER 1995, when Anitra first joined SHARE as a shelter participant at the Catholic Community Services (CCS) location, the self-managed organization was only five years old. Begun in late November 1990 as part public protest and part survival tactic of a group of people experiencing homelessness, reminiscent of the Hoovervilles of the Great Depression,

SHARE's first Tent City emerged in a muddy parking lot next to the railroad tracks near the Kingdome just south of Pioneer Square.[43] Modeled after homeless self-managed housing efforts of previous eras in Seattle, including the multiple Hoovervilles and the even earlier Hotel de Gink ("Gink" being hobo slang for "poor unfortunate"), which opened in 1913 in the old Providence Hospital building downtown, SHARE had overcome local opposition and expanded to other locations like CCS.[44] SHARE's sister organization, WHEEL, joined forces with SHARE in 1993 to include a focus on the issues unique to homeless women. Anitra found herself drawn to the work of both of these organizations.

In describing her time at the SHARE CCS self-managed shelter site, Anitra recalls that they had use of a storage shed outside, where the shelter participants could each store one thirty-gallon garbage bag of their belongings so they did not have to carry it around all day.[45] The storage unit also held mats and blankets, which the shelter participants would take inside to set up for the night, packing them back into the shed in the morning before they left for the day. She notes that they had use of the small kitchen and that many of the shelter participants were into Star Trek like she was, helping to create an immediate community bond.

All shelter participants had to sign up for various duties like cleaning, security, and weekly community meetings. They were encouraged to get involved in advocacy efforts around homelessness and poverty. Anitra started spending time during the day at the Street Life Art Gallery, a self-managed creative space started by one of the founders of SHARE.[46] Anitra met, became friends with, and eventually married one of the art gallery's leaders, Wes Browning, who got her involved with *Real Change*, an anti-poverty newspaper. She says that soon after she began her involvement with the gallery and *Real Change*, "I composed my second poem: 'Out of limbo I come to find myself / scattered across the pavement / creating from found objects a life.'"[47]

Anitra stayed at the SHARE CCS shelter site until the beginning of February 1996, when her DESC case manager, Debbie Shaw, got her into supportive housing in Pioneer Square at the Union Hotel. Of moving into her new apartment, Anitra says with characteristic humor and candor, "That first week or so I would dance around the apartment naked. I could cook for myself. I could eat anytime I wanted to. And it was silent. You never get silence when you're homeless."[48] She quickly adds, "A lot of people—women especially—you go from being surrounded by people pretty much 24/7 to being alone in your apartment, and the first couple of weeks, it's great. Then you're isolated."[49] She points out that her friends could not easily visit her in her new apartment, and she could not visit her friends still experiencing homelessness in the traditional homeless shelters and feeding programs.

Anitra did not have time to be isolated, given her involvement in many community organizations. By then, she had started a writing group and a computer training program for homeless women. "Talking about community, Debbie Shaw, the caseworker from DESC, got me my lithium, got me on to State disability, got me on track to get Social Security, got me into housing. But she couldn't have kept me going for four months all alone. It was the community that I found in SHARE and WHEEL and *Real Change*. And the writing group that kept me going. And once I was in housing, kept me stable."[50]

ANITRA FREEMAN MARRIED Wes Browning, also formerly homeless, and they currently live together in an apartment in the

International District in Seattle. Anitra is involved with many homeless advocacy groups and programs, including SHARE/ WHEEL, *Real Change*, and DESC. Despite internal leadership and external controversies and challenges, SHARE's various tent cities, which expanded into the earliest tiny house villages, constitute the longest-lasting self-managed temporary housing in the country.[51]

In 2000, Anitra was a founding member of WHEEL's Women in Black group. In the fall of 2020, after the murder-suicide of Lisa Vaugh and Travis Berge, Anitra was with Women in Black on the steps of City Hall, where they held cardboard signs with Travis's and Lisa's names. Anitra recalls that two of Lisa's friends were "just extremely upset, grabbing Travis's name card and tearing it up. . . . You've got to take your anger out on somebody."[52] Lisa's friends were upset that Travis, who had physically abused and murdered Lisa, was being remembered at the vigil alongside Lisa. Anitra told me that no bronze leaf memorial has been added for Travis Berge since no one has requested it.

When asked what motivates her to stay so active with the WHEEL Women in Black group, Anitra says, "The community of grief. If I did stay at home in that grief, it probably would kill me. But when you share grief, it's a healing experience instead. It builds the community. Doing it in front of City Hall, and going into City Hall, and testifying at City Hall, and saying, 'I'm Anitra Freeman. I stand with the Women in Black. These are how many people have died on your doorstep. You have to act.'"[53] Expanding on this, she states,

There's something about grief and death that our psychological reaction is to withdraw, and we curl around our pain. . . . But we need to grow out of that now. Sharing with, being at the vigil, being in the community has helped me bear this without going into a depression, going to the hospital. . . . No wonder people try to forget the homeless experience. No wonder people try not to think about other people as human like me, because it's almost too much. And yet, we have to if we're going to survive. . . . We've got to bear it, come out of the numbness and bear our pain, bear each other's pain.[54]

AS FOR ANITRA'S perspective on what contributed to her homelessness, she points to the combination of personal vulnerabilities within larger structural, systems-level factors. With regard to her exit from homelessness, she credits her access to a community health center, access to a source of basic income through disability and Social Security, access to subsidized housing, and connections with the wider community as key factors that "got me out of homelessness and that keep me out of homelessness."[55] She adds,

I might have had the same personal problems if there was social justice, economic justice, environmental justice, and everything the peace and justice community is struggling for. But would I have become homeless even with the same personal problems? I would have had more teeth left because I could have gotten dental care even during the times when I had no money. My physical health would have been better, and I would probably live longer. I probably would have still spent the rest of my life as a poster child for codependence, but I wouldn't have parts of my body that will never relax again, because when you're homeless you're scared all the time—you're scared while you're asleep.[56]

Anitra has developed metaphors for the causes of homelessness: "I have often said that people have personal problems, of course, but personal problems don't cause homelessness. Personal problems don't dig the hole in the sidewalk; they just influence who is going to fall into it. It's systemic factors that create the hole."[57] More recently, when I asked about her metaphor of the hole in the sidewalk, with her head thrown back in a hearty laugh she said,

> Yeah. I've expanded that a bit. There's a chasm at the edge of town. There's a big cliff at the edge of town, and the people living and working downtown hardly ever see it. A lot of them don't even know it's there. But the people who get pushed out to the edge of town for whatever reason—maybe they're people of color, maybe they don't speak English, maybe they're immigrants, maybe they're LGBT, maybe they're uncomfortable to be around because they act all weird, or maybe they drink too much or shoot up, whatever—people who get pushed to the edge of town end up going over the cliff.[58]

And she adds, "Homelessness is not going to change until you change the whole system."[59]

Notes

1. Desiree Hellegers, *No Room of Her Own: Women's Stories of Homelessness, Life, Death, and Resistance*, Palgrave Studies in Oral History (New York: Palgrave Macmillan, 2011), 80–81.
2. Anitra Freeman, Skid Road Oral History, interview by Josephine Ensign, October 25, 2022.
3. Freeman, Skid Road Oral History interview.
4. Jessica E. Bielenberg et al., "Presence of Any Medical Debt Associated with Two Additional Years of Homelessness in a Seattle Sample," *Inquiry: A Journal of Medical Care Organization, Provision and Financing* 57 (December 2020): 46958020923535, https://doi.org/10.1177/0046958020923535; Jessica Lipscomb, "Medical Debt Biggest Cause of South Florida Homelessness, Survey Says," *Miami New*

Times, October 5, 2017, https://www.miaminewtimes.com/news/medical-debt-ranks-no-1-cause-of-south-florida-homelessness-survey-says-9724408; Jessica Mogk et al., "Court-Imposed Fines as a Feature of the Homelessness-Incarceration Nexus: A Cross-Sectional Study of the Relationship between Legal Debt and Duration of Homelessness in Seattle, Washington, USA," *Journal of Public Health (Oxford, England)* 42, no. 2 (June 4, 2019): e107–19, https://doi.org/10.1093/pubmed/fdz062.

5. BenWaitingClips, "Women Surviving Homelessness Part One—Flying Focus Video Collective," YouTube video, 2014, https://www.youtube.com/watch?v=RnmAbSn5Ezk.

6. Hellegers, *No Room of Her Own,* 81.

7. Freeman, Skid Road Oral History interview.

8. "Anitra's Web: My Experience with Homelessness, Bipolar Disorder, & Activism," Anitra.net, accessed October 1, 2022, http://anitra.net/homelessness/real/mystory.html.

9. Vincent J. Felitti et al., "Relationship of Childhood Abuse and Household Dysfunction to Many of the Leading Causes of Death in Adults: The Adverse Childhood Experiences (ACE) Study," *American Journal of Preventive Medicine* 14, no. 4 (1998): 245–58, https://doi.org/10.1016/S0749-3797(98)00017-8; Karen Hughes et al., "The Effect of Multiple Adverse Childhood Experiences on Health: A Systematic Review and Meta-analysis," *Lancet Public Health* 2, no. 8 (August 1, 2017): e356–66, https://doi.org/10.1016/S2468-2667(17)30118-4.

10. Michael Liu et al., "Adverse Childhood Experiences and Related Outcomes among Adults Experiencing Homelessness: A Systematic Review and Meta-analysis," *Lancet Public Health* 6, no. 11 (November 1, 2021): e836–47, https://doi.org/10.1016/S2468-2667(21)00189-4.

11. Milad Parpouchi, Akm Moniruzzaman, and Julian M. Somers, "The Association between Experiencing Homelessness in Childhood or Youth and Adult Housing Stability in Housing First," *BMC Psychiatry* 21, no. 1 (March 8, 2021): 138, https://doi.org/10.1186/s12888-021-03142-0; Elizabeth Radcliff et al., "Homelessness in Childhood and Adverse Childhood Experiences (ACEs)," *Maternal and Child Health Journal* 23, no. 6 (June 1, 2019): 811–20, https://doi.org/10.1007/s10995-018-02698-w.

12. Anna Patrick, "Did You Miss This Week's Panel on Racism and Homelessness? Here Are Some Highlights," *Seattle Times*, June 26, 2020, https://www.seattletimes.com/seattle-news/homeless/did-you -miss-this-weeks-panel-on-racism-and-homelessness-here-are-some -highlights/.
13. Hellegers, *No Room of Her Own*, 84.
14. Hellegers, *No Room of Her Own*, 86.
15. Freeman, Skid Road Oral History interview.
16. Freeman, Skid Road Oral History interview.
17. Freeman, Skid Road Oral History interview.
18. Freeman, Skid Road Oral History interview.
19. "Anitra's Web."
20. Hellegers, *No Room of Her Own*, 81.
21. Freeman, Skid Road Oral History interview.
22. Freeman, Skid Road Oral History interview.
23. Freeman, Skid Road Oral History interview.
24. Casey Martin, "For Some without a Home, Sea-Tac Airport Is a Source of Shelter," *Seattle Times*, January 17, 2023, https://www .seattletimes.com/seattle-news/for-some-without-a-home-sea-tac -airport-is-a-source-of-shelter/.
25. Freeman, Skid Road Oral History interview.
26. Hellegers, *No Room of Her Own*, 81–82.
27. Hellegers, *No Room of Her Own*, 82.
28. Hellegers, *No Room of Her Own*, 82.
29. George Orwell, *Down and Out in Paris and London* (San Diego: Mariner Books, 1972), 129.
30. Daryn H. David, Lillian Gelberg, and Nancy E. Suchman, "Implications of Homelessness for Parenting Young Children: A Preliminary Review from a Developmental Attachment Perspective," *Infant Mental Health Journal* 33, no. 1 (2012): 1–9, https://doi.org/10.1002/imhj.20333.
31. Sylvia Novac et al., "Supporting Young Homeless Mothers Who Have Lost Child Custody," in *Finding Home: Policy Options for Addressing Homelessness in Canada*, ed. J. David Hulchanski et al. (Canadian Observatory on Homelessness, 2009), https://www.homelesshub.ca /resource/41-supporting-young-homeless-mothers-who-have-lost -child-custody.
32. Hellegers, *No Room of Her Own*, 82.

33. Hellegers, *No Room of Her Own*, 82.
34. Hellegers, *No Room of Her Own*, 83.
35. Hellegers, *No Room of Her Own*, 83.
36. Freeman, Skid Road Oral History interview.
37. William Evans et al., "Housing and Urban Development–Veterans Affairs Supportive Housing Vouchers and Veterans' Homelessness, 2007–2017," *American Journal of Public Health* 109, no. 10 (October 1, 2019): 1440–45, https://ajph-aphapublications-org.offcampus .lib.washington.edu/doi/full/10.2105/AJPH.2019.305231.
38. "Anitra's Web."
39. "Anitra's Web."
40. Hellegers, *No Room of Her Own*, 83.
41. Hellegers, *No Room of Her Own*, 83.
42. "Anitra's Web."
43. Ronald K. Fitten, "The Bonds of Poverty—Tent City Knots Homeless into a Community," *Seattle Times*, December 3, 1990, https://archive .seattletimes.com/archive/?date=19901203&slug=1107581.
44. Sinan Demirel, "Hotel de Gink (Seattle)," HistoryLink.org, June 13, 2002, https://www.historylink.org/File/3849.
45. Freeman, Skid Road Oral History interview.
46. Real Change staff, "Street Life Gallery," *Real Change*, August 1, 1994, http://www.realchangenews.org/news/1994/08/01/street-life-gallery.
47. Hellegers, *No Room of Her Own*, 84.
48. Freeman, Skid Road Oral History interview.
49. Freeman, Skid Road Oral History interview.
50. Freeman, Skid Road Oral History interview.
51. "Tent City 4 Division," SHARE/WHEEL, accessed October 1, 2022, http://www.sharewheel.org/tent-city-4/tent-city-4-division; "Early Jolt: Tent City Divorces SHARE," *Seattle Met*, November 15, 2012, https://www.seattlemet.com/news-and-city-life/2012/11/early-jolt -tent-city-divorces-share; Daniel McCraw et al., "Rebuttal to Seattle Times Interview with Jason Johnson," *Real Change*, March 10, 2021, https://www.realchangenews.org/news/2021/03/10/rebuttal-seattle -times-interview-jason-johnson.
52. Freeman, Skid Road Oral History interview.
53. Freeman, Skid Road Oral History interview.
54. Hellegers, *No Room of Her Own*, 91.

55. BenWaitingClips, "Women Surviving Homelessness Part One."
56. Hellegers, *No Room of Her Own*, 80.
57. Hellegers, *No Room of Her Own*, 80.
58. Freeman, Skid Road Oral History interview.
59. BenWaitingClips, "Women Surviving Homelessness Part One."

CHAPTER 8

Roll On

⬤　⬤　　⬤　　⬤　　⬤　　⬤　　⬤　　⬤　　⬤　　⬤　　⬤　　⬤　　⬤　　⬤　　⬤

> *They know that in the eyes of the law, they are*
> *homeless. But who can live under the weight of that*
> *word? The term "homeless" has metastasized*
> *beyond its literal definition, becoming a terrible*
> *threat. It whispers:* Exiles. The Fallen. The Other.
> Those Who Have Nothing Left.
>
> —JESSICA BRUDER, *NOMADLAND*, 203

"THE LAST THING YOU OWN when you're losing everything you own is probably your vehicle, so that becomes your home."[1] Jenn Adams knows this from six years living in her Seattle van starting in 2007. "I've lived in three different vans and a doorway," she said in a recent interview I had with her. She talked about her experience and current work as an advocate and peer outreach worker to vehicle residents in Seattle.[2]

I had my own experience resorting to living in my car and in an abandoned shed for six months in my hometown of Richmond, Virginia, when I was a young adult.[3] The topic of vehicle residency as a unique form of homelessness has long been of interest to me. I wanted to explore more of the nuances of vehicle residency from the perspective of a woman with a much longer experience than me and one based here in Seattle.

Vehicle residency has been called "the fastest-growing sub-population of homeless people in the US," although federal officials still do not measure rates of vehicle residency.[4] The number of vehicle residents in Seattle and King County more than tripled between 2012, when vehicle residency was first included in local homelessness counts, and 2020.[5] During the COVID-19 pandemic, vehicle residency grew exponentially. Why is vehicle residency such a large and growing part of homelessness, especially on the West Coast? How does vehicle residency differ from other forms of homelessness? What effective programs are there for people living in their vehicles? And why has vehicle residency become so controversial that it has been called the "third rail" in discussions about homelessness?

BORN AND RAISED in Bellingham and Mount Vernon, Washington, north of Seattle and close to the US-Canada border, Jenn has lived most of her adult life in Seattle. She comes from a large, supportive family; her mother was a nurse, and her father was a commercial fisherman. As a child, she was taught the value of hard work, starting with field work picking strawberries and spinach in the flat agricultural areas of Mount Vernon, and then working with her father fishing in the cold waters of the Salish Sea and Pacific Ocean. The death of a younger brother marked her childhood. About this, she says, "Everyone who is homeless fails the ACE test," referring to measures of adverse childhood events. After attending Skagit Valley College, Jenn moved to Seattle, where she worked as a car detailer, as an insurance adjuster at Pier 91 overseeing import and export vehicles, and even in the "crazy industry storing other people's stuff," where she "learned a lot about people," including the amount of meaning people place on their personal and family items.[6]

While working to help run other people's businesses, Jenn bought a house in 1991 for $79,000. But then a relationship soured and became abusive, and as she says, "I became homeless because I had a stalker, and I told him 'no.' If it can be that easy, then it can happen to anyone. It's not just the paycheck thing." She points to the "shame wrapped around homelessness" as the reason she did not reach out to her family for help. She did not want them to know of her situation, saying that when she told them about her homelessness after she had become housed again, they were angry at her. "If you don't have any kind of safety net or family, or you already come from generational traumas, then nobody knows what to do. Then you get this shame and blame, and we're blaming the victim."[7]

Jenn speaks of this experience while she was homeless, saying, "I realized that very few people listened to me, to us. They othered me. There's so much shame wrapped around homelessness." She adds that she felt that people were saying or thinking, "We don't want to see you. We want you gone. We want you moved out of our sights and waterfront views."[8] This internalized shame and stigma for people experiencing any form of homelessness is all too common and is a result of our society's (and our own individual) sorting of people into desirable and undesirable, the worthy and unworthy poor. For people experiencing homelessness this stigma and "othering" is reinforced through daily interactions with housed people, with service providers, and even with other homeless people, who may say things such as, "At least I'm not a homeless junky; I'm better than those people." Or, as can be the case for vehicle residents who may consider themselves houseless but not homeless, "At least I'm not that homeless bum on the street." Alexander, a fisherman and vehicle resident in Ballard's "car colony" in 2005, puts it this way: "Us in that truck is better than us on a doorstep somewhere."[9]

As described by Jenn above, "social exclusion" is defined by the *Oxford English Dictionary* as "exclusion or isolation from the prevalent social system and its rights and privileges, especially as a result of poverty or membership in a particular group."[10] People experiencing homelessness are, and historically have been, among the most visibly socially excluded. As Peter Cockersell, a psychologist in the United Kingdom working with people experiencing homelessness, states, "Homelessness is a powerful indicator of social exclusion because it involves the lack of a very fundamental resource in our society, a home; and that lack or loss leads to other losses, such as warmth, shelter, stability, and makes accessing other important resources, from social status through to healthcare, education or work, very difficult."[11] Cockersell is writing about social exclusion in a country with more social supports, including public housing and a national health care system, than we have in the United States. The shame, stigma, and fallout from being socially excluded, without effective interventions, contribute to a decline in quality of life and chronic stress for that person, leading to poor health and early death. In high-income countries like the United States, the mortality rate for men experiencing homelessness is eight times higher than that for the average man; for women experiencing homelessness, the mortality rate is twelve times higher.[12]

ALTHOUGH IT IS likely impossible to eliminate the practice of social exclusion within society and the provision of health care, there are exemplary programmatic and policy interventions. In the United Kingdom, they have the health care charity Pathway, which works with the National Health Service to create teams to provide what they term "inclusion health" for people who have been socially excluded. The groups of people they focus their services on are the homeless, asylum seekers, Gypsies ("Roma" being a preferable term here in the United States), Travelers, ex-prisoners, and sex workers. These groups of people are simultaneously stigmatized and romanticized to the point of fetishizing their lifestyles in the media and popular imagination.[13]

Pathway employs care navigators with the lived experience of homelessness and other forms of social exclusion, referring to them as experts by experience.[14] In the United States, lacking a national health care system, we have the national HCH Council supporting the work of providers in the various national HCH programs scattered throughout the country. It is important to recognize that individual and community resistance and resiliency building, including through self-help, self-managed programs like SHARE/WHEEL, buffer the negative effects of social exclusion. Moreover, these efforts operate outside of any formal health care and social support institutions.

Jenn Adams points to the self-help and mutual-aid movements she was part of as helping her survive her years of homelessness in Seattle: "It was the things that I saw and the people that I saw that weren't getting the help that they needed, especially mental illness and substance abuse. . . . I started reaching out to people, and bringing people water, and telling them that they were worthy."[15]

She tells the story of one Thanksgiving during her time of homelessness when she handed out twelve sleeping bags on her bicycle, getting two or three at a time and taking them to people. "That was fun, though, because it was exciting to me to be on my bicycle and riding in the wind and knowing that I was helping somebody. It gave me purpose, and as soon as I realized that I liked that, and that I could help people, I couldn't stop, and I haven't stopped. . . . It helped my psyche."[16] Although Jenn did not make an explicit link to this fact, research indicates that helping other people, when not done to such excess that it becomes detrimental to the giver, lowers stress-related cortisol levels and counters depression for the person doing the giving.[17]

In reflecting on her time living in her vehicle and then on the streets in Seattle, Jenn talked about her depression and alcohol use. "I think I got in a rut of depression. Homelessness can be really hard on the psyche." She added, "I had an addiction, but it was alcohol, and it was more I think I was trying to drown. Went to treatment once. Walked away. Next June, it will be eleven years [of sobriety]." Jenn had a job the entire time she was homeless. "I was landscaping because I didn't have to take a shower all the time. You do what you have to do in the environment that you're given. I never gave up. Never once. I was probably the happiest homeless person there was."[18]

Contributing to Jenn's happiness was the sense of community she felt with other vehicle residents and people experiencing various forms of homelessness in the Ballard area of Seattle, where she lived. She told me about a cold, rainy night in Seattle when her van broke down. No one would stop to help her, so she found five homeless people she knew, and they helped her push her van to the side of the road until she could get it fixed. "We come out at night," she explained, because vehicle residents try to remain inconspicuous during the day.[19]

WHILE HOMELESS, JENN DEALT with the effects of a chronic health condition, multiple sclerosis (MS), an autoimmune neurodegenerative disease with a high prevalence in the Seattle area.[20] First diagnosed in 1996 while she was housed and in her thirties, her first symptom of MS was going blind in her left eye in the span of an hour. It took three days and many tests before a medical specialist at the UW Medical Center diagnosed her with optic neuritis caused by MS. Later on, likely brought on by the chronic stress of homelessness, Jenn's MS flared. "I was having a hard time walking and stuff while I was homeless. Hence, the bike." Unfortunately, when she sought health care again, she was told that they could not find her previous medical records with the workup for the diagnosis of MS. "I was really taken back by that. I had never had that kind of experience and was really horrified. I told my story throughout the street, and I started hearing a lot of other stories on the street about the inadequacy of homelessness health care."[21]

People with medical conditions, especially those with mobility issues like Jenn, along with families and people with pets, often choose vehicle residency over emergency shelters or outdoor living when they have a vehicle. Mounting medical debt can lead to homelessness, including for vehicle residents.[22] In a conversation I had recently with Marty Hartman, founder and director of Mary's Place, providing multisite family shelters and housing in the Seattle area, she spoke of the number of people she knew who had sick children and who lived in their vehicles in and around Seattle Children's Hospital in Northeast Seattle, near the UW campus.[23] They lived there to be close to medical care for their child and because they did not want to stay in crowded shelters. In 2016, Mary's Place worked with Children's Hospital and Amazon to open Popsicle Place, a shelter for medically fragile children and their parents.[24] Popsicle Place is located downtown in one of the modern buildings of Amazon's headquarters. During the pandemic, when used vehicles were scarce, Marty reports that many homeless families lived in rental moving vans as a form of affordable and temporary housing.

In western states, including Washington, extreme weather events linked to climate change, especially wildfires and drought, are displacing more people, many of whom resort to vehicle residency, at least for a while. This situation is reminiscent of the Oakies and Rubber Tramps displaced during the Dust Bowl. Then as now, Seattle was home to both economic and climate refugees. The Rubber Tramps of the Dust Bowl era were, of course, not only economic refugees but also climate refugees. Their modern-day counterparts—climate and water refugees, people fleeing extreme drought conditions and fire-plagued regions of the western parts of our country—are steadily increasing in Seattle.

As the June 2021 heat dome extreme weather event proved to us, even the maritime, typically mild-climate area of Seattle is not immune to the effects of climate collapse. Unsheltered homeless people and others living in poverty and social isolation are at the highest risk of being severely affected by extreme weather events, as evidenced by the statistics on deaths attributed to the heat wave.[25] And, as civil rights lawyer Sarah Rankin points out, people living displaced and unsheltered are disproportionately from historically marginalized and vulnerable groups.[26]

DURING THE SIX YEARS that Jenn was a vehicle resident, she lived in the Ballard neighborhood of Northwest Seattle along the Ship Canal and near the shores of Puget Sound. The area where she lived was dubbed a "car colony," with at least fifty cars, vans, trucks, and buses parked in the boatyard district near Ballard Bridge. Rick Reynolds, director of Operation Nightwatch, an outreach program for people experiencing homelessness, said of the Ballard car colony, "It's the city's new rolling slum."[27] Jenn lived there because of the homeless and social services that were located in the area. She also lived there to be near Puget Sound. "I have to be near water, no matter where I am in life, so the water was there to keep me at peace and keep me calm so I could help other people."[28]

Ballard has long been a working-class neighborhood, with docking and repair shops for commercial fishing vessels east of the Ballard Locks in Salmon Bay. More recently, Ballard has been developed with large, modern houses and condominiums replacing the modest bungalows. Jenn sought out faith-based and secular food and social support services in the Ballard area, memorizing the schedules and locations of the various services and writing information on flyers to hand out to people she knew. "I was so excited for people to get things. I'm like a cheerleader for people." She also learned more about Seattle's parking enforcement regulations, including the scofflaw beginning in 2011 that required owners of vehicles parked on city streets to move them every seventy-two hours or risk ticketing, towing, and impoundment. There are also laws in Seattle limiting the parking of RVs to streets in industrial zones.[29]

While still living in her vehicle, Jenn met and began working with the Scofflaw Mitigation team—renamed the Vehicle Residency Outreach team—started by local activists Jean Darcy and Rev. Bill Kirlin-Hackett with the Interfaith Taskforce on Homelessness. The Vehicle Residency Outreach team coordinated with the city's parking enforcement department and with volunteer lawyers so that team members could do outreach to vehicle residents before they were ticketed and had their vehicles and belongings taken away. Working against vehicle residents are the growing number of punitive rules and regulations aimed at limiting vehicle residency in certain areas of King County, many of these spurred on by business owners and community members complaining of the presence of vehicle residents in their neighborhoods. Some business owners grew so frustrated with what they saw as the city's inaction that they illegally placed large concrete barriers on the streets in front of their business locations.[30] With vehicle residency growing much faster than outreach and advocacy groups can handle, and with the increase in criminalization of poverty and homelessness, people living in their vehicles continue to face obstacles.

ONE MAN WHO FACED and then overcame many of these obstacles while living in his vehicle in Seattle, and who helped challenge the parking enforcement penalties for vehicle residents, is Stephen Long. Although Jenn says she never interacted with Stephen, since he was living in Pioneer Square while she was living in Ballard, she also credits the Long case with improving legal protections and civil rights for vehicle residents. Ethnoarcheologist Graham Pruss, a regional and national expert on vehicle residency, worked with some of Stephen Long's lawyers at Columbia Legal Services as they were defending his rights, first at the city level and then on to the King County and even Washington State levels.

Stephen Long, an Indigenous man and member of the Confederated Salish and Kootenai Tribes of Flathead Nation, was evicted from his Seattle apartment in 2014 for being behind on his rent. At fifty-four years old at the time and thinking back to his earlier and happier years living and traveling around the West in his vehicle, Stephen held on to and lived in his truck, a 2000 GMC Sierra 2500. He worked as a general laborer. Since he had various jobs in the area south of Pioneer Square, including working as a cleaner for Quest Stadium, Stephen parked and lived in his truck nearby. He parked his truck near other vehicle residents and close to a homeless day center, where he sought supportive services. In October 2016, when his truck had engine trouble, precluding him from moving it around on the city streets, it was towed and impounded by the city-contracted Lincoln Towing Company. Stephen slept under a tarp and in a chair at a homeless day center the night he found his truck towed. He continued to live on the streets while he fought to regain his truck and the tools and personal possessions that were inside it, including warm coats and a laptop computer.

In order to get his truck back, a city court charged Stephen Long a $946.61 impoundment fee, which he could not pay, so they put him on a $50-per-month payment plan. Lawyers with Seattle's Columbia Legal Services took on Stephen Long's case, a case that wound through the city courts and then to King County Superior Court and to the State of Washington Court of Appeals. Since Stephen Long had been living in his truck, his lawyers successfully invoked homestead protections under the Washington Constitution and the frontier-era Homestead Act. The city reimbursed Long's payments for parking tickets and impounding of his truck, and he regained possession of it and his other belongings.[31]

Ironically, the original Homestead Act of 1862, enacted by the US Congress and adopted first by the Washington Territorial Legislature and then by the Washington Legislature in 1895, was intended to spur settlement of the western frontier areas of what was to become the United States. The purpose of the Homestead Act was also to protect people's homes and property against the fallout of economic downturns caused by the development of capitalism in our country.[32] In effect, it was aimed at preventing widespread homelessness. But the settler-colonial settlement protections were only for white men and not for women or Indigenous people.

Stephen Long would not have been considered eligible under the Homestead Act of that time, yet that racist and antiquated law protected him. In 1993, Washington State expanded the Homestead Act to cover not just homes but also cars and vans. Graham Pruss is currently on the Washington State Legal Advisory Committee tasked with "creating a set of recommendations based upon the Long ruling to change towing and impound processes across the state of Washington to protect vehicle residents. . . . We've been able to protect people's vehicles under the Homestead Act. Now we're enshrining that into law and creating those protections across the state."[33]

WHEN I ASKED JENN what people or organizations helped her when she was living in her van or on the street, she immediately mentioned the nonprofit group Heroes for the Homeless, started and run by Tricia Lapitan, a Seattle city attorney. At the time, Tricia worked as the program manager for the newly launched Seattle Municipal Court's Seattle Community Court Program for repeat offenders of low-level crimes. She was struck by the level of homelessness among her clients. "Most of them were there because they stole food, or shoes. . . . I thought, why don't we just feed them? Why do they need to go to jail? They need something to survive."[34] So Tricia began handing out juice boxes and sandwiches to people in doorways on her walk into work.

Beginning in 2006, Heroes for the Homeless had groups of volunteers who went to homeless encampments, including where vehicle residents were, and handed out sandwiches and water bottles. They also handed out two thousand cupcakes just in February, the way that Tricia chose to celebrate her birthday.[35] Jenn remembers getting hard-boiled eggs from their volunteers and storing the eggs in a drawer in her van, which, most of the time, was "like an icebox" owing to having no insulation. She appreciated the eggs because Bastyr University's naturopaths had told her that she needed to eat "closer to raw" to help with her MS.

She says she did not mind the volunteers with Heroes for the Homeless knocking on the door of her van. "They would come around with little bags of food. That's where I got my hugs from . . . food and hugs and hard-boiled eggs," she says with a smile.[36] Linking back to her comments on the shame and stigma that accompanied homelessness, she characterizes the unconditional and welcomed hugs and the hard-boiled eggs brought to her by Heroes for the Homeless volunteers as significant support for her. After a pause in our conversation, Jenn adds, "You don't think that a stranger tapping on your window is going to affect you." Countless times over the decades that I have worked with people experiencing, and exiting, homelessness, I have heard similar stories about the outsized meaningfulness of nonjudgmental volunteers showing up regularly with essential, welcomed items, like sandwiches.

Jenn also mentions the outreach workers from REACH. "REACH was out there. REACH was everywhere. REACH was helping my friends, but I didn't need REACH. At least I didn't think so."[37] She states that REACH helped many of her friends "in addiction to harder drugs," whereas she was drinking alcohol, "but it wasn't a big crutch." She adds that it is a common misperception that all homeless people are on drugs. "Is it the drugs or was it the depression from homelessness and the easy access to drugs? Because once you're homeless, the dealers are standing right there [saying] 'this will take the pain away.'"[38]

The Bridge Care Center in an industrial and commercial fishing area of Ballard greatly impacted Jenn. Her contact with them came when they handed out clothes, hygiene kits, and blankets several times a month from a bus stop at a busy intersection in the center of Ballard. She told her friends about their services and began volunteering to help them when they got their own building from a fisheries company. She says she did not ask them about volunteering but just showed up regularly to help, even assisting them with fixing a leaky roof. They stepped up their support for her when she landed in the hospital again, only this time it was for a severe injury.

ALTHOUGH JENN LIVED in her van for most of her time homeless, her main form of transportation was her bicycle. This helped with her MS-related mobility issues and saved on the cost of gas for her van. But then, in 2013, she had an accident "where I was hit by a car, and I shattered my pelvis in two places. I had no insurance." She was admitted to Swedish Hospital on First Hill, where social workers signed her up for Medicaid. When the social worker asked what else they could do for her, Jenn replied, "A house would be nice." Instead, they sent her across Puget Sound to Bremerton for three months, where she underwent rehabilitation services for her broken pelvis while staying in a nursing home. Back in Seattle, people at the Bridge Care Center kept her van and belongings safe while she was gone.

Seemingly a person not prone to wallowing in self-pity, Jenn used her time in the nursing home to dream up innovative programs to help more people like herself experiencing homelessness. "I had this dream that we could do more; that we could create this program where we could pick people off the street and we could give them a little internship." When she was released from the Bremerton nursing home, she returned to Seattle, living in her van and then on the streets for another year, before moving into permanent housing. But she also worked with the folks at the Bridge Care Center to make her dream into a reality. She helped them start a program called Advocate Representing the Community (ARC), and she was the first ARC intern.

Jenn worked as an ARC intern while living homeless on the streets. The ARC internship came with a six-month stipend and mentoring through the Bridge Care Center, a ministry of Quest Church. ARC interns "figure out one thing they want to do for the community," the homeless community. One intern got a water fountain installed in Ballard for the use of everyone. Another intern worked on a list of meals that could be safely handed out to people experiencing homelessness. Through her involvement in the ARC program, Jenn exited homelessness in 2014 and has been stably housed ever since. She says that some of her friends and others experiencing homelessness saw how much the ARC program helped her and lined up to do the internship, resulting in more people getting housed.

Besides her involvement in the Bridge Care Center while still living on the streets, Jenn also began volunteering with the WHEEL Women in Black, along with Anitra Freeman and others. "I think the final straw that got me from somebody trying to help other people to, oh, my gosh, I really need to do something, was the amount of people I saw die on the street . . . that's probably the most horrific part of what I saw was good people dying, for no other reason than they'd given up hope." Too many times, vehicle residents are found dead in their vehicles after friends or outreach workers sound the alarm and bring in police officers to check on their status—people like the man Jenn found dead in his RV.

GRAHAM PRUSS, WHO WORKED in 2013 as one of Seattle's first vehicle residency outreach workers for the city while he was waiting to start graduate studies at the UW, recounts the story of a man he calls Michael. Graham was the city's only paid vehicle residency outreach worker, tasked with reaching out to the city's then estimated fifteen hundred vehicle residents, urging them to relocate before the city's planned "displacement" or sweeps of areas. Of this he says, "I didn't feel right about being part of any effort to force people to move, but I was providing probably the only advance notice of these displacements." When working with a group of vehicle residents in the Ballard area, where Jenn had lived in a van and now lived on the streets, he kept knocking on the RV where Michael lived. Pruss knew Michael from his volunteer work with the Bridge Care Center's meal program. Michael never responded to his knocks, and Graham asked parking enforcement not to ticket or tow Michael's RV. "I have this vivid memory of his windshield wiper sitting an inch off the glass from all the tickets wedged underneath it."

After two months, when city officials told Graham they were towing Michael's RV, Graham enlisted the help of Jenn Adams, who knew the area and the vehicle residents from her six-plus years living there. When Jenn looked through one of the RV's windows, she saw Michael inside—or rather, she saw Michael's body inside. The coroner determined that he had died of natural causes and had been dead inside his RV for three months. He had no obituary, but his death was included in the WHEEL / Women in Black remembrance project.

Deaths such as Michael's spurred both Jenn and Graham to work on upstream, policy-level solutions to vehicle residency as a form of homelessness. As Graham puts it, "A lot of the outreach I did felt like a Sisyphean task: one step forward, two steps back. Michael's death led me to work for change on a much larger scale."[39] One of the larger-scale projects that Graham and Jenn have worked on is the safe parking program.

ALTHOUGH NOT AN overall solution to vehicle residency, safe parking programs are an evidence-based model that can help vehicle residents avoid legal issues over where they park.[40] Safe parking programs also help connect vehicle residents with case management and services. As legal researchers at Seattle University conclude, although safe parking programs can never be the ultimate solution, "vehicle residents' immediate need for safe, legal, and reliable parking, especially overnight, cannot be overstated."[41]

Seattle was an early adopter of the safe parking program model, often called safe lots, with the first safe lot in the city opening in 2010. Graham Pruss worked on that project and became its vehicle residency outreach worker. Jenn Adams currently works as a vehicle residency outreach worker for the University Heights (U Heights) Safe Lot program in the U District, which opened at the beginning of the pandemic in 2020. Critics of Seattle's safe parking programs point to what they view as their high cost.[42]

Safe lots are typically connected with faith-based organizations and are for passenger vehicles only. Many unofficial safe lots have existed for a long time, with churches and other places having their own parking lots and allowing people to stay there for a while. Currently, U Heights hosts ten parking spaces, with many spaces given to students (including those from the nearby UW), elders, and families. People utilizing the Safe Lot program go through a screening process and have to own their vehicles. The vehicles must be in good working condition and have up-to-date insurance and license and registration. The U Heights Safe Lot program partners with the Gathering Church, formerly University Temple Methodist Church. People from the Gathering provide some meals and gift cards, and they stock the outdoor community refrigerator and pay for guests' membership to the nearby University Family YMCA, where they can shower and use the gym facilities. U Heights provides case management for the ten parking spaces. U Heights also provides large, wheelchair-accessible portable toilets; a tiny house equipped with Wi-Fi, chargers, and a microwave that vehicle residents can use; and access to laundry facilities inside their building. U Heights leadership hoped to expand its services to include parking spaces for RVs on the UW's main Seattle campus. City officials under Mayor Harrell blocked this effort.

Not surprisingly, given the stringent requirements, a high percentage of vehicle residents staying in safe lots like at U Heights move rapidly into housing. Most of the safe lot residents have jobs, are going to college, or qualify for rapid rehousing, especially for the elderly and families. Safe lots only work for some vehicle residents, especially since safe lots typically require residents to move their vehicles off the lot during the day. This requirement means that the vehicles must be in good working condition and have sufficient gas for driving around. And not all vehicle residents can afford to keep their vehicles in good working condition and pay for a license and registration, or pass or want to undergo the required screening.

Jenn Adams works as a vehicle residency outreach worker at the U Heights Safe Lot program and for the U Heights Vehicle

Outreach team focusing on North Seattle. A second team from U Heights focuses on vehicle residents in South Seattle. The outreach teams connect with vehicle residents to build rapport and offer a variety of health, social, and legal support services. Jenn told me, "People in vehicles have a little bit more ownership and pride in what they have—that they have something—so they don't normally consider themselves homeless. Maybe unhoused, but not necessarily homeless." She added that housed people often think that vehicle residents are messy since their vehicle is the only place to store what matters to them. "It looks like you're a hoarder because you have your grandmother's album and your dog's ashes."[43]

Jenn spoke of her approach as an outreach worker to vehicle residents: "I try to come alongside those people and say, 'Hey, I'm right here. I've been there. I've done this . . .' And try to come in with a human approach, and then walk with them."[44] She adds that it does not work to insist that people change. Through her work at the U Heights Safe Lot program, she has helped a UW student who lost her apartment, had to drop out of school, and lived in her car until she could relocate. She was too embarrassed to tell her parents. Jenn also helped an older man who had lost his house and was living in his vehicle. He "just wanted to be nomadic and didn't have the information on how to do that." Through her work with Graham, she connected this man with places he could live on Bureau of Land Management public lands once he obtained a permit. Some vehicle residents prefer parking their vehicles and living out of them in places where they can blend in more, including in rural areas.

Graham adds that most vehicle residents want to settle down someplace, like a house or an apartment, but that there are many people, especially ones living in RVs (which are essentially mobile homes), who want to continue living in their vehicles in a location with sufficient hygiene facilities and where they will not be chased off by police or neighborhood vigilantes. A subset of vehicle residents are the rising number of retirees, families, and other people living in RVs and traveling to temporary jobs, like at Amazon fulfillment centers, as depicted in *Nomadland*.[45] Bob Wells, a sixty-six-year-old vehicle resident referred to as "the guru for nomads on a tight budget," founder of the annual Rubber Tramp Rendezvous in Arizona, and featured in *Nomadland*, points to the 2008 mortgage collapse, economic fallout from the COVID-19 pandemic, and effects of climate change as causes for the increase in vehicle residents. "We're going to be a planet on the move," he says.[46]

Graham talks about what he terms the "nomadic turn," by which he means "systemic displacement that is forcing people to mobilize. We're seeing more and more people turning to mobile, adaptive forms of housing in response to larger structural issues," including the subprime mortgage crisis of 2008 and the effects of climate change.[47] Graham is working with a group of people on the idea of "supportive parking focused on larger vehicles and [that] provides long-term residency, similar to a low-income or subsidized mobile home park."[48]

VEHICLE RESIDENCY IS increasing in urban areas like Seattle and in suburban and rural areas of King County and elsewhere. As pointed out by CHAZ/CHOP protestors in the summer of 2020, due to the gentrification of the Central District in Seattle, Black families have been forced out of their homes, and many are moving farther south into South Seattle and adjacent places in King County like Kent and Auburn. Dr. Ben Danielson, a pediatrician who ran the Odessa Brown Clinic in the Central District for decades, says that this is contributing to the suburbanization of poverty.[49] Some of the displaced people from the Central District and other neighborhoods in Seattle become vehicle residents or live doubled up with friends or relatives, at least for a time.[50] This displacement disconnects people from their established health care and social service supports, which are concentrated in Seattle. In addition, vehicle residents moving to suburban areas still face legal barriers. A study by the Seattle University School of Law found that, across all jurisdictions in Washington State, Seattle had the highest number of ordinances criminalizing vehicle residency, followed by Auburn and Kent.[51] Many business owners and housed people view vehicle residency as threatening their safety, health, property values, and community cohesion.

JENN ADAMS EMPHASIZES that finding her path out of homelessness took her a while. "I'm not here because I went straight from homelessness to helping. . . . There's four or five years of therapy there. There's several mentors that guided me." She adds that in her current work she is supported by mentors and supervisors who help her stay "within the boundaries that I need to be able to do this work in a healthy way so it doesn't affect my MS, so it doesn't affect me, and that I'm the best person I can be when I go out there to help people." She thinks that people having the lived experience of homelessness brings a necessary perspective, but she adds, "I think it's important, if we're going to do lived experience, that we don't do lived experience just on its own. It can't be like that. It has to have a support system."[52]

Jenn points to the relationship between childhood trauma and social exclusion's negative effects, saying, "I have some people that are five generations out here. Five generations homeless. We should be ashamed of that . . . we should be ashamed of walking by somebody and not looking at them . . . that's so damaging to people. . . . Just look at them and smile. Make them feel better." Jenn ended our interview by saying, "If everybody smiled at me while I was homeless, I wouldn't have been homeless that long."[53]

Besides smiles and other efforts at practicing social inclusion at the individual level and using experts by experience like Jenn in both direct service and policymaking, what can be done to intervene earlier to prevent or shorten the duration of homelessness, especially for teens and young adults?

Notes

1. Jenn Adams, Skid Road Oral History, interview by Josephine Ensign, January 12, 2023.
2. Adams, Skid Road Oral History interview.
3. Josephine Ensign, *Catching Homelessness: A Nurse's Story of Falling through the Safety Net* (Berkeley, CA: She Writes Press, 2016).
4. Thacher Schmid, "Displaced: Graham Pruss on Why More People Are Living in Cars and RVs," *Sun*, October 2021, https://www .thesunmagazine.org/issues/550/displaced?fbclid =IwAR1OqQ2VXPlpvvQOEEeHILBxkAfrVfjOilD7k6767uj4h8U7Yd-0PVpLMn8o.
5. Schmid, "Displaced."
6. "Jennifer Adams," LinkedIn, accessed February 4, 2023, https://www .linkedin.com/in/jennifer-adams-765b60181/.
7. Adams, Skid Road Oral History interview.
8. "Jen Adams," Facing Homelessness, July 30, 2022, https:// facinghomelessness.org/posts/tag/Safe+Parking+Lot.
9. Danny Westneat, "If Car-Camping Colony Isn't News, Then Times Are Worse Than We Think," *Seattle Times*, December 23, 2005, https://www.seattletimes.com/seattle-news/if-car-camping-colony -isnt-news-then-times-are-worse-than-we-think/.
10. *Oxford English Dictionary Online*, s.v. "social (adj. and n.)," accessed February 2, 2023, https://www.oed.com/view/Entry/183739.
11. Peter Cockersell, *Social Exclusion, Compound Trauma and Recovery: Applying Psychology, Psychotherapy and PIE to Homelessness and Complex Needs* (London: Jessica Kingsley, 2018), 14.

12. Robert W Aldridge et al., "Morbidity and Mortality in Homeless Individuals, Prisoners, Sex Workers, and Individuals with Substance Use Disorders in High-Income Countries: A Systematic Review and Meta-analysis," *Lancet* 391, no. 10117 (January 2018): 241–50, https://doi.org/10.1016/S0140-6736(17)31869-X.
13. Schmid, "Displaced."
14. Serena Luchenski et al., "What Works in Inclusion Health: Overview of Effective Interventions for Marginalised and Excluded Populations," *Lancet* 391, no. 10117 (2018): 266–80, https://doi.org/10.1016/S0140-6736(17)31959-1.
15. Adams, Skid Road Oral History interview.
16. Adams, Skid Road Oral History interview.
17. S. Han, K. Kim, and J. A. Burr, "Stress-Buffering Effects of Volunteering on Salivary Cortisol: Results from a Daily Diary Study," *Innovation in Aging* 2, no. S1 (November 11, 2018): 75, https://doi.org/10.1093/geroni/igy023.283.
18. Adams, Skid Road Oral History interview.
19. Adams, Skid Road Oral History interview.
20. "Washington Is a Hotbed for Three Dangerous Diseases," *Seattle Magazine*, May 11, 2011, https://seattlemag.com/news/washington-hotbed-three-dangerous-diseases/.
21. Adams, Skid Road Oral History interview.
22. Westneat, "If Car-Camping Colony Isn't News."
23. Marty Hartman, Skid Road Oral History, interview by Josephine Ensign, December 12, 2022.
24. Allison Williams, "Marty Hartman, the Single-Minded Homelessness Crusader," *Seattle Met*, January 31, 2018, https://www.seattlemet.com/news-and-city-life/2018/01/marty-hartman-single-minded-homelessness-crusader.
25. John Ryan, "2021 Heat Wave Is Now the Deadliest Weather-Related Event in Washington History," KUOW, July 19, 2021, https://www.kuow.org/stories/heat-wave-death-toll-in-washington-state-jumps-to-112-people; David Kroman, "Who Was Most Harmed during Seattle's Heat Wave?," Crosscut, July 1, 2021, https://crosscut.com/news/2021/07/who-was-most-harmed-during-seattles-heat-wave.
26. Thacher Schmid, "Vehicle Residency: Homelessness We Struggle to Talk About," *Nation*, November 11, 2021, https://www.thenation.com/article/society/homelessness-vehicle-residency-housing/.

27. Westneat, "If Car-Camping Colony Isn't News."
28. Adams, Skid Road Oral History interview.
29. Amanda Zhou, "Seattle to Increase Parking Enforcement Aimed at RV Dwellers," *Seattle Times*, May 31, 2022, https://www.seattletimes.com/seattle-news/homeless/seattle-to-increase-parking-enforcement-aimed-at-rv-dwellers/.
30. Erica C. Barnett, "'Eco Blocks' Are Concrete Signs of Seattle's Failure to Address RV Homelessness," PubliCola, July 1, 2021, http://publicola.com/2021/07/01/eco-blocks-are-concrete-signs-of-seattles-failure-to-address-rv-homelessness/.
31. "Seattle Judge Rules a Homeless Man's Truck Was His 'Home,' and That Has City Officials Worried," *Los Angeles Times*, March 10, 2018, https://www.latimes.com/nation/la-na-seattle-homeless-20180310-story.html.
32. "City of Seattle v. Steven Long," *Columbia Legal Services* (blog), accessed January 18, 2022, http://columbialegal.org/impact_litigations/city-of-seattle-v-steven-long-2/.
33. Graham Joseph Pruss, Skid Road Oral History, interview by Josephine Ensign, December 16, 2022.
34. Tricia Lapitan, Skid Road Oral History, interview by Josephine Ensign, March 6, 2023.
35. Lapitan, Skid Road Oral History interview.
36. Adams, Skid Road Oral History interview.
37. Adams, Skid Road Oral History interview.
38. Adams, Skid Road Oral History interview.
39. Schmid, "Displaced."
40. Tyrone Ray Ivey, Jodilyn Gilleland, and Sara Rankin, "Hidden in Plain Sight: Finding Safe Parking for Vehicle Residents," *SSRN Electronic Journal*, May 2018, https://doi.org/10.2139/ssrn.3173221.
41. Ivey, Gilleland, and Rankin, "Hidden in Plain Sight," 41.
42. Danny Westneat, "Parking Spots for the Homeless in Seattle, Finally. But at a Thousand Bucks a Month?," *Seattle Times*, October 18, 2019, https://www.seattletimes.com/seattle-news/politics/parking-for-the-homeless-in-seattle-finally-but-at-a-thousand-bucks-a-month/.
43. Adams, Skid Road Oral History interview.
44. Adams, Skid Road Oral History interview.
45. Jessica Bruder, *Nomadland: Surviving America in the Twenty-First Century* (New York: W. W. Norton, 2017).

46. Sarah Tory, "Where Do Public Lands Factor into the Homelessness Crisis?," *High Country News*, October 1, 2021, https://www.hcn.org/issues/53.10/south-public-lands-where-do-public-lands-factor-into-the-homelessness-crisis.
47. Schmid, "Displaced."
48. Schmid, "Displaced."
49. Benjamin Danielson, Skid Road Oral History, interview by Josephine Ensign, November 2, 2015.
50. Sydney Brownstone, "A Shower, Beds for the Kids and 'French Toast Wednesdays': New Blessings for a Grateful Eastside Family," *Seattle Times*, November 30, 2019, https://www.seattletimes.com/seattle-news/eastside/fftn-hopelink-an-eastside-family-living-in-their-van-once-felt-invisible-now-their-kids-see-what-others-dont/.
51. Jessica So et al., "Living at the Intersection: Laws & Vehicle Residency," Homeless Rights Advocacy Project, May 8, 2016, https://digitalcommons.law.seattleu.edu/hrap/5.
52. Adams, Skid Road Oral History interview.
53. Adams, Skid Road Oral History interview.

CHAPTER 9

Doorway

· · · · · · · · · · · · · · · · · · ·

> *These are our young people, from our community.*
> *They are part of us.*
>
> —DELLA HUGHES

"WHAT WOULD IT TAKE FOR you to live here?" A middle-aged man, an urban designer from a Boston design firm, asked me this question on a cold, rainy January day in 2018 as I stood in a bland, fluorescent-lit UW School of Law conference room. He pointed to a large printout spread across the conference table. The printout was a design mock-up of the U District around the UW's main Seattle campus. The UW contracted the design firm he worked for to develop a master plan for the area, especially the area around the twenty-two-story UW Tower, the main administration building, which was next to the planned University Street light-rail station projected to open in a few years. The U District was slated to be up-zoned, allowing the construction of numerous thirty-three-story high-rise apartment buildings in the area around the UW Tower under the 2017 Mandatory

Housing Affordability rezoning process in Seattle.[1] With this up-zoning and new light-rail station, the U District was slated to become a city within a city.

I wore full rain gear. Dripping wet from my bicycle ride through the hard rain to this meeting, I looked from the man's face to the map, back to his face again, trying to figure out what was behind this question. I decided that it was imprudent to tell him that I referred to the UW Tower, then the tallest building in the U District, as the Tower of Sauron. The building had been the Safeco Insurance Company headquarters, with a ninety-six-foot-long reader board, which in the 1970s had proclaimed, "Big Brother is Watching."[2] In 2018, the UW Tower was still the tallest building in the U District, and I always felt I was under its watchful purple and gold eye.

Disgruntled from my efforts to gain access to the law school building, due to it now being locked and with only School of Law faculty, staff, and students having access, I looked at him for a moment, perplexed at his odd question, and asked, "What do you mean?" While I do not remember his exact response, I remember realizing that this meeting was not about what I had thought it was for: finding a good location for a U District community café—the Doorway Café—aimed at reducing youth homelessness, including among our students, a place to help them navigate to services they wanted and needed. The idea was that it would be a community café geared toward youth yet open to everyone, with another aim of reducing the stigma associated with homelessness and social exclusion, as well as involving community members in supporting all of our young people.

I had become the director for the Doorway Project, championed by Rep. Frank Chopp, Democrat of the Forty-Third District of the Washington State House of Representatives, a district that includes the U District. The Doorway Project was funded by the state of Washington with a budget of $1 million for two years and with the purpose of developing a navigation center for homeless youth in the U District. I had been invited to this meeting with the urban planners because of my role with the Doorway Project. When UW administrators asked me to lead this project, starting in the summer of 2017, I was excited about the possibility of doing something innovative and community based to address upstream prevention and early intervention for teen and young adult homelessness—a project using applied research and participatory community-based research methods in support of practical program design. I was excited to draw on UW resources to design and implement a positive program to address homelessness and housing insecurity among young people, including our students. A university-wide survey of students on housing and food insecurity was underway to help document this need. In my early naive, idealistic phase, I viewed the Doorway Project as the final capstone of my almost three-decade-long academic and homelessness program planning career. On that rainy January day, six months into the project, and specifically with the personal question from the Boston urban planner running through my head, my idealistic phase ended.

As the meeting with the urban designer unfolded, I realized that he was showing me plans for "revitalizing" the U District. He specifically wanted to know how they could get rid of what they termed the "problematic alleyway" adjacent to the UW campus, near the almost block-long University Temple United Methodist Church (U Temple), where the ROOTS Young Adult Shelter, TeenFeed, Friday Feast, Urban Rest Stop, and People's Harm Reduction Alliance's (PHRA) needle exchange were located.

The ROOTS Young Adult Shelter, founded in 1999 as Seattle's first overnight shelter for young adults ages eighteen to twenty-five, had been located in the U Temple dining hall area since it began. TeenFeed, an evening meal for homeless teens and young adults at various churches in the U District, was started in 1987 by several UW Medical Center nurses. In 1996, Sinan Demeril started a feeding program, Friday Feast, in the U District, first at University Baptist Church and then, in 2000, moving it to U Temple. Sinan, then a sociology graduate student at the UW, started Friday Feast in memory of his mother, a Muslim who "always communicated to me that one of the pillars of Islam was to do charity, or some kind of engagement in helping people who are poor."[3] Sinan rallied his fellow sociology graduate students to do something less theoretical and more practical. The Urban Rest Stop, providing restrooms, showers, and laundry facilities to people of all ages experiencing homelessness, was colocated with ROOTS. And PHRA, purportedly our country's largest needle exchange program, started in 1989 by Bob Quinn and then run by Shiloh Murphy (now Jama), set up harm reduction supplies on a table in the alleyway beside U Temple.[4] Shiloh had been a homeless teen and heroin user in the U District in the 1990s; he continues to be an active user.[5] Quinn died in 2012 of suicide at the age of fifty-four.[6]

THE URBAN DESIGNER asked what it would take for me to want to live in the U District, ostensibly because I was considered a desirable resident, as in not being homeless. Instead of the meeting being about finding a good location for the Doorway Café, the subtext was, "How can we navigate homeless youth away from the U District? And how can we navigate these programs serving homeless youth and adults away from the U District central core?"

Through my two years at the helm of the UW Doorway Project, I learned firsthand just how politically fraught and frustrating it is when attempting to solve even one small aspect of
homelessness in Seattle. I learned how policies geared toward
youth homelessness would have unintended negative consequences when the young people most affected are left out of the
design, implementation, and evaluation phases. I learned how
the UW both addresses and contributes to an increase in homelessness in the U District, including housing insecurity and
homelessness among its students. I wondered whether the UW,
a public university, ostensibly an institution for the public good,
was more of a bully than a resource, especially for issues like
homelessness.

HIRED IN DECEMBER 1994 by the UW School of Nursing to be
an assistant professor before completing my doctorate in public
health at Johns Hopkins University in Baltimore, I was attracted
to the job mainly because of the innovative, positive work with
homeless youth being done by Nancy Amidei in the UW School
of Social Work. My clinical work then, as well as my dissertation research, was with homeless teens in Baltimore.[7] Nancy, a
can-do, glass-is-half-full sort of person, had started a monthly
U District–University Partnership for Youth (PFY) meeting in
the U District in 1993. Nancy was spurred on by a petite fire-
brand of a person, Josephine Archuleta, who helped start several Seattle emergency shelters for women and children and
worked as a homeless advocate for decades. As Nancy recounts
it, Josephine showed up one day in Nancy's office in the School
of Social Work and said, "The University of Washington is the
biggest neighbor in the neighborhood, and when it comes to

homelessness, you people aren't even at the table. You should be ashamed."[8]

While working with Josephine, Nancy sought to bring people from the UW and the U District together to have conversations and problem-solve as a group. Their focus was on the considerable number of homeless teens and young adults living in the U District, likely attracted to the youth-oriented culture, and not attracted by, as detractors claimed, the few services that existed for them in the U District. At that time, most social services were provided through and at the many churches on and near the main street, University Way, referred to as the Ave. The churches provided space either rent-free or at a reduced rent for the social services, such as ROOTS Young Adult Shelter at U Temple. Even then, a combination of aging church buildings and congregations, along with increasing real estate values of the U District church properties, strained faith-based resources for providing social services while they upheld their mission to help those less fortunate.

During my two-day UW job interview, I attended a U District–University PFY meeting in a board room in the School of Social Work. The UW School of Social Work is the university classroom building closest to the Ave. Nancy brought and passed around a large bag of assorted, individually wrapped chocolates and helped facilitate a discussion among those present. Homeless young people were at the table and actively involved, as were homeless youth service providers, neighborhood police Community Service officers, and some business owners and residents from the U District. That day they discussed one of the PFY's initiatives, the Donut Dialogues, which were facilitated meetings between homeless youth and SPD officers. Nothing close to a meeting of this kind had ever happened in my five years working with homeless youth in Baltimore. The atmosphere of the PFY meeting added to my view of Seattle as a more progressive and hopeful city than either Baltimore or Richmond, Virginia, where I had previously lived and worked on homelessness issues, as well as where I had become homeless.

Even though there were no other UW staff besides Nancy and me at this first meeting I attended, I was encouraged by her enthusiasm and by the fact that young people experiencing homelessness were not simply at the table but actively involved in the conversations. This was intentional. As Nancy put it in an interview I had with her, "Almost immediately, partly because in the work that I had done in the past related to poverty and welfare and hunger kinds of issues, I always felt strongly that you needed to have the voice of the people most affected. You don't just have the fancy people with the big degrees deciding what's good for the people who are having a bad time. You get them at the table—it's got to be a two-way street—and they have to be part of making decisions, because otherwise the decisions aren't going to work."[9] Nancy's statement echoes the "nothing about us without us" slogan of disability rights groups, expanding to additional policymaking decisions affecting marginalized populations.[10]

I was drawn to the hopefulness, energy, and creativity of teens and young adults and the emphasis on more upstream prevention and early intervention of homelessness. Nancy Amidei and the PFY were among the main reasons I accepted the UW job offer and moved from Baltimore to Seattle in late 1994.

ONCE I SETTLED IN SEATTLE, I began volunteering and then working as a nurse practitioner at the Forty-Fifth Street Youth

Clinic, a twice-a-week evening drop-in clinic for homeless teens and young adults ages twelve to twenty-six, located in a converted fire station in Wallingford, just west of the U District. In an interview for a UW School of Nursing magazine article soon after I moved to Seattle, I was quoted as saying, "I am drawn to the underserved and to 'outsiders.' I like the challenge of working through the barriers of preconceived notions to get at the teen underneath."[11] When this article was published, I was struck by the fact that the journalist left out of the article my description of difficulties I had had as a teen, including severe depression, as being reasons why I was drawn to this work. I purposefully left out mention of my experience of homelessness as a young adult, mostly because I had so much internalized shame about that time of my life. The message I received from the interviewer's reaction to what I had said and the omission in the article was that, as a faculty member, I should keep such lived experience and personal information private, especially if I wanted to obtain tenure. Apparently, sharing this sort of information was unseemly and unprofessional.

At that time, I was a single mother of a young son. I had significant student debt. I needed this UW job, so I remained silent on my lived experience of homelessness. I stopped being silent after obtaining tenure and went public with my story in 2016 with my memoir, *Catching Homelessness: A Nurse's Story of Falling through the Safety Net*. Even though it was named the UW Health Sciences Common Book for academic year 2016–17, I received passive-aggressive and outright aggressive feedback from various UW faculty members. Comments such as "Oh, you're so brave, I'd never do that," "Why exactly were you homeless?" "Your book isn't academic enough so it doesn't count as a real publication," and "You're not like other homeless people" were dismissive of my lived experience. I felt the effects of the stigma and shaming associated with homelessness in new and unsettling ways.

THROUGH MY WORK at the Forty-Fifth Street Youth Clinic, I learned firsthand the importance of having clinic-based paid peer outreach workers, young people with the lived experience of homelessness who could connect with teens and young adults on the streets and in shelters, build trust, and aid in connecting young people to needed health care services. In my previous clinical work on the East Coast, I had not encountered people in this role. Sarah Lippek, a clinic-based peer outreach worker at the time and who has the lived experience of homelessness as an adolescent, is now a civil rights attorney based in Seattle. Besides working on the case of vehicle resident Steven Long, defending his rights after his truck was towed away in Seattle, she works on aspects of juvenile status offense reform.[12]

Around the time I first met and worked with Sarah at the Forty-Fifth Street Youth Clinic, Washington State enacted legislation called the "Becca Bill" to give parents and guardians legal control over teenage runaways and school truants, termed "at-risk youth."[13] Once this not-so-progressive legislation took effect in 1995, Washington State quickly became the country's leading jailer of children.[14] The Becca Bill and its rippling adverse effects for young people and providers complicated my view of Seattle and Washington State as being progressive places to work and live.

Under the Becca Bill, children ages eight to eighteen could be picked up and placed in crisis residential centers and juvenile detention centers just for status offenses like school truancy, running away from home, or spending too much time on the streets—even if they had not committed any crimes like robbery, drug possession, or prostitution. Children could be involuntarily committed to locked inpatient psychiatric and substance use treatment centers by their parents and guardians. Service providers, such as those working at overnight shelters, those working at youth drop-in centers, and, in some circumstances, health care providers, were mandated by law to report suspected runaway homeless young people eighteen years old and younger to authorities.

The Becca Bill was named after Rebecca Ann Hedman, known to her family as Becca and to her street friends as Misty. She was the adopted daughter of a family in Tacoma, Washington, just south of Seattle. By age twelve, Becca had begun to run away from home repeatedly and was prostituted on the streets in Seattle, Tacoma, and then Spokane, Washington, where her parents had placed her in a residential treatment center for crack cocaine use. When she was thirteen years old, a thirty-two-year-old man in Spokane picked her up from the streets, paid her for sex in a hotel room, and then killed her with a baseball bat, throwing her body into the Spokane River. Becca had been sexually abused by her biological mother at six months of age and again at age five by an older adopted brother. Though her adoptive parents claimed they had sought individual and family therapy for her, psychological scars from these significant adverse childhood events likely contributed to her running-away behaviors, substance use, and vulnerability to being prostituted on the streets.

Even years later, as more effective programs and policies were implemented for commercially sexually exploited children (CSEC), advocates and case managers for CSEC young people often encouraged their placement in juvenile detention. Their rationale was that the lives of CSEC young people were in such great danger that at least they were safe in juvenile detention. There they could receive health care services and case management to help connect them with needed services once released. During the year that I worked in the King County Juvenile Detention Center helping young people write poetry, I heard the stories, especially from young girls, of their histories of childhood sexual abuse; their time in multiple foster care placements, often with exposure to more abuse; and then living on the streets and being prostituted, and not seeing a way out of that life.

Over the following decades, foster care and homeless youth advocates, like social worker Jim Theofelis, worked hard to enact changes to the Becca Bill. Changes to the Becca Bill in the 2023 Washington State legislative session now exempt shelters from being mandated to contact the teen's parents or guardians if there is a compelling reason not to, including when the teen is seeking gender-affirming or reproductive health care.[15] Although the Becca Bill is slated to expire in 2024, when it was first enacted in 1995, as I was beginning my work in Seattle, it sent chills through the entire youth-serving community, as well as through homeless teens who heard about or experienced its effects.[16]

ON THE FOGGY MORNING of Friday, April 7, 1995, I sat in an uncomfortable wooden pew in the large sanctuary of the University Congregational Church (UCC) in the heart of the U District at the corner of Forty-Fifth Street and Sixteenth Avenue Northeast. Dust motes floated in the air, illuminated by the muted light filtering through the tall, non-stained-glass windows. A large, gold-painted cross hung in the chancel at the front. Churches made me uncomfortable since I had had significant conflicts with the conservative Christian organization Cross-Over Clinic, where I had worked in Richmond, Virginia. They had tried to prevent me from referring women to abortion services and wanted me to pressure HIV-positive patients to repent of their sins. But in Seattle I realized the outsized importance of the city's more progressive faith-based organizations in combatting homelessness and related issues like hunger and low-income housing.

Nancy and the PFY, with grant funding from the UW School of Law, convened a two-day community planning event held at the UCC titled "Street Youth: Solving the Puzzle: A Gathering of the University and the Community in a Partnership for Youth." As Nancy put it, the title was chosen to reflect that street youth are not a "problem" and that, "as a community, we are likely to have 'the pieces,' we just have to figure out how to put them together."[17] This can-do, positive attitude permeated all of the events, beginning with the opening keynote address by Della Hughes, executive director of the National Network of Runaway and Youth Services based in Washington, DC. In her speech, Hughes pointed to recent research showing that about 76% of youth on the streets of Seattle and King County came from these same communities.[18] She admonished all of us as audience members to look at institutions and organizations within our community to find and address causes of youth homelessness.

A panel to discuss innovative programs for homeless youth included people from YouthCare (a major homeless-youth-serving agency in Seattle), the Forty-Fifth Street Youth Clinic, and the University District Youth Center (UDYC). UDYC was, and still is, located in an old two-story house next to UCC's parking lot. It functions as a drop-in youth center using volunteers from local churches, the UW, and civic groups. CCS ran UDYC until 2016, when YouthCare took it over.

With the effects of the Becca Bill in mind, one outcome of the community planning event was starting a GED program at the UDYC. Obtaining a GED helps young people apply for and receive an emancipation designation for homeless youth ages sixteen and older. Another planning event outcome was the MedRest

Program, a medical respite for homeless young people ages eighteen to twenty-five. A few years after the community planning event, I received Group Health funding for MedRest and ran the program for two years in conjunction with YouthCare, the Forty-Fifth Street Clinic, Harborview Medical Center, and the UW's Adolescent Medicine Division of the Department of Pediatrics. MedRest was designed to care for homeless young people who were too sick or injured to be in a regular shelter or on the streets but did not necessitate hospitalization. While MedRest was a successful pilot program, it proved too expensive and labor-intensive to be sustainable.

Directly related to the Doorway Project's community café model, another outcome of the "Solving the Puzzle" planning sessions was the plan to develop a multipurpose community center in the U District, "to serve the entire community, but with an emphasis on homeless youth," and to help "bridge the gap between youth culture and adult culture."[19] The planning group's ambitious timeline was to obtain funding, secure a site in the U District, and open the community center by September 1996. Barriers this planning group identified included "UW's possible desire to control the project" and "competition from similar services/other groups."[20] The multipurpose community center did not come to fruition. The planning group's identified barriers proved to be correct and insurmountable. Those identified barriers were prescient and pertinent twenty-two years later when I wrote the Doorway Café project grant and began work with a multidisciplinary team to plan and implement the project.

SUNDAY, DECEMBER 3, 2017, dawned cloudy. Months of planning meetings had gone into this day, our first Doorway pop-up café and community planning event at U Heights, the community center in the U District. As I drove my car, packed with participatory research supplies, to the event, I rehearsed my opening address and proper pronunciation of the names of the various VIPs and the Doorway Project team members I would introduce. I knew that various news reporters would be there to cover the event. Nervous about how the event would go, I recognized that I did not have full support from Lisa Kelly, a UW School of Law professor (a professor I had been strongly encouraged by UW administrators to have on the Doorway team), and her students. Neither did I have support, especially for the community café model, from Melinda Giovengo, the CEO and president of Youth-Care, our community agency partner for the Doorway Project. Less than five years later, Melinda would leave YouthCare amid internal racial and leadership style turmoil.[21] I had both respect for and wariness of Melinda; she had steered YouthCare during a time of tremendous growth in services.

Social worker Charlotte Sanders, a former colleague of mine from the Forty-Fifth Street Youth Clinic, and graduate students from the UW School of Public Health and Landscape Architecture were on our team. Nursing, social work, and public health were a natural interprofessional fit. The Landscape Architecture graduate student was forced on me by UW leaders, but she became useful in the visual design of the Doorway Café. The UW School of Law was not a good fit. From my perspective, people in the School of Law did not understand or value community health or participatory research methods. This tension and lack of cohesion between members of the professional schools on the Doorway Café planning team proved problematic. The School of Law dropped out for year two of the project.

Despite these early tensions on the Doorway team, our first pop-up café and participatory community research efforts were successful.[22] We had a pay-it-forward food truck, coffee and hot chocolate, tents with various social service providers sharing re-sources, and a tent for community mapping.[23] The community mapping was a useful participatory research design method I used in my research with homeless teens in Baltimore.[24] The Baltimore teens had enjoyed the community mapping so much that they kept asking to do more.

At the Doorway pop-up café, large pieces of paper were spread over tables. The paper had hand-drawn maps of the central U District, including the UW campus. We provided stickers and colored markers and asked participants to add their ideas as to where the Doorway Café should be located and what it should contain. We also asked participants to mark places on the map that they felt were healthy and unhealthy, safe and unsafe, and we asked them for their reasoning behind these designations.

Soft rain began to fall as Representative Chopp gave his re-marks. He commented on the rain, saying it was a good reminder of why we needed a warm, dry indoor space for the Doorway Café as a welcoming place for homeless young people. Although he did not include this in his speech, I knew he was working hard to pressure the UW administration to designate building space in the U District for the Doorway Café. Even then, the UW owned a sprawling amount of land and buildings outside of the main campus. The UW has had a long-standing reputation for being a real-estate-hungry land-grabber in the community. At the same time, since the UW is the largest employer in Washington State, the UW's continued expansion was largely tolerated. With Rep-resentative Chopp's influence and tenaciousness, I was optimis-tic that a café space would be found by the end of our first year.

OUR DOORWAY PROJECT team members continued an iterative participatory design effort with young people experiencing homelessness, with input on what the Doorway Café should look like, what services to include, and how to make it a welcoming place both for them and for the wider community. In collaboration with social service agencies, we developed a Doorway Project website with resources for homeless youth, including for homeless UW students. At the same time, I faced resistance from leaders at YouthCare, who were equal partners in the Doorway Project funding from the state. YouthCare leaders, understandably, wanted more of the state funding for the Doorway Project to support their existing programs. A series of tense meetings ensued where people aired these differences in perspectives and directions for the Doorway Project. People, including me, jockeyed for control over the project direction and the project budget. Representative Chopp and people from the Office of Homeless Youth at the state level wanted periodic progress reports, which I wrote and submitted.

By the spring of 2018, when we held a day-long community charrette at U Heights, similar to Nancy Amidei's "Solving the Puzzle" community planning sessions at UCC back in 1995, I felt hopeful that the Doorway Project could move past its first year's growing pains. Feedback from homeless young people at the Doorway events emphasized that they wanted a space like the Doorway Café. They also admonished our team members about how they had been repeatedly disappointed by people, including groups of UW researchers, asking them what they wanted in terms of services, writing reports that went on shelves in someone's office, and never delivering on promises. I vowed to myself that we would deliver on our promise of a youth-designed and youth-centric U District community café.

I told people—and myself—that leading the Doorway Project was exciting and daunting. It was exciting because it was such an outward, public-facing project, one that was working with the population of young people experiencing homelessness, a population that I love. It was exciting in that I was able to combine my academic self with my more activist self. And it was exciting in that I was able to talk with a variety of people about the real-life "wicked problems" of homelessness and how we could work toward ending youth homelessness.

Simultaneously, the Doorway Project was daunting in that it was a large, messy, unwieldy, and ambitious project that could go wrong in so many ways. It was daunting in that my leadership of the project had me more in the public spotlight and open to criticism from many different angles. It was daunting in that I strove to work effectively yet authentically with radically different people and across multiple sectors. I constantly had to code-shift my language and the angle of my message, if not the actual message itself. It was daunting in that I enjoyed the leadership position. It was daunting and frustrating in the role confusion felt and communicated by many of the people working on the project. It was daunting in that my ego was in this, and I knew from experience that that could get messy, derail me from the work, and become unhealthy. I could fall into the trap of founder's syndrome.[25] It was daunting in that I knew I might enjoy working on it so much that I could have a difficult time letting go of the project, or seeing it evolve into something else entirely. It was daunting in how time-consuming it was. The daunting aspects of the Doorway Project quickly outweighed the exciting elements.

This recounting of events and the politics involved with the Doorway Project is my story. There are multiple stories from everyone involved with this complex project. One of my strengths is the ability to envision creative, outside-the-box thinking, program planning, and problem-solving. I am not as skilled at or, frankly, as interested in managing large teams and coordinating

program implementation details. I also did not have the pa-
tience to deal with the mutating, multilayered, and nuanced
politics involved with starting and running the Doorway Project. I began to plan for when, how, and to whom to hand off the
leadership of the project.

AT THE END of a hot, humid August day in 2019, inside a wood-
paneled, large-windowed, second-floor auditorium of the 1903
elementary school turned community center of U Heights, I sat
at a long table on a raised platform at the front of a packed room
of people. At that point, I was two years into leading the Doorway Project. Jenn Adams was an audience member working with
vehicle residents through the Scofflaw Mitigation team, renamed
the Vehicle Residency Outreach team. The room smelled of old
chalk dust combined with human sweat. With me at the table
were five others: city council members Abel Pacheco and Teresa
Mosqueda; Tyreesha Jenkins, a young Black artist with the lived
experience of homelessness, including vehicle residency; Rev. Bill
Kirlin-Hackett, director of the Interfaith Task Force on Homelessness and their outreach program for vehicle residents; and
Graham Pruss, then a UW anthropology doctoral student focusing on vehicle residency.

Titled "Understanding and Responding to Vehicle Residency
in Our Community: A U District Community Conversation," this
was a public event with "a panel of experts and those with lived
experience." For an hour, we discussed vehicle residency and the
possibility of U Heights sponsoring a Safe Lot program in their
parking lot in the near future. City council member Teresa
Mosqueda is a Labor Democrat first elected in 2017, who focuses
on health and housing inequities. At the forum, Mosqueda spoke
of the increasing number of "environmental refugees" and "water

refugees" coming to Seattle to escape environmental threats like fires, droughts, and fiercer and more frequent hurricanes. Although she did not make this connection in her remarks, they conjured up memories of the environmental refugees of the Dust Bowl era, the *Grapes of Wrath*–type families traveling in ragged vehicles in search of jobs. The older and more derogatory term "Rubber Tramps" had been invoked again.

I spoke of my lived experience of homelessness, including vehicle residency, as a young adult, as well as of the number of UW students living outside or in their vehicles. A May 2019 UW survey of students found that between 1,527 and 2,046 students had experienced some form of homelessness in the past twelve months.[26] I also spoke of the number of women whom I had encountered in my clinical work at EGH, a women's day shelter just blocks away from U Heights. Some of the women at EGH were elderly, even into their eighties, and lived in their vehicles. Sometimes the Lutheran church where EGH is located would allow the women to park in their parking lot, but only for short periods of time. I advocated for U Heights to open a Safe Lot program and to give priority to the elderly and to students. Other people advocated for that as well, along with priority for families living in their vehicles. Despite the COVID-19 pandemic, the U Heights Safe Lot program opened in the spring of 2020, serving UW and other students, the elderly, and families.

LATER THAT AUGUST of 2019, at the end of two years of steering the Doorway Project, I decided that it was time for me to hand over the project to a colleague, preferably a BIPOC colleague given the racial and ethnic disproportionality of homeless youth. Seema Clifasefi, a colleague from the UW School of Medicine and Harborview Medical Center, agreed to take over the leadership.

Seema is someone with deep community roots in harm reduction research and who is better than I at navigating the politics of a complex project. What they call Doorway 2.0 has monthly community advisory board meetings, a youth book club, and a youth training partnership program with the U District Food Bank's rooftop garden. The Doorway Café, though, as was the case for the PFY's desired multipurpose youth-centric community center back in 1995, remains a concept that has yet to be implemented.

Simultaneously, in the summer of 2019, members of Pearl Jam, along with the then Seattle mayor Jenny Durkan, King County executive Dow Constantine, and major area philanthropists like Microsoft and the Raikes Foundation, announced a plan to end youth homelessness by June 2021.[27] They called it the "End Youth Homelessness Campaign" and infused federal funds combined with $1.2 million from philanthropy, hiring LaMont Green as the director. Green is Black and has the lived experience of youth homelessness in the Seattle area. Green resigned a year later, saying that campaign staff members had been laid off or reassigned. Allegations of racism and other sources of strife between the campaign staff, county officials, and YouthCare as the main homeless-youth-serving agency in the area emerged. The campaign was suspended after a year of planning and gap analyses and, not surprisingly, without having ended youth homelessness in King County. The campaign effort was turned over to Marc Dones, CEO of the RHA, who said that the campaign is "on my radar but not yet embedded in any specific planning activity."[28] As of the spring of 2024, the campaign remains defunct.

THE U DISTRICT has undergone massive changes in the past three years.[29] As of the spring of 2023, the UW Tower is no longer the tallest building in the area, since multiple thirty-three-story buildings now surround it. More tall buildings are being constructed. Towering cranes dot the skyline; dump and concrete trucks deepen potholes in the streets. In the summer of 2021, U Temple Church was reduced to a pile of bricks.[30] ROOTS Young Adult Shelter moved from U Temple to just north of the UW campus, oddly enough, on fraternity row. PHRA now operates in an alleyway adjacent to Christ Episcopal Church, closer to the U Heights Center. Teen Feed operates out of other U District churches that remain in the area. The Friday Feast, tied to ROOTS Young Adult Shelter, serves boxed meals weekly from an alleyway behind the UW School of Social Work. The Urban Rest Stop, the only restrooms open to people experiencing homelessness in the U District, has been displaced and closed.

The UW campus was locked down during the COVID-19 pandemic when all teaching went virtual. Sally Clark is a former Seattle City Council member and now the UW vice president for Campus Community Safety.[31] According to Sally, people experiencing homelessness broke into campus buildings and even set up camps in some of the university's lab spaces during the pandemic lockdown.[32] Even when the campus reopened for in-person classes in the fall of 2021, access to most UW buildings was restricted and remains that way. In a recent interview, Sally told me that about half of all of the calls she gets are about homeless people on campus, sleeping in the underground parking lot on the main Seattle campus, getting into campus buildings, and even walking into classrooms while classes are in session.[33] Professors call her asking what they are supposed to do when confronted with such occurrences that disrupt their teaching.

Even the UW Health Sciences complex connected to the UW Medical Center remains locked, with a Husky card required to gain entry. This includes the Health Sciences Library, which had been open to patients, family members, and other community members searching for up-to-date health information. As a state-funded public institution, this change has made the UW Seattle campus even more unwelcoming and hostile to everyone, including students and people like me who teach there and try to access the library. To be fair, though, even the otherwise welcoming and community-minded U Heights building is now locked, due to similar security issues. That they house several preschools makes their decision more palatable. But with school and university mass shootings occurring with increased frequency across our country, for people like Sally who are tasked with campus safety, restricting access to campus buildings makes sense. That most school and campus mass shootings are perpetrated by current or former students, and not by homeless people, complicates this issue.

The UW administration defends its continuing limited access to campus buildings by stating that it is due to the vague, opaque, and ominous-sounding "security issues." Some of these security issues are real, since the university has made cuts to building maintenance, security staffing, and its own campus police force, but much of it seems to be a convenient way to exclude homeless people from having access to the UW buildings, including restrooms. At the same time, the UW hosted SHARE/WHEEL's Tent City 3 on campus in the winter of 2023. The self-managed tent encampment was located behind Husky Stadium next to the Waterfront Activities Center. A smaller encampment than usual, likely due to its windswept location, it was cordoned off with temporary wire fencing completely covered with purple plastic banners emblazoned with "UW" and depictions of students studying and doing science experiments.

Is the UW a resource or a bully when it comes to interfacing with urban issues like homelessness? After almost thirty years of working at the UW on homelessness issues, I think that it is a bit of both. But with academia in general, including public universities like the UW, becoming more business focused and less mission driven, the bullying tendencies are increasing, sometimes cleverly hidden behind the facade of caring about marginalized populations, including our university students.

Notes

1. Shaun Kuo, "A Skyline by UW—U District Development Spree Part 2," Urbanist, July 2, 2021, https://www.theurbanist.org/2021/07/02/a -skyline-by-uw-u-district-development-spree-part-2/.

2. Paul Dorpat, "Seattle Neighborhoods: University District—Thumbnail History," HistoryLink.org, June 18, 2001, https://historylink.org/File /3380; josephineensign, "University Bullies," *JOSEPHINE ENSIGN* (blog), February 10, 2013, https://josephineensign.com/2013/02/10 /university-bullies/.

3. Sinan Demirel, Skid Road Oral History, interview by Josephine Ensign, February 23, 2017.

4. Eric M. Johnson, "Largest U.S. Needle Exchange Tries Free Meth Pipes in Seattle," Reuters, sec. Healthcare & Pharma, May 14, 2015, https://www.reuters.com/article/us-usa-drugs-seattle -idUSKBN0NZ11U20150514.

5. Rick Anderson, "Seattle Activist Plans Mobile Drug Haven to Encourage Safe Use," *Los Angeles Times*, January 11, 2016, https://www .latimes.com/nation/la-na-heroin-on-wheels-20160111-story.html; Ross Reynolds and Hannah Burn, "'Heroin Saved My Life': Shilo Murphy Stands Up for Drug Users," KUOW, October 24, 2018, https://www.kuow.org/stories/heroin-saved-my-life-shilo-murphy -stands-drug-users.

6. Brendan Kiley, "RIP Bob Quinn," Stranger, November 6, 2012, http://slog.thestranger.com/slog/archives/2012/11/06/rip-bob-quinn; Steven Dolan, "Remembering Bob Quinn, Needle-Exchange Founder," *Daily*, November 14, 2012, https://www.dailyuw.com/news /remembering-bob-quinn-needle-exchange-founder/article _38598267-f9b5-55bf-a11b-6b04885ddba8.html.

7. Jo Ensign, "Health Issues of Homeless Youth," *Journal of Social Distress and Homeless* 7, no. 3 (1998): 159–74, https://doi.org/10.1023

/A:1022931628497; Jo Ensign and Joel Gittelsohn, "Health and Access to Care: Perspectives of Homeless Youth in Baltimore City, U.S.A," *Social Science and Medicine* 47, no. 12 (1998): 2087–99, https://doi.org/10.1016/S0277-9536(98)00273-1.

8. Nancy Amidei, Skid Road Oral History, interview by Josephine Ensign, June 16, 2015.

9. Amidei, Skid Road Oral History interview.

10. James I. Charlton, *Nothing about Us without Us: Disability Oppression and Empowerment* (Berkeley: University of California Press, 1998).

11. Anne Devine, "Ensign Focuses on Health Care Needs of Homeless Teens," *Connections*, Spring 1996.

12. "City of Seattle v. Steven Long," Columbia Legal Services, accessed January 18, 2022, http://columbialegal.org/impact_litigations/city-of-seattle-v-steven-long-2/; SORC (@SOreformcenter), "Check Out Our Most Recent Blog Post Featuring Starcia Ague and Sarah Lippek: Http://Statusoffensereform.Org/Blog/Guest-Blog/the-Becca-Bill-20-Years-Later-How-Washingtons-Truancy-Laws-Negatively-Impact-Children Https://T.Co/97DTACnXPM," Twitter, November 6, 2015, https://twitter.com/SOreformcenter/status/662728159343677440; see also https://modelsforchange.net/publications/842/The_Becca_Bill_20_Years_Later_How_Washingtons_Truancy_Laws_Negatively_Impact_Children.pdf.

13. Alison G. Ivey, "Washington's Becca Bill: The Costs of Empowering Parents," *Seattle University Law Review* 20, no. 1 (1996): 125–56; "Truancy and At-Risk Youth Programs," King County, accessed October 21, 2019, https://www.kingcounty.gov/courts/superior-court/becca.aspx.

14. SORC (@SOreformcenter), "Check Out Our Most Recent Blog Post."

15. Claire Withycombe, "With 10 Days to Go, Some Bills Fall by the Wayside in Olympia," *Seattle Times*, April 14, 2023, https://www.seattletimes.com/seattle-news/politics/with-10-days-to-go-some-bills-fall-by-the-wayside-in-olympia/.

16. Melissa Santos, "'It's an Issue of Liberty': WA Will Stop Jailing Kids Who Run Away or Skip School," Crosscut, May 9, 2019, https://crosscut.com/2019/05/its-issue-liberty-wa-will-stop-jailing-kids-who-run-away-or-skip-school.

17. Nancy Amidei, "Street Youth: Solving the Puzzle" (Seattle, WA, April 1995).

18. Amidei, "Street Youth."

19. Amidei, "Street Youth."

20. Amidei, "Street Youth."

21. Sydney Brownstone, "YouthCare CEO to Step Down after Protest, Racial Turmoil inside Homelessness Organization," *Seattle Times*, July 15, 2021, https://www.seattletimes.com/seattle-news/homeless /youthcare-ceo-to-step-down-after-protest-racial-turmoil-inside -homelessness-organization/.

22. Scott Greenstone, "A Cafe Where No One Is Homeless: One Solution to Youth on Seattle Streets," *Seattle Times*, December 11, 2017, https://www.seattletimes.com/seattle-news/a-cafe-where-no-one-is -homeless-one-solution-to-youth-on-the-streets/; Kim Malcolm and Andy Hurst, "A Cafe to Solve Youth Homelessness? UW Is Getting Innovative," KUOW, October 24, 2018, https://kuow.org/stories/cafe -solve-youth-homelessness-uw-getting-innovative/.

23. Kim Eckart, "UW's Doorway Project Kicks Off Services for Homeless Youth," *UW News* (blog), November 27, 2017, https://www.washington .edu/news/2017/11/27/uws-doorway-project-kicks-off-services-to -homeless-youth/; "The Doorway Project & U-District Community Partners Community Resource Fair," Urban@UW, May 22, 2021, https://urban.uw.edu/news/the-doorway-project-x-u-district -community-partners-community-resource-fair/.

24. Paul J. Barry, Josephine Ensign, and Sarah H. Lippek, "Embracing Street Culture: Fitting Health Care into the Lives of Street Youth," *Journal of Transcultural Nursing* 13, no. 2 (2002): 145–52, https://doi .org/10.1177/104365960201300208.

25. "'Founder Syndrome': The Strong Personality Crippling My Charity," *Guardian*, sec. Voluntary Sector Network, April 12, 2017, https:// www.theguardian.com/voluntary-sector-network/2017/apr/12 /founder-syndrome-personality-crippling-charity.

26. Rachel Fyall, Christine Stevens, and Lynne Manzo, *Understanding Housing and Food Insecurity among University of Washington Students: An Internal Report* (University of Washington, May 10, 2019), https://evans.uw.edu/wp-content/uploads/2022/12/student _housing_and_food_insecurity_report_may2019.pdf.

27. Scott Greenstone, "King County Promised to End Youth Homelessness by June 2021. It Didn't," *Seattle Times*, June 6, 2021, https://www.seattletimes.com/seattle-news/homeless/king-county-promised-to-end-youth-homelessness-by-june-2021-it-didnt/.
28. Greenstone, "King County Promised."
29. Kuo, "Skyline by UW."
30. Kate OConnell, "Needle Exchange, Youth Shelter to Be Displaced as U-District Church Torn Down," KUOW, July 11, 2018, https://www.kuow.org/stories/needle-exchange-youth-shelter-be-displaced-u-district-church-torn-down; Katie Campbell, "'I Was Baptized Here. I Thought I'd Have My Memorial There.' University District Bids Adieu to Historic Church," KUOW, June 18, 2021, https://www.kuow.org/stories/i-was-baptized-here-i-thought-i-d-have-my-memorial-there-university-district-bids-adieu-to-historic-church.
31. "Advancing Safety at UW, in the Community and Beyond," *UW News* (blog), September 27, 2022, https://www.washington.edu/news/2022/09/27/advancing-safety-at-uw-in-the-community-and-beyond/.
32. Sally Clark, Skid Road Oral History, interview by Josephine Ensign, April 13, 2023.
33. Clark, Skid Road Oral History interview.

CHAPTER 10

Welcome In

· · · · · · · · · · · · · · · · · ·

> *Somewhat the way it happens today on a vast*
> *scale: if the poor spill over, wash up against the*
> *borders of prosperity, the wealthy get frightened*
> *and turn violent.*
>
> —ELENA FERRANTE, *FRANTUMAGLIA: A WRITER'S*
> *JOURNEY*

> *Compassion fatigue n. Originally US: apathy or*
> *indifference towards the suffering of others or to*
> *charitable causes acting on their behalf, typically*
> *attributed to numbingly frequent appeals for*
> *assistance.*
>
> —*OXFORD ENGLISH DICTIONARY*, DRAFT ADDITION,
> APRIL 2002

SPRING MORNING SUNLIGHT FILTERED through the banks of floor-to-ceiling windows into the corner office in the old four-story mid-century modern UW Alumni House Building on Forty-Fifth Street near the Ave and the former U Temple Church, still a fenced-off hole in the ground. Fusty carpeting mingled with bakery smells from the large box of doughnuts on the conference table just outside the office. Traffic noise from the city buses and dump trucks going by on the streets below rattled the windows and drowned out nearby conversations of office workers.

It was March 21, 2023, the beginning of Spring Break for UW students, which made the sidewalks below uncharacteristically empty. I was there to interview Don Blakeney, the executive director of the U District Partnership (UDP), a nonprofit organization partially funded by the U District Business Improvement Area.[1] Don sat behind his desk wearing a purple UW sweater. I quipped about his clothing's UW branding. He laughed and mentioned that their outreach staff members all wore UW-logoed attire. Even though they do not officially work for the UW, the UW does invest in UDP, and both parties like to highlight that affiliation. Large maps of the U District hung on the wall behind Don's desk. Highlighted areas on the maps demarcated the central business district for which he is responsible. A bright pink U District Cherry Blossom Festival poster hung on the wall beside the maps. Don's bicycle occupied a corner of his office.

In Don's words, UDP's main purpose is "to look after the U District."[2] They manage event planning, like for the Cherry Blossom Festival and the U District Street Fair; economic development for the area; the somewhat nebulous-sounding "urban vitality"; and a Clean and Safe program. The Clean and Safe program focuses on removing graffiti, pressure-washing sidewalks, and controlling rats. Don mentioned that the city of Seattle installed bioswales in the U District as part of its Rain Wise program to reduce contaminated rainwater runoff from buildings into Puget Sound. These depressions in the ground for rainwater runoff "became this beautiful home for rats." The intersection of Forty-Fifth Street and the Ave in the alleyway behind restaurants has one of our city's highest concentrations of rats. He added that the once-numerous homeless teens and young adults in the U District, back when I first moved here in 1994, used to call themselves the Ave Rats, adopting, deflecting, and challenging a negative stereotyping moniker. It cannot feel good to call yourself a rat.

UDP also focuses on public safety, with paid "public realm ambassadors" walking through the business areas of the U District, helping visitors, including visitors to the UW campus, with wayfinding and checking in with businesses—a program called "Eyes on the Street." On my way into this meeting, I had observed one of UDP's team members, clad in a UW sweatshirt, checking on several people wrapped in blankets lying in store doorways along the Ave. In 2021, UDP added a homeless outreach team, partnering with REACH to have social worker David Delgado, a seasoned outreach worker with the lived experience of homelessness, work as the neighborhood care coordinator in the U District. A monthly homeless census in the U District area served by UDP finds between seventy-five and a hundred people living outside in tents or doorways, although this count does not include vehicle residents.[3] David calls his current position "assertive neighborhood outreach worker."[4] He describes what he does and why he does it, stating, "After hearing so many complaints coming from the businesses about the unhoused, and so much anger with the police in the neighborhood, I decided to give businesses my card and invited them to call me during the day if it's not an immediate safety issue."[5]

David uses de-escalation techniques to diffuse situations, oftentimes offering the homeless person something they want, like coffee or a cigarette, engaging them in a conversation while moving them away from the business that called him to complain. David tries to connect homeless individuals with shelters and other services. His options are more limited if he is working with someone with an acute behavioral health crisis. "One option is to access the Direct Crisis Response team, but it usually takes them weeks to come look for the person . . . the other option is

the Crisis Center Downtown, but I'm not allowed to call and refer people to the crisis center as an outreach worker."[6] Only police officers or medical staff from hospitals are allowed to admit
people into the crisis center. David reports that he works with
many homeless people in crisis who have had such bad experiences with the police and hospitals that "they often walk away
without getting any help."[7]

Don and other people, like longtime Seattle-based youth substance use counselor Johnny Ohta, report that the U District is
now seeing a higher prevalence of middle-aged chronically
homeless adults with severe behavioral health issues, as well as
higher levels of street-level violence.[8] Some of this violence is
from random physical assaults by homeless people with escalating behavioral health issues, but often the violence is perpetrated by housed people, including street gang members selling
drugs. Their buyers include our UW students. Don and Johnny
point to these changes as leading to fewer homeless teens and
young adults wanting to spend time on or near the Ave. Johnny
also says, "The real deal is the prevention of adult chronic homelessness. You get this window of time to engage with youth before they hit their mid-20s."[9] When homeless teens and young
adults become twenty-five or twenty-six, they age out of homeless youth services and risk becoming chronically homeless
adults with more entrenched behavioral and physical health issues.[10] People like Johnny Ohta, who has the lived experience of
substance use and has worked with Seattle homeless youth for
twenty-seven years, are, unfortunately, rare. The work is emotionally challenging and poorly compensated, leading to high
burnout rates and staff turnover. These same issues plague frontline staff members working with homeless adults. Given the
normal adolescent and young adult developmental tasks, including identity formation and building trusting, mature relation-

ships, this staff turnover is particularly problematic for homeless teens and young adults in overcoming trauma, homelessness, and behavioral health problems.

With all of the current changes in the U District, Don speaks of the opportunity to do things better, by "using geography as a powerful lens." "For Seattle, we're the next place that's inventing a dense urban environment."[11] He did not mention that Seattle is among the top three most gentrifying major cities in the United States, the U District being part of that controversial trend since it displaces a disproportionate number of low-income and BIPOC people.[12] Don adds that partnering with REACH workers who get to know homeless people in the U District moves public-facing conversations about homelessness from "oh, it's overwhelming" to something solvable. Don references his time working with the Times Square Association in New York City during the Great Recession, when groups such as Common Ground reduced the number of homeless people in that area to just one man named Heavy.[13] Of course, a significant difference in terms of homelessness between New York City and Seattle is that New York City has a law requiring shelter for all homeless people.[14] New York's shelter law is being challenged now by the increasing number of newly arrived migrants, refugees, and asylum seekers needing shelter.[15] Don states, "Focusing on the person and the place helps us in a way that helps the community and keeps it from being this abstract thing that we can fight about. It just takes the politics right out of it."[16]

POLARIZING DISCOURSE ABOUT homelessness helps no one, particularly not people who are experiencing homelessness or who have experienced homelessness. As Don alludes to, having more opportunities for homeless people to be known by their names and to share their stories if they want helps put a face on homelessness. A By-Name List is a data tool to assist with more effective case management and linking people with housing and other services.[17] It has been used successfully by communities in reducing youth homelessness.[18] The US Department of Veterans Affairs pioneered this approach in significantly reducing homelessness among veterans.[19] This fact is behind the movement for a names list of all people experiencing homelessness in Seattle and King County, while acknowledging the herculean task of naming all forty-thousand-plus people experiencing homelessness in King County in a twelve-month time period.

The other purposes of the By-Name List are to document the specific needs—and hopefully also strengths—of people experiencing homelessness, to help give people the dignity they deserve and to be known by more than just a number on a "problem list," and to welcome them into housing and social services that match their desires. It was also related to Rex Hohlbein's Facing Homelessness program and his current spin-off project *You Know Me Now*, the podcast featuring stories of people living homeless in Tent City 3 and elsewhere in Seattle.[20]

REX HOHLBEIN, A SUCCESSFUL Seattle architect who, in 2010, had his office in Fremont near the Burke-Gilman Trail and the adjacent Fremont Canal Park, began having coffee breaks and lunch in the park with people experiencing homelessness. As Rex puts it, "I was having meetings in my office, designing homes worth millions of dollars, while people just outside were struggling, with nothing to their names."[21] Jenn Adams, who was a vehicle resident living nearby and remembers this time, says that Rex "was right across from the duck walk, and he used to walk from million-dollar houses and doing architectural stuff, and then he'd have lunch with Dinkus or some of the other guys who were down there. . . . That was such a natural, beautiful way to make things, to create. He let things happen naturally. That's a lot of what we need to do with what's going on now."[22]

Dinkus McGank, previously a logger from the Olympic Peninsula, was forty-nine years old and lived outside when Rex took his photograph in 2011. People commented on how much Dinkus resembled Robin Williams, with a similar wry, lopsided grin. After a logging accident, Dinkus had been medevaced to Harborview Medical Center, but then he began drinking to ease his back pain and ended up on the streets of Seattle. Later, at age fifty-two, Dinkus moved into permanent supportive housing at the Pacific Hotel downtown, run by Plymouth Housing. After he moved into housing, Dinkus told Rex he was lonely being away from his street family and friends. But Dinkus got sober and stayed housed until he died a few years later.[23]

Rex progressed from having coffee and lunch with people like Dinkus living in homelessness outside his office to inviting them into his office to use the restroom, get water, charge their phones, or dry off after spending the night outside in the rain. Rex states, "I was seeing a side of homelessness that the negative stereotype had never shown me, and I was struck by the fact that if [the] community saw the same beauty I was seeing, that was being shared with me, that we would all rush in and want to end the struggling and suffering of people that were going through homelessness."[24] Then, Rex set up a Facebook page to match homeless people's needs for material goods, like tents or sleeping bags, or services, like vehicle repairs, to people from the general public who would provide these items. Rex took black-and-white photographs of homeless people and posted them on Facebook alongside their stories as told to him.[25] Jenn recalls that when she first met Rex, she did not trust him. "I thought, who is this guy taking pictures of everybody? Why is he doing this? What nefarious thing is he trying to do?"[26] She laughs and adds, "He's done so many interviews with people who aren't here anymore. Without that documentation, we wouldn't have some of that."[27]

Karina Wallace was living in her car with her boyfriend when she made the request to Rex for beading supplies to make rosaries. She says, "We didn't know how a person that didn't know us could care and want to help . . . he showed us we could live a different life. For once, it seemed like someone believed in us."[28] With Rex's help, Karina and her boyfriend accessed services and entered permanent housing. Today, Karina is housed. She worked as the community programs coordinator for Facing Homelessness.

In 2014, at his wife's urging, Rex founded the nonprofit Facing Homelessness. They had a Facing Homelessness office in U Temple in the U District, alongside ROOTS Young Adult Shelter and other social services. They started the Just Say Hello initiative to encourage people not to shun those experiencing homelessness whom they may encounter on the streets. To smile and say hello, as Jenn Adams points out, is vitally important for homeless people to feel seen and included in the community at some fundamental level. Facing Homelessness opened a Window of Kindness, providing hot soup and meals, sleeping bags, coats, and other items to homeless people who stopped by. It grew so popular that they moved it to the Quaker University Friend's Meeting building near Peace Park and the U District P-Patch community garden, where it was until 2024.

Not content to stop there, and using his architectural skills, Rex and his architect daughter, Jenn LaFreniere, started Facing Homelessness's BLOCK Project. Countering NIMBY (not in my backyard) voices with YIMBY (yes, in my backyard), the BLOCK Project identifies homeowners in Seattle who are interested in having a 125-square-foot house built in their backyards and matches them with homeless people who want to live there. The houses are considered to be detached accessory dwelling units. A community vetting process occurs first, getting the entire neighborhood behind the new tiny house and formerly homeless neighbor. Facing Homelessness volunteers build the house off-site and then help install it in less than a month, keeping the cost of each unit to $75,000. In contrast, building traditional affordable housing units in Seattle starts at $300,000. Upward of 75% of Seattle is still zoned for single-family homes (renamed neighborhood residential housing), with its racist roots. This severely limits land eligible for new traditional low-income housing.[29] In 2023, the Washington State Legislature passed a bill to allow more "middle housing" like accessory dwellings, duplexes, and even fourplexes on land throughout the state zoned for single-family dwellings.[30] However, exclusive, wealthy, "common interest" communities and buildings with homeowner associations are excluded from this rezoning.[31]

People who want to live in the BLOCK homes are screened by Seattle agencies, like the Chief Seattle Club and Mary's Place, which help provide ongoing case management and linkage to health care. In this way, the BLOCK homes are a form of permanent supportive housing. As of the end of 2022, the BLOCK Project had built and installed fifteen homes in Seattle, and they have provided over ten thousand nights of stable housing to residents who were homeless.[32]

Facing Homelessness was scaling up the production and installation of BLOCK homes. They are hoping that more Seattle homeowners will sign on to host a tiny home on their property.[33] During the pandemic, they developed a pilot project to provide the BLOCK house kit to other organizations, with the Indigenous NDN Collective in South Dakota building a twenty-plus-cottage community.[34] The modular tiny homes are built to be energy-efficient and environmentally friendly, using invasive species juniper for the exterior, wool for insulation, and cork for the flooring.[35] People can live in the BLOCK homes indefinitely or use the housing as a stepping stone to other forms of permanent housing.[36]

Although the BLOCK Project tiny homes are far from being able to eliminate homelessness in Seattle, they are a vital part of the solution. They can help counter the harmful social exclusion and stigma experienced by people living homeless. Jenn says that she knows people who live in the BLOCK Project homes. "What a great thing, to put a tiny house in the middle of the block, where the whole neighborhood knows and can jump in and help with the garden and get to know the person, and make this sense of community so that they can grow and become a beautiful part of society."[37]

WHY IS IT so difficult for many of us to have and sustain compassion and empathy for people experiencing poverty and homelessness? Is it due to "compassion fatigue," which, as the *OED* definition points out, is akin to burnout from the numbingly repeated appeals for assistance? Not surprisingly, given our country's "pull yourself up by the bootstraps" myth, this term originated in the United States. In terms of homelessness, especially in places like Seattle, where homelessness appears to be intractable and growing despite many well-intentioned efforts by individuals, groups, philanthropies, and government entities, could compassion fatigue be precisely because of this overwhelming surfeit of compassion?

One reason for compassion fatigue in the Seattle area has to be the growing number of wealthy and extremely wealthy people who live here. In 2022, thirteen Washington residents made the global billionaires list, people such as Jeff Bezos (until his late 2023 move to Florida to avoid capital gains taxes) and Bill Gates and their ex-wives, Mackenzie Scott and Melinda French Gates. Most of these thirteen people live in the Seattle area, mainly in the Eastside cities of Kirkland, Redmond, and Bellevue.[38] In Kirkland in 2021, the top 5% of households had an average income of more than $1 million.[39] People higher on the socioeconomic ladder tend to have diminished empathy for people living in poverty and more interest in maintaining the status quo, especially if they live in gated, socioeconomically homogenous communities.[40] Research through the Harvard Implicit Association Test indicates a pervasive pro-wealthy/anti-poor bias, especially pronounced for people in higher socioeconomic strata and for men. Researchers point to the effects of the widespread beliefs in the United States in upward mobility despite the evidence against it.[41]

Attempting to make Seattle a fairer place for everyone, Seattle City Council member and socialist and economist Kshama Sawant helped shepherd in a $15-per-hour minimum wage in Seattle in 2015.[42] Seattle's minimum wage increased to $18.69 for most workers in 2023 and remains the highest in the country. Some economic analyses point to this high minimum wage as modulating income inequities in Seattle, at least for people who earned less than the city's median wage.[43] Other analyses of the effects of the minimum wage hike performed by UW researchers with funding from the city counter these findings.[44]

Income and wealth inequality have long existed in Seattle as throughout the United States, but these inequalities rose in the early days of the COVID-19 pandemic. As downtown Seattle Amazon headquarters and the Microsoft Seattle and Redmond campuses heeded county public health advice to have their employees work remotely from home, lower-income people working in restaurants and other nonessential work lost their jobs. Other low-income workers deemed essential such as grocery workers, who are more likely to be BIPOC and living in crowded housing, had higher exposures to illnesses and deaths from COVID-19.[45] This deepened already existing income and wealth inequities, including racial inequities.[46]

Local, state, and national efforts to address the economic fallout of the pandemic, including eviction moratoriums, rental assistance, housing vouchers, paid sick and caregiving leave, Medicaid continuity and Affordable Care Act subsidies, expansion of food stamps, and child tax credits, helped modulate the disproportionate economic effects of the pandemic on people in lower socioeconomic levels but did not eliminate inequities. Most of these social safety net measures have ended or will soon end.[47] Because of the strengthening, if only temporary, of the social safety net, child poverty in the United States was cut by more than half.[48] That fact would seem to be cause for celebration. Instead, the conservative backlash rhetoric blamed high unemployment rates on the increase in the government's social safety net, claiming that government "handouts" made people lazy and motivated people to stay out of the workforce. In his recent book *Poverty, by America*, Matthew Desmond writes about why this backlash occurred: "Perhaps it's because we've been trained since the earliest days of capitalism to see the poor as idle and unmotivated."[49] Child poverty rates in the United States for 2023 have doubled since the ending of many pandemic-era health and social supports.[50]

Through the leadership of council member Teresa Mosqueda and connecting with council member Kshama Sawant's longstanding but unsuccessful "Tax Amazon" campaign, in 2020 the Seattle City Council passed the JumpStart payroll tax, a tax on high-earning workers at places like Amazon and Microsoft.[51] Withstanding lawsuits, the JumpStart payroll tax still stands.[52] In 2021, it brought the city $231 million, but much of that new revenue went to the city's General Fund for ongoing pandemic relief efforts and not as much as was planned for housing and homelessness issues.[53] With pandemic emergency federal funding streams drying up and the effects of inflation, City of Seattle government officials currently face tough choices on more progressive taxation like through the JumpStart payroll tax.[54]

Another reason for people's compassion fatigue over homelessness in Seattle and King County is summarized by Nicole Macri in an interview I conducted with her in the summer of 2022. Nicole, who is the deputy director for DESC and Washington State representative for the Forty-Third District alongside Rep. Frank Chopp, stated, "People sometimes call it compassion fatigue that residents are generally well intended and want to help but they're just tired of there not being faster solutions."[55] She adds that there is a community backlash in the Seattle area and nationally, with people saying, "Well, you did Housing First. There's still homeless people. There's more homeless people than ever before, so it must not work."[56]

WHY IS HOMELESSNESS in Seattle and King County getting worse despite all the innovative, evidence-based local policy and program solutions like Housing First? Are we doing it all wrong and, through a twisted sense of compassion, creating more of a problem with homelessness than we solve? What can we do differently to have a greater impact on homelessness?

The high cost of housing in the Seattle area is often cited as a major contributor to housing instability and homelessness. For 2022, a worker in the Seattle area would have had to make at least $39.31 an hour to be able to afford a two-bedroom apartment at fair market rate; that is equivalent to someone making our higher minimum wage having to work 2.7 full-time jobs to be able to afford the apartment.[57] Almost 50% of Seattle residents are spending more than the recommended 30% of their income on housing and so are at risk of losing their housing and possibly becoming homeless.[58] The racial disparities of housing insecurity, as with homelessness in the Seattle area, are striking.[59] High-impact nonprofits led by BIPOC people in the Seattle area, such as Africatown Community Land Trust, Communities Rise, and the Urban League of Metropolitan Seattle, are working on local solutions.

One of the biggest problems we have is that more people enter homelessness than successfully and permanently exit homelessness. This includes people who were formerly homeless and moved into subsidized housing, but when the subsidies ended and they were expected to pay the full rent, they became homeless again.[60] A recent Bill and Melinda Gates Foundation–funded project, the Puget Sound Family Homelessness Initiative, had the goal of cutting family homelessness in half through coordinated entry, rapid rehousing, and flexible funding to match a family's needs. Researchers found that the inflow of families into homelessness more than doubled from 2012 (3,145) to 2019 (6,469). The project's outflow increases and their successes in helping families exit homelessness were offset by a larger increase in the inflow.[61] Most of this outcome is likely because the pipeline into homelessness is much bigger than the available exits out of homelessness.

Common claims, especially from more conservative-leaning people, are that homelessness is caused by a drug problem or a mental illness problem and that these are exacerbated by an overly permissive, progressive populace in certain urban areas like Seattle or San Francisco.[62] People point to the high rates of homelessness in cities along the West Coast, including Seattle, Portland, San Francisco, and Los Angeles, as being a direct result of these being heavily Democratic-leaning areas. Researchers, service providers, and policymakers push back against these simplistic and judgmental assessments. At the same time, cities like Seattle are facing increased public backlash against their enactment of more lenient drug policies that many people see as contributors to visible homelessness and public drug use, including on public transportation. In September 2023, the Seattle City Council passed a law to make public drug use and possession a gross misdemeanor punishable by up to 180 days in prison and a $1,000 fine; people with two prior drug convictions can get up to 364 days in prison. This new Seattle law is in alignment with a 2023 state drug possession law.[63]

Recent statistical analyses done by UW researcher Greg Colburn and data scientist Clayton Paige Aldern and presented in their book *Homelessness Is a Housing Problem: How Structural Factors Explain US Patterns* look at variations in rates of homelessness for multiple metropolitan areas in different regions of the United States. They examined the data to see whether the variance in homelessness rates could be explained by mental illness, drug use, poverty, climate, level of public assistance, and socioeconomic mobility. For instance, some observers also claim that the West Coast has such high rates of homelessness because of the milder climates of the urban areas in this geographical region. Their research findings indicate that the driving forces behind the variability of homelessness across the United States are the cost and availability of rental housing. The researchers point out that their findings support the conclusion that homelessness is caused more by an excess of affluence than by poverty. For affluent coastal cities like Seattle, with a scarcity of affordable housing, the consequences of being in poverty are much higher—consequences that can lead to homelessness.[64]

AS DANIEL MALONE, executive director of the DESC, told me in an interview I had with him, not everyone wants to believe these analyses and research conclusions. Daniel says, "I hear a lot of reaction to 'Oh, my god, the left just wants to act like this is just a market-driven homelessness problem, and they just ignore that the guy on the sidewalk is out of his mind on fentanyl and meth.'"[65] Nicole Macri also told me of conversations she has had with members of the public about the causes of homelessness. "There is a camp of people who believe that it is a housing problem and another camp that believes, no, this is a drug problem."[66] Nicole does not find the debate fruitful. "I think it's true we have a housing problem. And it's true we have a drug problem. For many people who need housing, they also need a lot of support to address the impacts of their substance use."

Infighting among public and private agencies providing homelessness services is another reason for there not being more progress on solving our regional homelessness crisis. The list of infighting, at least the instances that become public knowledge, is long and growing: the RHA and Mayor Harrell sparring over encampment sweeps, which they call cleanups;[67] the RHA and the Low Income Housing Institute (LIHI) sparring over the legitimacy of tiny house villages as a form of noncongregate shelter and a step toward permanent housing;[68] and, most recently, the RHA, in collaboration with the Lived Experience Coalition headed by LaMont Green, being accused of mismanagement of FEMA funds to pay for homeless people to stay in hotels, causing hundreds of formerly homeless people to face eviction from hotels back into homelessness.[69] Cynics, especially ones on the sidelines of the homelessness world, are all too eager to point fingers at their least favorite politician, agency, or policy and say, "I told you so." While vilification of people and agencies may feel good to the villifier, it is ultimately divisive and destructive. Extremism on both the left and the right of the political spectrum is dangerous.

IT HAS ALWAYS struck me that while people in Seattle and King County are good at coming up with innovative, evidence-based programs, we could be better at scaling up those programs. Is there a need for more political will to scale up innovative, evidence-based policies and programs? Evidence-based programs, like Housing First, are expensive and take so long to permit and construct buildings that it is difficult to increase them relatively quickly. Is the problem exacerbated by NIMBYism, such that residents and business owners successfully prevent programs like Housing First, Safe Lot programs, and the new King County Crisis Care Centers from being added to their communities? Graham Pruss points out that programs like the Safe Lot program can only serve a limited number of vehicle residents. "They are not built as scalable models, the low levels of success mean that they don't get scaled," he told me in an interview.[70]

In my experience, another reason for the lack of progress on homelessness in the Seattle area is the culture of lengthy decision-making. When I first moved to Seattle from Baltimore, one of my most difficult cultural adjustments was transitioning from the East Coast, with its more streamlined, top-down decision-making, to the Seattle area's lengthy, process-heavy attempt at egalitarian decision-making. An Orwellian example from my UW work was sitting through seemingly endless community health faculty meetings where people argued over the decision-making process—and that was with an outside paid facilitator trying her best to pull us together to come to a decision—about decision-making.

Admittedly, some of my UW-based experience can be chalked up to the particularly fossilized and absurd ineptitude of academia, but I've been in many similar non-academia-related meetings, such as those for the King County Ten-Year Plan to End Homelessness. Launched in 2005 and with monthly subgroup meetings, like the one on youth homelessness I was part of, the Ten-Year Plan to End Homelessness created many recommendations but was largely unsuccessful. Ten years into the plan, homelessness in King County had increased significantly.[71] While I understand and, to a certain degree, applaud our area's attempt to be egalitarian, an overreliance on this approach leads to delays in making sound and timely decisions that affect people's lives. Not having a more organized approach to decision-making wastes time and money and delays critical evidence-based interventions from helping more people who are suffering.

Notes

1. Tisa Somsap, "U District Partnership Welcomes New Leader, Don Blakeney," *Daily*, February 16, 2021, https://www.dailyuw.com/news/u-district-partnership-welcomes-new-leader-don-blakeney/article_e9277a5a-701c-11eb-8f99-5fb6406cbaa9.html.
2. Don Blakeney, Skid Road Oral History, interview by Josephine Ensign, March 21, 2023.
3. Blakeney, Skid Road Oral History interview.
4. David Delgado, "Word from the Street: David Delgado's Keynote Speech," *Real Change*, September 22, 2021, https://www.realchangenews.org/news/2021/09/22/word-street-david-delgado-s-keynote-speech.
5. Delgado, "Word from the Street."
6. Delgado, "Word from the Street."

7. Delgado, "Word from the Street."
8. Johnny Ohta, Doorway Project, interview by Josephine Ensign, January 31, 2018; Blakeney, Skid Road Oral History interview.
9. Allegra Abramo, "Johnny Ohta's 'There-for-Everything' Care for Seattle's Homeless Youth Is Rare—and He Does It on a Bike," Crosscut, September 27, 2019, https://crosscut.com/news/2019/09/johnny-ohtas-there-everything-care-seattles-homeless-youth-rare-and-he-does-it-bike.
10. Abramo, "Johnny Ohta's 'There-for-Everything' Care."
11. Blakeney, Skid Road Oral History interview.
12. Gene Balk, "Seattle Is the Third Most Gentrifying U.S. City—but That Might Not Be as Bad as You Think, Study Finds," *Seattle Times*, July 24, 2019, https://www.seattletimes.com/seattle-news/data/seattle-ranks-near-top-for-gentrification-but-that-might-not-be-as-bad-as-you-think-study-finds/.
13. Julie Bosman, "Times Square's Homeless Holdout, Not Budging," *New York Times*, sec. New York, March 29, 2010, https://www.nytimes.com/2010/03/30/nyregion/30heavy.html.
14. Gabriel Poblete and Rachel Holliday Smith, "Mayor Adams Wants to Reassess New York's Right to Shelter. Can He?," City, September 19, 2022, https://www.thecity.nyc/2022/9/19/23357320/right-shelter-eric-adams-asylum-homeless.
15. Bobby Caina Calvan, "New York City Further Tightens Time Limit for Migrants to Move out of Shelters," AP News, September 23, 2023, https://apnews.com/article/new-york-migrants-shelter-time-limit-a028edfe8b2cee99eaadf07f423a6f6a.
16. Blakeney, Skid Road Oral History interview.
17. "Definitions," KCRHA, accessed April 29, 2023, https://kcrha.org/resources/definitions/.
18. Tim Meliah, "Lessons from Walla Walla County's Success Reducing Youth Homelessness," *Seattle Times*, August 25, 2022, https://www.seattletimes.com/opinion/lessons-from-walla-walla-countys-success-reducing-youth-homelessness/.
19. William Evans et al., "Housing and Urban Development–Veterans Affairs Supportive Housing Vouchers and Veterans' Homelessness, 2007–2017," *American Journal of Public Health* 109, no. 10 (October 1, 2019): 1440–45, https://ajph-aphapublications-org.offcampus.lib.washington.edu/doi/full/10.2105/AJPH.2019.305231.

20. See https://www.youknowmenow.com.

21. Sheila Cain, "Rex Hohlbein Moved from Upmarket Architecture to Helping Seattle's Poorest Rebuild," Crosscut, September 23, 2019, https://crosscut.com/2019/09/rex-hohlbein-moved-upmarket -architecture-helping-seattles-poorest-rebuild.

22. Jenn Adams, Skid Road Oral History, interview by Josephine Ensign, January 12, 2023.

23. Facing Homelessness, "This Is Dinkus McGank. He Is 49 Years Old," Facebook, accessed April 23, 2023, https://www.facebook.com /HomelessInSeattle/photos/a.376595449052371/267038016674782/ ?type=3&av=100080082161604&eav =AfaqVdAIWIWy5jJ9XW3DP0iGWuQIIZxHTncdaV4szDlrA8seqy- CvKWcv3VDLIGahI6w.

24. Rex Holbein, Skid Road Oral History, interview by Josephine Ensign, February 21, 2024.

25. Heather Hansman, "These Stirring Portraits Put a Face on Homeless- ness," *Smithsonian Magazine*, June 15, 2015, https://www .smithsonianmag.com/innovation/these-stirring-portraits-put-face -on-homelessness-180955495/.

26. Adams, Skid Road Oral History interview.

27. Adams, Skid Road Oral History interview.

28. Cain, "Rex Hohlbein Moved."

29. Katherine Shaver, "Single-Family Zoning Preserves Century-Old Segregation, Planners Say. A Proposal to Add Density Is Dividing Neighborhoods," *Washington Post*, November 20, 2021, https://www .washingtonpost.com/transportation/2021/11/20/single-family-zoning -race-equity/; Rick Mohler, "Rick Mohler: A Reckoning with Single- Family Zoning's Impact on Racial Equity—and on Architects' Liveli- hood," *Architect*, September 18, 2020, https://www.architectmagazine .com/practice/rick-mohler-a-reckoning-with-single-family-zonings -impact-on-racial-equityand-on-architects-livelihood_o; David Gutman, "Is This the Year WA Ends Single-Family Zoning?," *Seattle Times*, February 24, 2023, https://www.seattletimes.com/seattle-news /politics/is-this-the-year-wa-ends-single-family-zoning/.

30. David Gutman, "WA Senate Passes Bill Allowing Duplexes, Four- plexes in Single-Family Zones," *Seattle Times*, April 11, 2023, https:// www.seattletimes.com/seattle-news/politics/wa-senate-passes-bill -allowing-duplexes-fourplexes-in-single-family-zones/.

31. David Gutman and Daniel Beekman, "Single-Family Zoning Ban Exempts Some Wealthy Seattle Enclaves," *Seattle Times*, April 23, 2023, https://www.seattletimes.com/seattle-news/politics/was-new-ban-on-single-family-zoning-exempts-some-of-seattles-wealthiest-neighborhoods/.

32. Stacy Kendall, "Seattle's BLOCK Project Is Expanding," *Seattle Magazine*, April 17, 2023, https://seattlemag.com/tiny-house-big-moves/.

33. Kendall, "Seattle's BLOCK Project."

34. Kendall, "Seattle's BLOCK Project."

35. Jane Margolies, "Tiny Homes for the Formerly Homeless," *New York Times*, sec. Style, May 3, 2023, https://www.nytimes.com/2023/05/03/style/seattle-homeless-tiny-homes.html; "Block Houses, by Block Project," *Architect*, October 18, 2022, https://www.architectmagazine.com/project-gallery/block-houses_o.

36. Margolies, "Tiny Homes."

37. Adams, Skid Road Oral History interview.

38. Renata Geraldo, "Is Your Neighbor a Billionaire? 13 Call Washington Home," *Seattle Times*, April 7, 2023, https://www.seattletimes.com/business/13-washingtonians-make-global-billionaire-list-despite-wealth-drop/.

39. Gene Balk, "$1 Million-Plus Incomes Set One WA City Apart from Most of the Nation," *Seattle Times*, March 8, 2023, https://www.seattletimes.com/seattle-news/data/wa-city-one-of-only-6-in-u-s-where-top-5-percent-make-over-1m/.

40. Josephine Ensign, *Soul Stories: Voices from the Margins*, Perspectives in Medical Humanities (San Francisco: University of California Medical Humanities Press, 2018); Matthew Desmond, *Poverty, by America* (New York: Crown, 2023); Lydialyle Gibson, "Mirrored Emotion," *University of Chicago Magazine*, April 2006, https://magazine.uchicago.edu/0604/features/emotion.shtml.

41. Bradley Mattan and Jasmine Cloutier, "A Registered Report on How Implicit Pro-rich Bias Is Shaped by the Perceiver's Gender and Socioeconomic Status," *Royal Society Open Source* 7, no. 8 (August 26, 2020): 191232, https://doi.org/10.1098/rsos.191232.

42. Benjamin Wallace-Wells, "How the Minimum-Wage Movement Entered the Mainstream," *New Yorker*, March 31, 2016, https://www.newyorker.com/news/benjamin-wallace-wells/how-the-minimum

-wage-movement-entered-the-mainstream; Kirk Johnson, "Seattle Approves $15 Minimum Wage, Setting a New Standard for Big Cities," *New York Times*, sec. U.S., June 3, 2014, https://www.nytimes.com/2014/06/03/us/seattle-approves-15-minimum-wage-setting-a-new-standard-for-big-cities.html.

43. Mark C. Long, "Seattle's Local Minimum Wage and Earnings Inequality," *Economic Inquiry* 60, no. 2 (2022): 528–42, https://doi.org/10.1111/ecin.13053.

44. Daniel Beekman, "Sawant, UW Researchers Clash over Impact of $15 Minimum-Wage Law," *Seattle Times*, September 21, 2016, https://www.seattletimes.com/seattle-news/politics/sawant-uw-researchers-clash-over-impact-of-15-minimum-wage-law/.

45. Latoya Hill and Samantha Artiga, "COVID-19 Cases and Deaths by Race/Ethnicity: Current Data and Changes over Time," *KFF* (blog), August 22, 2022, https://www.kff.org/racial-equity-and-health-policy/issue-brief/covid-19-cases-and-deaths-by-race-ethnicity-current-data-and-changes-over-time/.

46. Elizabeth Turnbull, "Report Shows Racial Wealth Divide Growing in Seattle, Forum Will Explore Solutions," South Seattle Emerald, March 16, 2021, https://southseattleemerald.com/2021/03/16/report-shows-racial-wealth-divide-growing-in-seattle-forum-will-explore-solutions/; Emanuel Nieves and Madelaine Santana, *Racial Wealth Divide in Seattle* (Prosperity Now, March 2021), https://prosperitynow.org/sites/default/files/Racial%20Wealth%20Divide_%20Profile_Seattle_FINAL_3.2.21.pdf.

47. Claire Cain Miller and Alicia Parlapiano, "The U.S. Built a European-Style Welfare State. It's Largely Over," *New York Times*, sec. The Upshot, April 6, 2023, https://www.nytimes.com/interactive/2023/04/06/upshot/pandemic-safety-net-medicaid.html.

48. Desmond, *Poverty, by America*, 81.

49. Desmond, *Poverty, by America*, 83.

50. Jennifer Ludden, "Child Poverty More Than Doubles—a Year after Hitting Record Low, Census Data Shows," NPR, sec. National, September 12, 2023, https://www.npr.org/2023/09/12/1198923453/child-poverty-child-tax-credi-pandemic-aid-census-data.

51. Daniel Beekman, "Seattle City Council Passes 'JumpStart' Tax on High Salaries Paid by Big Businesses," *Seattle Times*, July 6, 2020, https://www.seattletimes.com/seattle-news/politics/seattle-city

-council-passes-new-jumpstart-tax-on-high-salaries-paid-by-big
-businesses/.

52. Sarah Taylor, "Seattle's JumpStart Tax on Big Businesses' Salaries
Upheld by WA Court," *Seattle Times*, June 21, 2022, https://www
.seattletimes.com/seattle-news/seattles-jumpstart-tax-on-big
-businesses-salaries-upheld-by-wa-court/.

53. Angela King and Katie Campbell, "The New Jumpstart Payroll Tax
Raised More Than Expected. Is the Money Going Where It's Most
Needed?," KUOW, July 20, 2022, https://www.kuow.org/stories/the
-new-jumpstart-payroll-tax-raised-more-than-expected-is-the-money
-going-where-it-s-most-needed.

54. Guy Oron, "Will Seattle Choose to Tax the Rich or Cut Services?," South
Seattle Emerald, August 22, 2023, https://southseattleemerald.com
/2023/08/22/will-seattle-choose-to-tax-the-rich-or-cut-services/.

55. Nicole Macri, Skid Road Oral History, interview by Josephine Ensign,
July 29, 2022.

56. Macri, Skid Road Oral History interview.

57. "Out of Reach: Washington, 2022," National Low Income Housing
Coalition, accessed April 25, 2023, https://nlihc.org/oor/state/wa.

58. Turnbull, "Report Shows Racial Wealth Divide."

59. Nieves and Santana, *Racial Wealth Divide*.

60. Anna Patrick, "Here's How 2 Seattle Women Found Their Strength
While Homeless," *Seattle Times*, May 14, 2023, https://www
.seattletimes.com/seattle-news/homeless/heres-how-two-seattle
-women-found-their-strength-while-homeless/.

61. *A Decade of Innovation: Lessons from the Puget Sound Family
Homelessness Initiative* (Bill and Melinda Gates Foundation,
January 2021), https://local.gatesfoundation.org/wp-content/uploads
/2021/01/Gates-FHI-White-Paper-FINAL.pdf.

62. Michael Shellenberger, *San Fransicko: Why Progressives Ruin Cities*
(New York: Harper, 2021).

63. Josh Cohen, "Seattle City Council Passes Law to Prosecute Drug Use,
Possession," Crosscut, September 19, 2023, https://crosscut.com
/politics/2023/09/seattle-city-council-passes-law-prosecute-drug-use
-possession.

64. Gregg Colburn, *Homelessness Is a Housing Problem: How Structural
Factors Explain U.S. Patterns* (Oakland: University of California
Press, 2022).

65. Daniel Malone, Skid Road Oral History, interview by Josephine Ensign, July 14, 2022.
66. Macri, Skid Road Oral History interview.
67. Sarah Taylor, "Seattle Mayor Does Damage Control after Leaked Criticism of Homelessness Agency, City Council," *Seattle Times*, August 31, 2022, https://www.seattletimes.com/seattle-news/politics /seattle-mayor-does-damage-control-after-leaked-criticism-of -homeless-agency-city-council/.
68. Erica C. Barnett, "Tiny-House Funding Debate Reveals Fractures over Future of Homelessness System," PubliCola, April 4, 2022, https://publicola.com/2022/04/04/tiny-house-funding-debate -reveals-fractures-over-future-of-homelessness-system/.
69. Erica C. Barnett, "As Homeless Agencies Bicker over Blame, Time Runs Out for Hundreds Living in Hotels," PubliCola, April 10, 2023, https://publicola.com/2023/04/10/as-homeless-agencies-bicker-over -blame-time-runs-out-for-hundreds-living-in-hotels/; Amanda Zhou, "After Financial Collapse of Shelter, Homelessness Authority Scrambles for Housing," *Seattle Times*, April 22, 2023, https://www .seattletimes.com/seattle-news/homeless/after-financial-collapse-of -shelter-homelessness-authority-scrambles-for-housing/.
70. Graham Joseph Pruss, Skid Road Oral History, interview by Josephine Ensign, December 16, 2022.
71. Josephine Ensign, *Skid Road: On the Frontier of Health and Homelessness in an American City* (Baltimore: Johns Hopkins University Press, 2021), 201.

CHAPTER 11

Way Home

. . . .

> *When Emily Dickenson writes, "Hope is the thing*
> *with feathers that perches on the soul," she*
> *reminds us, as the birds do, of the liberation and*
> *pragmatism of belief.*
>
> —TERRY TEMPEST WILLIAMS, *REFUGE: AN UNNATURAL*
> *HISTORY OF FAMILY AND PLACE*

ONE OF THE QUESTIONS THAT I had at the beginning of this book project, and a question I posed to the people I interviewed, was this: in terms of homelessness, what lessons have we learned from the combination of the COVID-19 pandemic and the 2021 extreme heat event, and which of these lessons can and should we carry forward?

On March 23, 2020, Governor Jay Inslee issued an emergency "Stay Home, Stay Healthy" order for Washington State.[1] This emergency order highlighted the urgency of implementing emergency measures for people without a home. A major lesson we learned at the start of the pandemic was that the large, crowded, congregate shelter model we had relied on in the past was a bad idea from a public health perspective. In April 2020, King

County officials moved more than seven hundred people from congregate emergency shelters into hotel rooms that were empty as a result of the pandemic. Concurrently, officials de-intensified the remaining shelters, meaning that they created more space between where each shelter resident slept to decrease the risk of transmission. Since the US community spread of what became known as COVID-19 was first discovered in the Seattle area, people working on health and homelessness issues in other parts of the country looked to Seattle and King County homeless service providers and policymakers for advice.

Recalling the rise of homelessness and tuberculosis in the 1980s, we were reminded of how quickly infectious diseases could spread in congregate shelter settings.[2] That we had to learn this lesson again with the novel coronavirus is dismaying. In addition, even before the pandemic, we had ample evidence that chaotic, oftentimes violence-filled traditional shelters are not trauma informed and lead to worsening mental health for clients and higher burnout rates for direct-service providers.

Longtime Public Health–Seattle & King County public health nurse Heather Barr, who has helped shelter staff reduce the risk of tuberculosis and other communicable diseases, also conferred with shelter staff on trauma-informed care, including on shelter environments. In an interview I had with her before the pandemic, she commented on the typical high noise levels in shelters and the cold, oppressive settings of many of them. She said, "How do we replicate or reflexively make environments look kind of like prison . . . or a harsh mental institution of yesteryear?"[3] She remembered that in the 1980s it was a "stated desire to not make places too comfortable. . . . I don't think anybody needs extra punishment when our society is sort of hung up on punishing people or blaming them for bad choices when really the array of choices a lot of people have are not—none of them are going to be especially great."[4]

A study done on the effects of King County's homelessness response during the COVID-19 pandemic found significant decreases in COVID-19 infection rates and in the spread of the infection among people who moved into hotels from shelters.[5] In the hotels, people had their own rooms, bathrooms, and support staff, as well as three meals a day delivered to them.[6] Social distancing and masking were required in elevators and lobbies. An evidence-based public health harm reduction approach was taken.

Qualitative research findings from these studies showed dramatic improvements in housing stability and in subjective measures of well-being. Residents of the hotels reported improvements in sleep, reductions in stress, and less exposure to interpersonal conflict and outright violence.[7] The reported reduction in interpersonal conflict was corroborated by data on calls to the SPD by unnamed but likely DESC staff working at their large congregate shelter for a five-month time period before the pandemic and then for five months after the move of people to hotels. Calls to the SPD fell by 75% in 2020 compared to 2019.[8]

Residents staying in the hotels under this program reported improved mental health and reduced alcohol and other substance use, which they attributed to their safer, calmer living situation. One resident said, "It has helped to re-establish my self-esteem and dignity. . . . It feels more like home. I have space to create things, not just exist."[9] Another resident said, "I'm starting to get my dreams back. You get to the point when you're homeless you don't even care."[10] Having access to their own bathroom and storage space in their room with a lockable door allowed people accustomed to being socially marginalized to step out of that, at least for a while. Of not having to carry around their belongings, one resident said, "I don't have to pack it around, which has been really nice to feel normal again." They added, "When you don't have to carry that stuff around, people, they don't judge you as being homeless or whatever. They look at you differently. It's been nice not to be judged like that."[11]

Service providers commented on the positive changes they saw in people experiencing chronic homelessness they worked with because of the move from shelters to hotel programs. In a summer 2022 interview I conducted with Noah Fey, director of DESC housing programs, he said, "By moving people into a space where they had that privacy, we saw people overnight start sleeping better, talking about how they're able to handle their hygiene needs differently, feeling better in terms of overall mental health, starting to plan for their future."[12] He added, "To see it happen overnight was just so remarkably profound that we immediately said, 'We're not going back. We are not going back to this crowded space.'"[13]

Since DESC's mission has always been to serve people experiencing homelessness who have the most profound needs, Noah said, "We didn't want to lose capacity in the system for high-needs people. . . . I think we're seeing that play out in the streets of Seattle right now, particularly for people with really high needs."[14] Noah was referring to the rise of people living unsheltered with severe behavioral health issues. Walking to his office at the Morrison Hotel on Third Avenue on the morning of our interview, I passed numerous tent encampments on the sidewalks near DESC.

BECAUSE OF THE otherwise clear successes of the decision to move people staying in shelters to hotels, leaders in King County quickly acquired additional hotels and other buildings as permanent supportive housing and not just as emergency, pandemic-driven shelters.[15] They have designated some of these buildings as emergency housing to help move people out of encampments or for people with other emergent needs, such as for diabetic people needing to store their insulin in a refrigerator of their own. As of June 2024, the new Health Through Housing initiative has sixteen buildings with 24/7 on-site staffing and supportive services, including linkages to behavioral health.[16]

Another shelter model that was shown to reduce the risk and spread of COVID versus traditional congregate shelter was tiny house villages. In the Seattle area, the largest provider of tiny house villages is the LIHI. In the spring of 2022, when I talked with Sharon Lee, the executive director of LIHI and longtime housing advocate, she told me that they were operating sixteen tiny house villages. They have since added three new ones. Altogether, they serve over sixteen hundred people annually.[17] A few of these villages are outside of Seattle and King County, in places like Tacoma, Olympia, and Bellingham. She said that they could set up each village for $600,000, which she equated to the cost of two apartment units. Each tiny house is eight feet by twelve feet, with doors that lock and a heating system. Residents have access to toilets, showers, laundry facilities, a community kitchen, and a community activities space within the village. They have special population tiny house villages. One village is for women, one is for mainly BIPOC people, and several are reserved for families. Sharon told me that during the first two years of the COVID-19 pandemic, only fourteen of the hundreds of LIHI tiny house village residents contracted COVID. These residents were isolated in their tiny homes while being provided with supportive services, and there was no documented spread of infection within the villages.[18]

A significant policy change related to health through housing and spurred on by the COVID-19 pandemic was the Apple Health and Homes (AHAH) Act championed by Rep. Frank Chopp during the 2022 Washington State legislative session.[19] I was on the health care planning subcommittee for this bill and testified in favor of it to the members of the House Health Care and Wellness Committee, then chaired by Rep. Eileen Cody (Democrat from Seattle). Through my small role, I gained a greater appreciation of the political strategies for passing such progressive legislation related to health and homelessness.

When I interviewed Representative Chopp after the passage of the AHAH Act into law in the spring of 2022, he described how the concept has been around for a while but that it was challenging to implement owing to the different silos of Medicaid and housing. Medicaid does not pay for housing, only health care services. He connected Medicaid with a Washington State program, Foundational Community Supports (FCS), which evaluates people according to medical criteria and provides supportive housing. Representative Chopp said, "If you are homeless because of your medical condition, then you ought to have a home as part of your medical treatment." The qualifying medical conditions for FCS include mental illness, substance use disorder, and physical disabilities. Representative Chopp emphasized that this should be seen as an entitlement issue and not only as the vaguer statement that housing is a human right. He said, "Because if you put the issue in terms of health care, you have a different dynamic and a different discussion than if it's just housing homeless, affordable housing."[20]

Rep. Nicole Macri was cosponsor of the bill. In my discussion with her in the summer of 2022, I reflected on the relative ease with which this bill gained bipartisan support, including from more conservative legislators in rural parts of the state.

Referring to the work of Representative Chopp on the AHAH bill, Representative Macri said, "He was able to get, I think, colleagues of ours who are more conservative, who historically have had pretty stigmatizing views of people experiencing homelessness, and really shift the narrative by talking about people living with disabilities, particularly people living with mental illness, and relating that to people's own personal experiences."[21]

I asked Representative Macri how much of this bipartisan and rural support for the bill was because of the effects of the COVID-19 pandemic. She replied, "I think [that] probably played a lot into it. I think the increases in opioid dependence in rural areas of the state, and the exacerbation of behavioral health challenges that we've seen through the pandemic, really influenced people's thinking."[22] She added, "And that homelessness is now visible in areas where we haven't seen it before, including rural areas. I think that legislators felt like, well, if I can get a solution that works in my area and it's not just an urban-specific one, maybe that helps my neighbors and constituents."[23] Representative Macri added that the AHAH Act passed almost unanimously, with only one "no" vote in the House. She said that it is now a national model in terms of policy.

Rural homelessness has always existed, even though it looks different from urban or suburban homelessness. It is easier to remain invisibly homeless in rural communities because of lower population density and because there are fewer shelters and social services for people living in homelessness in rural areas.[24] Service providers are points of contact for people experiencing homelessness and keep records of who and how many people come in for services. Transportation in rural areas is difficult for people living in poverty and homelessness. As social support services and public transportation were curtailed during the pandemic and the fentanyl crisis deepened, homelessness in rural areas worsened. Housing insecurity and homelessness—including vehicle residency—became more visible and dire even in rural areas because of the COVID-19 pandemic.

THERE HAVE BEEN changes in response to the double disaster of the COVID-19 pandemic and the summer 2021 heat dome along with exposure to smoke from wildfires, events that greatly impacted people experiencing homelessness. The Washington State Department of Health reported 150 excess deaths from the 2021 extreme heat event, with the elderly poor, people living homeless or in substandard housing, and outdoor workers, like farmworkers, most at risk.[25] A recent study by UW researchers looking at data on excess deaths, including from heat-related injuries like drownings, violence, and self-harm, found 159 excess deaths for the same event.[26] Seattle officials reported thirty deaths from the 2021 heat event, disproportionately affecting people experiencing homelessness.[27]

Researchers have found evidence that extreme heat causes psychological and physiological brain changes linked to anger and impulsiveness.[28] This puts a new spin on the phrase "hot-tempered." The UW researchers estimate that a similar extreme heat event will occur in the Pacific Northwest every five to ten years as a result of climate change.[29] To better prepare for these extreme heat events, Public Health–Seattle & King County officials, working with other King County departments and the King County RHA, have implemented the Extreme Heat Mitigation Strategy. This strategy includes establishing cooling centers and designating air-conditioned public libraries and Metro buses as heat shelters.[30] Air filtration systems are being added to aid in the reduction of the spread of airborne viruses, like the novel coronavirus, as well as wildfire smoke particles. In early May 2023, the Seattle area had its earliest heat wave on record, which is even more dangerous to medically vulnerable people, including those experiencing homelessness, whose bodies are not yet acclimated to hot weather.[31]

With the strain on our US health care system caused by the COVID-19 pandemic and the rise in homelessness in the Seattle area, hospitals have difficulty responding to additional stressors caused by extreme heat events. During another extreme heat event in Seattle at the end of July 2022, Representative Macri told me of her recent visit to Harborview Medical Center, our region's Level I trauma center. Harborview staff members described to her what they termed "difficult-to-discharge patients." She said, "These are patients who don't need acute care hospitalization, but they need continual care, probably in a long-term care setting, like a skilled nursing facility or assisted living, but it could be home care."[32] Not all of these difficult-to-discharge patients are homeless, but many are.

Of the hospital discharge planners Representative Macri said, "They describe the problem that we have all these people who don't need our hospital care, but they're here because we don't have a better place that can appropriately serve them. Which means that our inpatient folks are being squeezed and displaced because we have too many patients who don't need to be here . . . then the front door, usually through the emergency department, is getting backed up."[33] Harborview Medical Center operates a medical respite program, the Edward Thomas House, in Jefferson Terrace, Seattle Housing Authority's largest apartment building, which is across the street from the emergency department.[34] This program is for homeless patients not sick or injured enough to require hospitalization but who are too sick or injured to return to shelters or the street.[35] Both the medical respite program and Harborview's palliative care program for homeless patients—the first of its kind in the country— fill an important need but can only serve a limited number of homeless patients.[36]

When Macri visited Harborview Medical Center the day before our interview, all of the area hospitals were on alert because of the extended heat wave causing heat-related injuries. "The emergency room Medical Director said, 'This afternoon, we had no available ambulances to go on call in Seattle because they were all at emergency departments waiting to transition their patients to the ED,' but they struggle to do that because the hospitals are all backed up."[37] Representative Macri told me that at that moment she realized that our medical system is going through a crisis similar to what the behavioral health system has been in for years. She said, "So we have all these people who are homeless, living with severe behavioral health conditions. They are trying to get in the front door, usually through the crisis system, and the crisis system is totally overloaded and can't respond."[38]

Another lesson from the 2021 extreme heat event is a heightened awareness of the importance of parks, green spaces, and tree canopy—especially mature tree canopy—in urban areas of King County. Trees modulate temperatures, pollution, and even flooding. Mapping temperature differences throughout Seattle and King County during recent heat waves found up to a twenty-degree temperature difference between highly urbanized and industrialized areas with few green spaces and higher-income residential neighborhoods with dense tree canopy.[39] Correlating the temperature maps and the location of trees and green spaces in King County highlights significant inequities, with lower-income neighborhoods and those with higher BIPOC populations being impacted the most. These are also people and neighborhoods with less access to air-conditioning in their living spaces. This has led to tree equity efforts statewide.[40] Ironically, amid these efforts locally and throughout Washington State, the urban development occurring in the U District, which had included plans to open a new park near the UW Tower and the Link light-rail station, has had pushback from businesses and residents who say it will become a magnet for people living in homelessness.[41]

Cal Anderson Park, the site of the CHAZ/CHOP protests in the summer of 2020 and of the murder-suicide of Lisa Vach and Travis Berge, is now full of people walking their dogs, playing sports, or watching their children play on the playground (which is slated for an upgrade). These activities all occur during the day. At night, this park continues to be plagued by shootings.[42] Trees at Cal Anderson Park, planted according to original plans by John Olmstead during the City Beautiful movement beginning in 1903 in Seattle, are being protected or replaced if they are diseased or damaged.[43] The only remnants of the CHAZ/CHOP protests include the large BLM mural painted on the Pine Street pavement near the park. In late December 2023, the city removed the BLM community garden.[44] The large BLM sign painted on the park building near the community garden has been removed. The pump house where Travis Berge killed himself remains closed off with fencing and barbed wire.

The city/county fight for control of the troubled City Hall Park in Pioneer Square ended in October 2022, with the city of Seattle maintaining ownership. This was at the urging of Pioneer Square residents and social service agencies like the Chief Seattle Club, who worried that they would lose one of the few remaining green spaces in the neighborhood.[45] City Hall Park remained closed and fenced off until June 13, 2023, when it reopened to the public.[46] Seattle Parks and Recreation added a park ranger to monitor the park.

CRIMINALIZATION OF HOMELESSNESS is linked to increases in violence against people experiencing homelessness.[47] Besides anti-criminalization efforts by advocates, there is an increasing emphasis on preventing violence against people experiencing homelessness. Advocates have attempted to make people living homeless a protected class in terms of hate and bias crimes. At the federal level, there have been ongoing discussions about this issue and the need to document crimes against people experiencing homelessness beyond the advocacy work of the National Coalition for the Homeless. The Hate Crimes Statistics Act of 1990 requires the DOJ to collect data from law enforcement agencies about crimes showing prejudiced bias based on race, religion, sexual orientation, ethnicity, disability, gender, or gender identity.[48] In the Hearing before the Subcommittee on Crimes and Drugs of the Committee of the Judiciary on September 29, 2010, there was pushback from certain sectors about adding homelessness because of how expensive it is to investigate and prove a hate crime. Other people testified that they believed that people experiencing homelessness cause more violent crimes than they are victims of.

Beginning in December 2007, homelessness became a bias hate crime category in the city of Seattle, punishable as a Class C felony.[49] Homelessness is not a bias hate crime category in Washington State despite efforts to change this. Studies have shown that the Seattle homelessness hate crime law is not well-known by people experiencing homelessness or by social service workers working on homelessness.[50] In addition, the reporting of and follow-up for such hate crimes is such a cumbersome process that many victims of hate crimes do not report them even if they know about the law. In reading over the details of this Seattle hate crime legislation, it is interesting to note the use of language stating that it is a hate crime if someone purposefully physically harms a person or "causes physical damage to, or destruction of" that person's property because of his or her perception that the victim is homeless. While I am sure there is a fine legal line within these issues, it would appear that city-sponsored encampment sweeps cause damage and destruction of property of the encampment residents—whom city officials know, of course, are homeless.

BRUCE HARRELL WAS elected mayor in November 2021, largely on a campaign promise to clean up Seattle and get tough on homelessness. His administration has made good on this campaign promise, at least to the extent of conducting numerous sweeps of homeless encampments throughout the city. The activists with Stop the Sweeps constantly send out social media appeals to block these sweeps. And they take and post photographs and video clips of SPD officers and sanitation crews doing sweeps. Mayor Harrell has used the term "Housing First" to describe the encampment "cleanups."[51] This is an odd and likely politically expedient use of the term, since Housing First in Seattle has solid support from most policymakers.

I asked Noah Fey about this when I met with him at DESC. He said, "Most definitely, the term Housing First gets used in ways that don't appear to be tied to the underpinning principles that really make the model both meaningful in how it's been designed, but also the evidence-based model it is. You can't pick and choose from the principles and still think it's the evidence-based program."[52]

There is mounting evidence that encampment and vehicle residency sweeps, or displacements, harm people experiencing homelessness.[53] A recent study on the health effects of sweeps on people experiencing homelessness who are injection drug users found that sweeps may substantially increase morbidity and mortality, mainly by worsening overdose and hospitalization rates and interfering with use of medications for opioid use disorder.[54] During the COVID-19 pandemic, when shelters closed or were at reduced capacity and we had public health evidence of how the novel coronavirus spread, the CDC issued the advice to halt encampment sweeps.[55] Mayor Jenny Durkan heeded this advice to a degree, at least during the first months of the pandemic. Then, as evidenced by the multiple clearances of the encampments at Cal Anderson Park, sweeps resumed.

Mayor Harrell and his administration have aggressively conducted encampment and vehicle residency sweeps. An April 2023 report from Mayor Harrell's office claims that since the city's Unified Care Team launch, and in partnership with the RHA, they had completed an estimated eight hundred encampment "site resolutions" (meaning sweeps or clearances) between mid-February and December 2022.[56] Through the combined efforts of the Unified Care Team and RHA, they made 1,831 referrals to enhanced shelters (meaning shelters with more behavioral health support) and tiny house villages.[57] The Mayor's Office claims that they have reduced the number of tents in Seattle by 42% since the winter of 2022 and have cut the number of RVs being used as housing in Seattle by 29% over the same time period.

When Deputy Mayor Tiffany Washington presented data from this report to the City Council, she said that many residents of these encampments wanted to move to tiny homes versus shelters, but there are not enough of these tiny homes to meet the need. *Seattle Times* columnist and social commentator Danny

Westneat reported that none of the council members criticized the mayor's report when Deputy Mayor Washington presented the findings. "After years of fighting about how to approach homeless encampments—with police teams, then navigation teams, then hope teams and now the United Care Team—our city of perpetual process reinvention finally seems to have hit on a formula that works," Danny Westneat wrote.[58] His optimism appears to be premature.

The ACLU of Washington sued the City of Seattle over the sweeps.[59] In June 2023, a King County Superior Court judge ruled that aspects of the city's approach to sweeps are unconstitutional. Specifically, the city's definition of "obstruction" as justification for swift encampment removals, including of vehicle residents, is too broad.[60] The ruling notes that through their encampment sweeps the city violates people's rights to privacy without due cause, which constitutes cruel punishment. As of October 2023 this court case is ongoing and the city's sweeps continue.[61] Concurrently, Seattle city attorney Ann Davison, along with other local and regional officials across the political spectrum, have petitioned the Supreme Court to overturn both the *Martin v. Boise* ruling and a similar ruling about outdoor camping in *Johnson v. Grants Pass*.[62] An increasing number of these same officials, even more progressive ones, are talking of ways to manage, not end, homelessness. Democratic governor Gavin Newsom of California said recently that although he initially supported the *Boise* ruling, he now thinks that it is causing a humanitarian crisis.[63]

Noah Fey told me, "I am not a fan of sweeps, but I'm not a fan of simply saying, 'We need to leave people where they are and leave them be.' Neither of those are good alternatives and neither of those are all that, I think, informed by what we know works for people."[64] I agree with him. He also spoke of the sense of community and safety expressed by many residents of encampments and how disruptive sweeps are: "There's already such a feeling of insecurity when you don't have a place to live. Losing it time and time again is inherently traumatic." When talking about the increased number of encampments in Seattle and King County, he said, "I'm equally frustrated as most neighbors—maybe not all neighbors—but I'm equally frustrated about the situation before us. I might disagree on what the solution is than most neighbors, but we should all agree it is unacceptable that people are living in tents in any city in America, let alone one that has the wealth that we have." Noah quoted someone he works with at the county as saying, "The state of homelessness is inherently unacceptable except for, of course, that we accept it."[65]

I FIND IT encouraging that there is a growing understanding of the importance of people with the lived experience of homelessness needing to be included in real, not token, ways in order to achieve more effective program planning and policymaking. An example of this is Marc Dones, a Black nonbinary person with the lived experience of homelessness and mental illness (bipolar disorder), being named the first director of the RHA. Dones, although controversial in his role, did lead the RHA for its first two years. People with the lived experience of homelessness, like Jenn Adams and David Delgado, have long been employed as outreach workers, but not many have become leaders like Marc and Derrick Belgarde, an Indigenous man and CEO of the Chief Seattle Club. Representation and visibility matter. They matter in informing better programs and policies. They matter in countering negative stereotyping and social exclusionary practices of people experiencing, or having experienced, homelessness.

A recurring issue in terms of people with the lived experience of homelessness working on some aspect of homelessness,
especially in direct service work, are the dangers of being re-
triggered, relapsing if clean and sober, not maintaining professional boundaries, or burning out. As I mentioned earlier, in
trauma work, there is the phenomenon of trauma mastery, of a
person being drawn to working with people in difficult situations similar to those they experienced and felt powerless to
control. In trauma mastery, people, frequently unconsciously,
return to sites of trauma wanting to "do it right" this time, to
have control and mastery of the situation.[66] Too often, this sets
people up for unreasonable expectations of themselves, coworkers, and their clients. As Jenn Adams said, it takes years of support and even therapy to gain perspective on one's own
experience of homelessness. She points to mentors and work
supervisors who check in with her, point out possible triggering
situations, and help her maintain healthy boundaries in her direct service work.[67]

In my discussion with Derrick Belgarde about the increased
focus on people with the lived experience of homelessness, he
said, "I'm a firm believer that lived experience should always
lead in any field. . . . The best ones are ones who can actually
relate."[68] He followed this by talking about the fact that there is
a spectrum of different types of homelessness that people experience. He says of these experiences, "They're all traumatic and
horrible and awful, but they're all totally different, and I'm only
an expert in one." He added, "There needs to be more diversity
in these decision-makings because they don't think about that.
I see a lot of the lived experience movement making grounds in
homelessness work today, but a lot of them, I don't think, come
from the type of homelessness we're trying to solve in the downtown core."[69]

The 2022 National Health Care for the Homeless Conference and Policy Symposium, in person for the first time since the pandemic, was held in the swanky Hyatt Regency Bellevue near a high-end shopping center at the beginning of May. The venue was ironic given the fact that Bellevue officials work hard, mainly through more aggressive policing and criminalization of homelessness, to keep the city sanitized, especially compared with Seattle. Inside the hotel, many research and policy presentations were about the negative public health effects of encampment sweeps and increased mortality rates among people experiencing homelessness from deaths of profound despair.

I attended the conference and spoke with David Peery, a Black lawyer from Miami, Florida, with the lived experience of homelessness during the Great Recession. David is the current cochair of the National Health Care for the Homeless Council's National Consumer Advisory Board. I asked him if members of the advisory board have conversations about what "counts" as someone with the lived experience of homelessness. He said that they follow a guideline of recent experience of homelessness within the past five years, or longer ago if the person has stayed involved in direct homeless service provision, like being a peer outreach worker, being a direct service provider, or being involved in policy and advocacy work on homelessness. "A lot of times people who were homeless become judgmental about currently homeless people—unless they understand trauma-informed care," he explained.[70]

OTHER REASONS I FIND for hope in terms of homelessness and housing insecurity in Seattle and King County include the recent passage of Social Housing Initiative 135 by voters in the city of Seattle.[71] The House Our Neighbors group that developed this social housing initiative came from grassroots community support in opposition to the Compassion Seattle charter amendment attempt in the summer of 2021. Social housing, a European model gaining momentum nationally, is publicly owned and permanently affordable, with cross-class communities of different income groups and democratically controlled renter leadership.[72] The Seattle Social Housing Public Development Authority board members have been selected and are tasked with developing and maintaining public affordable housing in Seattle.[73] Social housing proponents point to the Faircloth Limit, from the 1998 Faircloth Amendment of the federal government preventing any net increase in our country's public housing stock, and time limits for affordable housing units to remain affordable housing as being reasons to have more social housing options.[74]

An additional hopeful sign, especially related to youth homelessness, is the passage of legislation in the 2023 Washington State legislative session of funding for the Bridge Program. Longtime Seattle homeless youth advocate Jim Theofelis was involved in the development of this program.[75] The program is for homeless youth ages sixteen to twenty-four who have previously entered inpatient behavioral health treatment, have stabilized, and need a supportive community and place to live after inpatient discharge.[76] Too often, homeless young people discharged from behavioral health inpatient treatment end up on the streets owing to inadequate housing and support. Knowing Jim's track record of developing and implementing innovative and evidence-based programs, like the Mockingbird Family Model for foster care youth and A Way Home Washington working on upstream prevention of youth homelessness, I do not doubt that the Bridge Program will be successful.[77]

WHAT CAN PEOPLE with the lived experience of homelessness say about the contemporary landscape of homelessness in Seattle and King County? What can we learn from the voices and stories of people experiencing homelessness who met with tragic and preventable deaths, as well as from people with the lived experience of homelessness who have not only survived but are thriving? By this, I do not mean thriving in the up-by-the-bootstraps, rags-to-riches way of people like Steve Jobs, but thriving in the sense that they are housed, happy, and engaged in important work.

Lisa Vach's and Travis Berge's lives and deaths highlight the dysfunctional amalgam of our behavioral health and criminal justice systems. Charleena Lyles's and John T. Williams's stories and senseless killings by SPD officers underscore the effects of racism and disproportionate police violence against BIPOC people, people living in homelessness, and people with behavioral health issues. Then there are the hopeful stories like those of Derrick Belgarde, Anitra Freeman, Jenn Adams, and Derrick Delgado, all of whom attribute their survival of homelessness to finding different types of supportive communities and meaningful work: smiles, doughnuts, and hard-boiled eggs delivered by compassionate volunteers; access to affordable, comprehensive, and culturally congruent health care, including behavioral health care, and housing; connection to and involvement in self-managed housing and support services like SHARE/WHEEL; positive and ongoing outlets for the grief that accompanies homelessness, such as artwork, writing, and groups like the Homeless Remembrance Project; and work helping other people survive homelessness.

Matt Fowle, cofounder of HomelessDeathsCount.org, a community-based research project collecting nationwide data on mortality among people experiencing homelessness, talked with me about his work in the summer of 2022. He was completing his PhD at the UW Evans School of Public Policy, his dissertation being on the causes and consequences of racial inequality in homelessness in the United States.[78]

In talking about homeless mortality statistics, he said that all-cause mortality for people experiencing homelessness had increased across the United States over the past decade. In Seattle over the past five years, homeless deaths due to fentanyl and methamphetamine have increased, as have deaths due to heart disease, deaths due to exposure, and deaths due to environmental conditions. In 2022, King County saw a record-breaking 310 deaths of people experiencing homelessness.[79] For 2023, the number of people who died homeless in Seattle stands at 415.[80] Deaths of homeless women have tripled.[81] Fowle said, "I try to make the point that it is not just a case of deaths of despair. This is what I've been calling 'mortal systemic neglect.' This is that we have failed to invest in life-affirming institutions, like health care, like housing, like education. Instead, we have invested in institutions that really deal with death. The carceral system. Even, to an extent, the homelessness response system, especially shelters."[82] He adds, "We've invested in these institutions that promote death rather than preserve life. I think that's the hidden story that especially deaths among people experiencing homelessness really exposes."[83]

There are lessons within these stories and these statistics that point us as individuals, communities, service providers, and policymakers toward what works to remedy homelessness. We need to prioritize evidence-based programs and policies while being open to new, innovative programs and policies, especially ones led by people who have experienced different types of homelessness. We need to build on the positive changes that have come about in terms of how we address homelessness as a result of the public health crises of the COVID-19 pandemic and the effects of climate change. We need to stop accepting homelessness as an unfortunate part of our country's current situation and invest more, as Matt says, in life-affirming institutions and programs.

Notes

1. "Inslee Announces 'Stay Home, Stay Healthy' Order," Washington Governor Jay Inslee, March 23, 2020, https://www.governor.wa.gov /news-media/inslee-announces-stay-home-stay -healthy%C2%A0order.

2. "Prevention and Control of Tuberculosis among Homeless Persons Recommendations of the Advisory Council for the Elimination of Tuberculosis," MMWR, Centers for Disease Control and Prevention, April 17, 1992, https://www.cdc.gov/mmwr/preview/mmwrhtml /00019922.htm; Barron H. Lerner, *Contagion and Confinement: Controlling Tuberculosis along the Skid Road* (Baltimore: Johns Hopkins University Press, 1998).

3. Heather Barr, Skid Road Oral History, interview by Josephine Ensign, October 27, 2015.

4. Barr, Skid Road Oral History interview.

5. Gregg Colburn, Rachel Fyall, and Samantha Thompson, *Impact of Hotels as Non-congregate Emergency Shelters* (University of Washington and King County Department of Community and Human Services, Performance Measurement and Evaluation Unit, November 2020), https://kcrha.org/wp-content/uploads/2020/11/Impact-of -Hotels-as-ES-Study_Full-Report_Final-11302020.pdf.

6. Colburn, Fyall, and Thompson, *Impact of Hotels*.

7. Gregg Colburn et al., "Hotels as Noncongregate Emergency Shelters: An Analysis of Investments in Hotels as Emergency Shelter in King

County, Washington during the COVID-19 Pandemic," *Housing Policy Debate* 32, no. 6 (June 8, 2022): 853–75, https://doi.org/10.1080/10511482.2022.2075027.

8. Colburn et al., "Hotels as Noncongregate Emergency Shelters."
9. Colburn et al., "Hotels as Noncongregate Emergency Shelters," 14.
10. Colburn et al., "Hotels as Noncongregate Emergency Shelters," 18.
11. Colburn et al., "Hotels as Noncongregate Emergency Shelters," 19.
12. Noah Fey, Skid Road Oral History, interview by Josephine Ensign, June 24, 2022.
13. Fey, Skid Road Oral History interview.
14. Fey, Skid Road Oral History interview.
15. "Massive Health Through Housing Measure Approved by King County Council," King County, December 7, 2021, https://kingcounty.gov/council/mainnews/2021/December/12-07-Health-Thru-Housing.aspx.
16. "Health Through Housing," King County, accessed March 26, 2023, https://kingcounty.gov/depts/community-human-services/initiatives/health-through-housing.aspx.
17. "Tiny Houses," Low Income Housing, accessed May 2, 2023, https://www.lihihousing.org/tinyhouses.
18. Sharon Lee, "Tiny House Villages in Seattle: An Efficient Response to Our Homelessness Crisis," *Shelterforce* (blog), March 15, 2019, https://shelterforce.org/2019/03/15/tiny-house-villages-in-seattle-an-efficient-response-to-our-homelessness-crisis/.
19. "Apple Health and Homes Act Signed by Governor," Frank Chopp, March 30, 2022, https://housedemocrats.wa.gov/chopp/2022/03/30/apple-health-and-homes-act-signed-by-governor/.
20. Frank Chopp, Skid Road Oral History, interview by Josephine Ensign, May 16, 2022.
21. Nicole Macri, Skid Road Oral History, interview by Josephine Ensign, July 29, 2022.
22. Macri, Skid Road Oral History interview.
23. Macri, Skid Road Oral History interview.
24. Paul A. Rollinson and John T. Pardeck, *Homelessness in Rural America: Policy and Practice* (New York: Haworth Press, 2006).
25. Nadja Popovich and Winston Choi-Schagrin, "Hidden Toll of the Northwest Heat Wave: Hundreds of Extra Deaths," *New York Times*, sec. Climate, August 11, 2021, https://www.nytimes.com/interactive/2021/08/11/climate/deaths-pacific-northwest-heat-wave.html; John

Ryan, "2021 Heat Wave Is Now the Deadliest Weather-Related Event in Washington History," KUOW, July 19, 2021, https://www.kuow.org/stories/heat-wave-death-toll-in-washington-state-jumps-to-112-people; David Kroman, "Who Was Most Harmed during Seattle's Heat Wave?," Crosscut, July 1, 2021, https://crosscut.com/news/2021/07/who-was-most-harmed-during-seattles-heat-wave.

26. Joan A. Casey et al., "Excess Injury Mortality in Washington State during the 2021 Heat Wave," *American Journal of Public Health* 113, no. 6 (June 1, 2023): 657–60, https://doi.org/10.2105/AJPH.2023.307269; Elise Takahama, "New Count of WA's Past Heat Wave Deaths Gives a 'Warning to the PNW,'" *Seattle Times*, April 17, 2023, https://www.seattletimes.com/seattle-news/health/new-count-of-states-past-heat-wave-deaths-give-a-warning-to-the-pnw/.

27. "King County to Develop Its First-Ever Extreme Heat Mitigation Strategy to Prepare the Region for More Intense, Prolonged Heat Waves Caused by Climate Change," King County, June 24, 2022, https://kingcounty.gov/depts/dnrp/newsroom/newsreleases/2022/June/24-extreme-heat-mitigation-strategy.aspx.

28. Alden Woods, "Washington State's 2021 Heat Wave Contributed to 159 Excess Injury Deaths over Three Weeks," *UW News* (blog), April 6, 2023, https://www.washington.edu/news/2023/04/06/washington-states-2021-heat-wave-contributed-to-159-excess-injury-deaths-over-three-weeks/.

29. Casey et al., "Excess Injury Mortality."

30. "King County to Develop," King County.

31. McKenna Oxenden and Chris Cameron, "12 Million People Are Under a Heat Advisory in the Pacific Northwest," *New York Times*, sec. U.S., May 13, 2023, https://www.nytimes.com/2023/05/13/us/heat-wave-pacific-northwest-canada.html; Niko Kommenda, Naema Ahmed, and John Muyskens, "The Early Heat Wave Gripping the Northwest Is Rare—and Worrying," *Washington Post*, May 13, 2023, https://www.washingtonpost.com/climate-environment/2023/05/13/west-coast-early-heat/.

32. Macri, Skid Road Oral History interview.

33. Macri, Skid Road Oral History interview.

34. "Edward Thomas House Medical Respite," UW Medicine, accessed May 14, 2023, https://www.uwmedicine.org/practitioner-resources/refer-patient/medical-respite.

35. Scott Greenstone, "You're Homeless, but You Have to Leave the Hospital. Where Do You Go?," *Seattle Times*, December 24, 2018, https://www.seattletimes.com/seattle-news/homeless/sick-homeless -people-get-stuck-in-washington-hospitals-but-theres-a-solution/.
36. Sydney Brownstone, "She Didn't Want to Die Homeless. But in Seattle, There Were Few Places to Turn," *Seattle Times*, January 9, 2022, https://www.seattletimes.com/seattle-news/homeless/she -didnt-want-to-die-without-a-home-but-even-with-cancer-she-had -few-options-in-seattle/.
37. Macri, Skid Road Oral History interview.
38. Macri, Skid Road Oral History interview.
39. "Results of Heat Mapping Project Show Inequitable Impact of Hotter Summers, Will Inform Actions by King County and City of Seattle," King County, June 23, 2021, https://kingcounty.gov/elected /executive/constantine/news/release/2021/June/23-heat-mapping -results.aspx.
40. Isabella Breda, "Coming Soon to an Urban Area near You: More Trees," *Seattle Times*, April 14, 2023, https://www.seattletimes.com /seattle-news/wa-seattle-launch-campaign-to-plant-thousands-of -urban-trees/.
41. Don Blakeney, Skid Road Oral History, interview by Josephine Ensign, March 21, 2023.
42. Paige Cornwell, "2 Dead, 1 Critically Wounded in Shooting at Cal Anderson Park in Seattle," *Seattle Times*, April 29, 2023, https://www .seattletimes.com/seattle-news/law-justice/shooting-reported-at-cal -anderson-park-in-seattles-capitol-hill/.
43. William Wilson, *The City Beautiful Movement* (Baltimore: Johns Hopkins University Press, 1989).
44. Daniel Beekman, "City Removes Seattle's Black Lives Matter Garden at Cal Anderson Park," *Seattle Times*, December 27, 2023, https:// www.seattletimes.com/seattle-news/politics/city-removes-seattles -black-lives-matter-memorial-garden/.
45. David Gutman, "Why the Deal to Give Seattle's Troubled City Hall Park to King County Fell Apart," *Seattle Times*, October 14, 2022, https://www.seattletimes.com/seattle-news/politics/troubled-city -hall-park-will-remain-seattles-ending-plan-to-transfer-to-county/.
46. Ryan Packer, "City Hall Park Reopens after Nearly Two Years, Still a City Asset," Urbanist, June 14, 2023, https://www.theurbanist.org

/2023/06/14/city-hall-park-reopens-after-nearly-two-years-still-a
-city-asset/.

47. Esther Schrader, "'Banned from Public Spaces': Report Highlights
Criminalization of Homelessness," Southern Poverty Law Center,
March 8, 2024, https://www.splcenter.org/news/2024/03/08/banned
-public-spaces-report-highlights-criminalization-homelessness;
"Sheltering Injustice," Southern Poverty Law Center, accessed
March 17, 2024, https://www.splcenter.org/sheltering-injustice-report.

48. *Crimes against America's Homeless: Is the Violence Growing?*
Hearing before the Subcommittee on Crime and Drugs of the
Committee on the Judiciary, 111th Cong. (2011).

49. P-I staff, "Harassing Homeless Now a Crime in Seattle," Seattle
Post-Intelligencer, December 11, 2007, https://www.seattlepi.com
/seattlenews/article/Harassing-homeless-now-a-crime-in-Seattle
-1258388.php.

50. Melissa Alderson, Claudia Gross-Shader, and Jane Dunkel, *Review of
Hate Crime Prevention, Response, and Reporting in Seattle: Phase 2
Report* (Seattle Office of City Auditor, May 19, 2019).

51. "Bruce Harrel Unveils Homelessness Plans, Decries Lack of Action to
Help People out of Encampments as School Year Begins," Bruce
Harrell for Seattle Mayor, July 2021, https://www.bruceforseattle
.com/bruce-harrell-unveils-homelessness-plans-decries-lack-of
-action-to-help-people-out-of-encampments-as-school-year-begins
/#:~:text=Harrell%20also%20wants%20to%20see,Color%2C%20
LGBTQ%2B%20youth%20and%20others.

52. Fey, Skid Road Oral History interview.

53. "Encampment Sweeps: What They Are and the Harm They Cause,"
ACLU of Washington, January 11, 2023, https://www.aclu-wa.org
/story/encampment-sweeps-what-they-are-and-harm-they
-cause%C2%A0.

54. Joshua A. Barocas, Samantha Nall, and Sarah Axelrath, "Population-
Level Health Effects of Involuntary Displacement of People Experiencing Unsheltered Homelessness Who Inject Drugs in US Cities,"
JAMA 329, no. 17 (April 10, 2023): 1478–86, https://jamanetwork-com
.offcampus.lib.washington.edu/journals/jama/fullarticle/2803839
?guestAccessKey=f321ceca-78d6-4d55-bcc5-e7a775ce1152&utm
_source=For_The_Media&utm_medium=referral&utm_campaign
=ftm_links&utm_content=tfl&utm_term=041023; Laura Rabell,

"Study Shows Involuntary Displacement of People Experiencing Homelessness May Cause Significant Spikes in Mortality, Overdoses and Hospitalizations," National Health Care for the Homeless Council, April 10, 2023, https://nhchc.org/study-shows-involuntary -displacement-of-people-experiencing-homelessness-may-cause -significant-spikes-in-mortality-overdoses-and-hospitalizations/.

55. Teresa Wiltz, "Against CDC Guidance, Some Cities Sweep Homeless Encampments," Stateline, April 28, 2020, https://pew.org/2W4sXhq.

56. Jamie Housen, "One Seattle Homelessness Action Plan Posts Q1 Data Updates, plus 2022 Totals for Referrals and Site Resolutions," Office of the Mayor, April 26, 2023, https://harrell.seattle.gov/2023/04/26 /one-seattle-homelessness-action-plan-posts-q1-data-updates-plus -2022-totals-for-referrals-and-site-resolutions/.

57. Housen, "One Seattle Homelessness Action Plan."

58. Danny Westneat, "Seattle Says the Bad Times Are Easing. Do You Feel It?," *Seattle Times*, May 3, 2023, https://www.seattletimes.com /seattle-news/politics/seattle-says-the-bad-times-are-easing-do-you -feel-it/.

59. "Encampment Sweeps," ACLU of Washington.

60. Anna Patrick, "Parts of Seattle's Encampment Clearing Rules Are Unconstitutional, Judge Rules," *Seattle Times*, July 24, 2023, https:// www.seattletimes.com/seattle-news/homeless/parts-of-seattles -encampment-clearing-rules-are-unconstitutional-judge-rules/.

61. Greg Kim, "How One Case Changed the Way Cities Deal with Homelessness," *Seattle Times*, October 15, 2023, https://www .seattletimes.com/seattle-news/homeless/one-court-case-changed -how-west-coast-cities-deal-with-homeless-encampments/.

62. Kim, "How One Case Changed"; Shawn Hubler, "In Rare Alliance, Democrats and Republicans Seek Legal Power to Clear Homeless Camps," *New York Times*, sec. U.S., September 27, 2023, https://www .nytimes.com/2023/09/27/us/in-rare-alliance-democrats-and -republicans-seek-legal-power-to-clear-homeless-camps.html.

63. Hubler, "In Rare Alliance."

64. Fey, Skid Road Oral History interview.

65. Fey, Skid Road Oral History interview.

66. Laura van Dernoot Lipsky, *Trauma Stewardship: An Everyday Guide to Caring for Self While Caring for Others* (Oakland, CA: Berrett-Koehler, 2009).

67. Jenn Adams, Skid Road Oral History, interview by Josephine Ensign, January 12, 2023.

68. Derrick Belgarde, Skid Road Oral History, interview by Josephine Ensign, April 7, 2022.

69. Belgarde, Skid Road Oral History interview.

70. David Peery, National Health Care for the Homeless 2022 Conference and Policy Symposium, Seattle, WA, interview by Josephine Ensign, May 11, 2022.

71. jseattle, "Seattle 'Social Housing' Backers Declare Victory on I-135," *Capitol Hill Seattle* (blog), February 16, 2023, https://www .capitolhillseattle.com/2023/02/seattle-social-housing-backers -declare-victory-on-i-135/.

72. See https://www.houseourneighbors.org; Galen Herz, "Social Housing Is Becoming a Mainstream Policy Goal in the US," *Jacobin*, February 21, 2021, https://jacobinmag.com/2021/02/social-housing -public-affordable-california-maryland; Ally Schweitzer, "How European-Style Public Housing Could Help Solve the Affordability Crisis," NPR, February 25, 2020, https://www.npr.org/local/305 /2020/02/25/809315455/how-european-style-public-housing-could -help-solve-the-affordability-crisis.

73. Jesse Franz, "Meet the 13 People Appointed to Bring Social Housing to Seattle," *Seattle City Council Blog* (blog), April 28, 2023, https:// council.seattle.gov/2023/04/28/meet-the-13-people-appointed-to -bring-social-housing-to-seattle/; Anna Patrick, "Initiative 135, Seattle 'Social Housing' Ballot Measure Leading in Tuesday Vote Count," *Seattle Times*, February 14, 2023, https://www.seattletimes .com/seattle-news/homeless/initiative-135-seattle-social-housing -ballot-measure-leads-on-election-night/.

74. "What Is the Faircloth Amendment?," National Coalition for the Homeless, April 7, 2022, https://nationalhomeless.org/repeal -faircloth-amendment/; "Office of Capital Improvements," U.S. Department of Housing and Urban Development, accessed May 15, 2023, https://www.hud.gov/program_offices/public_indian_housing /programs/ph/capfund.

75. "About NorthStar Advocates," NorthStar Advocates, accessed May 4, 2023, https://northstaradvocates.org/about/.

76. Josh Cohen, "Seattle's Historic Pacific Hospital Could House Unsheltered Youth," Crosscut, April 28, 2023, https://crosscut.com/news

/2023/04/seattles-historic-pacific-hospital-could-house-unsheltered
-youth.

77. "Mockingbird Family™," Mockingbird Society, accessed May 4, 2023,
https://mockingbirdsociety.org/our-work/mockingbird-family; "A Way
Home Washington—Prevent and End Youth Homelessness," A Way
Home Washington, accessed May 4, 2023, https://awayhomewa.org/.

78. Matthew Z. Fowle, "The Color of Homelessness: The Causes, Repro-
duction, and Consequences of Racial Inequality in Homelessness"
(PhD diss., University of Washington ProQuest Dissertations
Publishing, 2022), https://search.proquest.com/docview/2729081192
?pq-origsite=primo.

79. Anna Patrick, "More Homeless People Died in King County in 2022
Than Ever Recorded Before," *Seattle Times*, January 16, 2023,
https://www.seattletimes.com/seattle-news/homeless/more-homeless
-people-died-in-king-county-in-2022-than-ever-recorded-before/.

80. Danny Westneat, "King County Setting Records for Homeless Deaths
Is Becoming Awfully Routine," *Seattle Times*, January 10, 2024,
https://www.seattletimes.com/seattle-news/king-county-setting
-records-for-homeless-deaths-is-becoming-awfully-routine/.

81. Guy Oron, "Advocates Call for New Shelter as Unsheltered Women's
Mortality Rate Triples," *Real Change*, August 23, 2023, https://www
.realchangenews.org/news/2023/08/23/advocates-call-new-shelter
-unsheltered-women-s-mortality-rate-triples.

82. Matthew Fowle, Skid Road Oral History, interview by Josephine
Ensign, July 26, 2022.

83. Fowle, Skid Road Oral History interview.

Epilogue

· · · · · · · · · · · · · · · · · ·

Home is where you are known.
You are not alone.
The key is tied
to the way out and the way home.

—JOSEPHINE ENSIGN, *SOUL STORIES: VOICES*
FROM THE MARGINS

TOWARD THE END of the sunny and warm Tuesday afternoon of April 25, 2023, I rode my bicycle from my home near Seattle Children's Hospital to Magnuson Park. The King County special election deadline approached, and I had my completed ballot to place in a voters' drop box. My route took me past a newly built tiny house village of attractive, Easter egg–colored cottages and then alongside Brettler Family Place 3, where Charleena Lyles had lived and been killed by SPD officers. Clusters of elementary school children walking home from school with their mothers filled the air with happy chatter.

In the six years since Charleena Lyles's murder, when so many systems of care had failed her and her children, what, if anything, has improved?

Just focusing on the mental health system overlapping with the carceral system, Washington State's efforts to overhaul its mental health system, although well-intentioned, have been delayed.[1] Beginning in 2018, Governor Jay Inslee vowed to improve the state's beleaguered mental health system, including building six civil psychiatric facilities throughout the state by 2023. As of April 2023, two of these new facilities had been built.[2] Some of this delay is because of the NIMBYism of residents of places like Auburn and Burien in South King County. They have blocked the building of these psychiatric facilities in their communities, to the detriment of everyone.

Meanwhile, Western State Hospital, Washington's largest inpatient psychiatric hospital, has been in the process of eliminating approximately two hundred beds, releasing psychiatric patients into communities ill equipped to care for them. In a scenario reminiscent of the mass deinstitutionalization of psychiatric patients who were mainly discharged to the streets in the 1960s through the 1980s, people with severe mental health issues are ending up homeless, including in Seattle. Most of these people live unsheltered, caught up in the traumatizing cycle of sweeps, jail time, and hospital stays. As with having to relearn the public health lesson that crowded shelters are bad for people's physical and mental health, are we now having to relearn the lesson that psychiatric deinstitutionalization without adequate community behavioral health resources leads to a disaster? While I am a proponent of appropriate civil rights protections for people with profound behavioral health issues, our current situation is untenable and inhumane.

Especially pertinent to what Charleena experienced in her final days as her mental health deteriorated, King County has no walk-in behavioral health crisis centers, so people end up being treated inadequately in emergency departments and jails, as happened to Charleena.[3] With the rising rates and pervasiveness of behavioral health issues throughout the United States, which worsened as a result of the effects of the COVID-19 pandemic, the need for crisis centers became clear to policymakers, service providers, and the general public. Such crisis centers are for anyone experiencing a behavioral health crisis. People can self-refer, or family and friends can bring a loved one in for care. Law enforcement officers and first responders can also drop people off at these crisis centers. Patients can receive psychiatric and substance use treatment, for as long as needed, and be evaluated for competency, thus diverting people from jail and emergency departments.[4]

The day I rode my bike past Charleena's last apartment, I was voting for the King County Crisis Care Centers levy, a nine-year levy on property tax to bring in an estimated $1.2 billion over nine years. I wondered whether these crisis care centers could have provided Charleena with the support she needed to stabilize and continue to be a great mother to her children, possibly avoiding the preventable tragedy of her being shot and killed by SPD officers in her own home.

The money from the levy will go toward building and operating five crisis centers throughout King County, with one of the crisis centers specifically reserved for young people. It would also fund training and retention for the behavioral health workforce, including more equitable wages.[5]

THE CRISIS CARE CENTERS levy passed by a healthy margin, and planning is underway to expand access to behavioral health outreach and other services even before the opening of the five crisis centers beginning in 2026 and extending to 2032.[6] As Rep.

Nicole Macri told me, "But now, in the policy realm, there's a lot of focus on crisis response. 'What are we doing about crisis response?' I'm like, 'We created the crisis.'"[7]

A FEW DAYS before I voted for the Crisis Care Centers levy, on a cloudy Sunday morning, I attended the Homeless Remembrance Project's rededication service in the U District. Fourteen bronze leaves of remembrance for people experiencing homelessness who died had been embedded in the sidewalk in front of the entrance to what had been the University Temple United Methodist Church. The leaves of remembrance had been removed to protect them from the heavy machinery expected to build the new market-rate student apartments on the land that had been the church. But the firm that bought the church property delayed building the apartment complex because of the pandemic, with the project on indefinite hold. The UW was trying to buy the land. So WHEEL and the Homeless Remembrance Project people decided to rededicate and relay on the sidewalks the bronze leaves, along with another leaf of remembrance that had been blocks north in front of an old Safeway building near the University Heights Center.

The area of the old church building was now a fenced-off giant hole in the ground, with graffitied walls in what had been the church basement, where ROOTS Young Adult Shelter, the Urban Rest Stop, the Friday Feast, and PHRA needle exchange had been located. The original cornerstone sign for the church still stood next to the sidewalk and behind the fence, moss and lichen creeping over it like a headstone. U Temple's former pastor, Rev. Pat Simpson, led the rededication service on the sidewalk around the leaves of remembrance. There were twenty of us in attendance, including Michelle Marchand and Anitra Freeman from

WHEEL. Former members of U Temple participated. Three undergraduate UW students were part of the service. They were doing a group project on the Homeless Remembrance Project for a geography course.

Pat opened the service with a brief ecumenical prayer and then read out each deceased person's name, to which we replied, "We remember you." After this, Pat encouraged attendees to say something about any of the fifteen homeless people if we had known them. Several people shared fond memories of Ed McClain, a longtime vendor of *Real Change* anti-poverty newspaper, who sold outside the old U District Safeway store. Pat spoke of Lorraine Wong, an Asian American woman who lit candles, participated in services, and took naps in the U Temple Chapel. One day in 2015, Pat found Lorraine unconscious on a back pew, and despite emergency measures, she died several days later down the street at the UW Medical Center. The woman's sisters asked for the bronze leaf of remembrance for Lorraine to be placed near the church, where she had sought and found sanctuary.

Despite the constant roar of city buses passing by on the street beside us and people walking around our group on the sidewalk, giving us furtive glances, the service sparked a place of quietude in me. Warm hugs from Anitra before and after the service helped, as did a recollection of her words to me months ago when I asked her why she stays so active with the WHEEL Women in Black group. She spoke of the importance of sharing grief in community and, as the Homeless Remembrance Project pamphlet says, "nurturing connections among people homeless and housed, living and dead."

WHAT DOES IT mean to be settled in an unsettling world? Is a nomadic or at least a seminomadic life in the face of climate change and its fallout, like the COVID-19 pandemic, a healthier lifestyle for people who do not need to be in one place all the time? Who are we to judge people's choices, especially choices that are adaptive to external circumstances beyond their control?

I asked myself those questions throughout the writing of this book. They echoed in my mind as I drove south on Interstate 5 from Seattle, through Portland, Oregon, and Redding, California, to the tiny town of Point Reyes Station next to the Point Reyes National Seashore. I was on my way to a two-week writing residency at the Mesa Refuge, directly on the San Andreas fault, where I completed the draft of this book. The subject of homelessness was foremost on my mind.

Along the way, I saw numerous tent encampments and vehicle residents clustered near urban areas beside the interstate. Around the town of Weed, California, destroyed by wildfire in 2022, I noticed many RVs parked along the roadside. Near the Point Reyes Station's public restrooms and city park, RVs and vans lined the shoulders of the street. Beside the shiny RVs of retirees, snowbirds, and other tourists were older RVs with broken windows reinforced with cardboard. Individuals, couples, and entire families are on the move to basic survival, to a sense of home.

While this nomadic turn may be more pronounced in the wildfire- and earthquake-prone West, it is occurring throughout our country, spurred on by the ending of pandemic-era social supports and climate change forces. When I interviewed Graham Pruss, he pointed out that a needs assessment has never been done on vehicle residents in Seattle, King County, Washington State, or the United States.[8] He knows from his research and advocacy work that many vehicle residents take pride in their RVs and vans and consider them their homes. There is a

movement to develop more stable, safe parking models like a mobile home park and treat them as a form of affordable housing.
Many vehicle residents refer to traditional shelters, permanent
supportive housing, and even tiny houses as "sticks and bricks"
housing. Graham says that these forms of housing, as opposed
to vehicle residency, prepare "people to be a renter, a tenant,
and pay a portion of their income to live."[9]

Graham states that in Seattle and King County and at the federal level, vehicle residency programs are "seen as an extension
of homelessness, as perpetuating homelessness . . . rather than
providing a stability, and really a Housing First model," where
people can "live in their vehicle while they connect with service
programs and health care as needed."[10] Graham refers to this as
a settled bias that local news sources, including the *Seattle Times*,
adhere to, portraying vehicle residents as a problem and a
scourge to be cleaned away.[11] This portrayal reinforces the image of the propertied and unpropertied classes in proximity and
conflict.

THE EXPERIENCE OF homelessness, with the grace of hindsight,
becomes a point of comparison when bad things happen.

We all have had so many losses because of the pandemic. Grief
upon grief. Some people, as well as some groups of people, have
experienced these losses much more so than others, and often
they had much less to begin with. As Derrick Belgarde told me
when describing different experiences of homelessness, it is not
a pain or loss or grief Olympics. The people I had the privilege
of getting to know through the research for this book have had
a multitude of losses that most of us cannot imagine.

However, I believe that we need to challenge ourselves to
imagine at least some of what homeless people have lived

through, in order for positive empathy leading to action to occur. The experience of homelessness rends the soul. It causes a loss and grief so profound that even combat veterans identify homelessness as the worst trauma in their lives. Think about that fact: the experience of homelessness, with all of the cascading negative effects of social marginalization that accompany it, is a worse trauma than actively being in the atrocious horrors of direct combat in wars.

Only through distance and reflection does my own experience of homelessness, now many decades in the past, along with my continued work as a nurse and policy advocate, deepen my empathy for people who experience homelessness of all kinds—even for people I struggle to have empathy for, like Travis Berge. Recognition of the role of trauma, including childhood trauma, in homelessness needs to be widened. So does recognition of the profoundly negative effects, including health effects, of social marginalization; of compound, complex traumas; and of grief. We need much more of an emphasis on preventing homelessness in the first place and supporting people to deal effectively with the traumas of and traumas contributing to homelessness. Providing safe, supportive housing is an essential component. Preventing child and youth homelessness needs to be a much greater priority. By helping children and young people experience a safe, stable home, they then have the foundation to thrive and to not go on to become chronically homeless adults.

There is an important balancing act involved with emphasizing the role of individual vulnerabilities, including traumas, in contributing to homelessness while viewing this within the essential larger context of structural inequities, including access to affordable housing and health care, as well as the effects of systemic racism. This balance includes acknowledging the long-lasting adverse effects of homelessness while also remembering that people have an amazing capacity for healing, for becoming leaders and change agents, especially when bolstered by adequate community support. People like Anitra Freeman, Derrick Belgarde, and Jenn Adams attest to this resilience and resistance. They are truly experts by experience.

My hope is that we will remember and apply lessons learned from the COVID-19 pandemic and from extreme climate change events in terms of care for especially vulnerable and socially excluded populations, including people experiencing homelessness. My hope is that together we will resist the cacophony of calls to petty divisiveness around the myriad issues of homelessness; instead, I hope we will listen to the voices of experts by experience and hold those voices close when interpreting "cold hard facts." This approach can help lead us past our biases and assumptions to make more deeply informed decisions affecting the lives of our unhoused, our unhomed, community members.

Notes

1. Esmy Jimenez, "How WA's Plan to Transform Its Mental Health System Has Faltered," *Seattle Times*, April 9, 2023, https://www .seattletimes.com/seattle-news/mental-health/how-was-plan-to -transform-its-mental-health-system-has-faltered/.
2. Jimenez, "How WA's Plan."
3. Jimenez, "How WA's Plan"; Josh Cohen, "King County to Vote This Month on a Levy for Crisis Care Centers," Crosscut, April 6, 2023, https://crosscut.com/politics/2023/04/king-county-vote-month-levy -crisis-care-centers.
4. Michelle Baruchman, Hannah Furfaro, and Esme Jimenez, "King County's Proposed Crisis Centers: How They Would Work, What They Would Cost You," *Seattle Times*, April 12, 2023, https://www .seattletimes.com/seattle-news/mental-health/king-countys -proposed-crisis-centers-what-they-are-how-they-would-work/.
5. "King County's Proposed Crisis Centers."
6. Taylor Blatchford, "Three Key Updates on King County's Crisis Care Centers," *Seattle Times*, March 4, 2024, https://www.seattletimes

.com/seattle-news/mental-health/three-key-updates-on-king-countys
-crisis-care-centers/; "Voters Approve Crisis Care Centers Levy—a
Generational Investment to Transform the Behavioral Health System
in King County," King County, April 28, 2023, https://kingcounty.gov
/elected/executive/constantine/news/release/2023/April/28-CCC
-levy-approval.aspx.

7. Nicole Macri, Skid Road Oral History, interview by Josephine Ensign,
July 29, 2022.
8. Graham Joseph Pruss, Skid Road Oral History, interview by Josephine
Ensign, December 16, 2022.
9. Pruss, Skid Road Oral History interview.
10. Pruss, Skid Road Oral History interview.
11. Pruss, Skid Road Oral History interview; Graham Joseph Pruss, "A
Home without a Home: Vehicle Residency and Settled Bias" (PhD diss.,
University of Washington, 2019).

Index

Photographs follow page 116 and are indicated in the index as *photo*.

Berge, Travis: arrests as repeat criminal offender, 35, 44–46, 51; background of, 41–43; CHAZ/CHOP and, 47–49, 67; DESC services and, 42, 48, 67, 72–73; KOMO news coverage of, 43–44, 46–47, 54, 56, 66–67, 76; Lisa's murder by, 18–19, 55, 83; Lisa's relationship with, 48–49, 54; memorial mention of, 82; mental illness and meth use of, 43, 45, 54, 56, 67, 76; no leaf of remembrance for, 83, 185; *Seattle Times* article after death of, 75–76; suicide after Lisa's murder, 18–19, 55, 277, 286; system failures in story of, 35, 56–57, 66, 75–76
Best, Carmen, 21–22, 52
Bill and Melinda Gates Foundation, 256
BIPOC (Black, Indigenous, and persons of color) people, 8; children attending predominantly white schools, 100–101; community-led development projects, 128; COVID-19 impact, 20, 71, 254; exclusion laws and, 125; extreme heat events and, 276–77; gentrification displacing, 247; as lower-income workers, 254; as Pioneer Square residents, 137; police killings of, 20, 94, 157; school to prison pipeline for youth of, 79; tiny house village for, 271. *See also* racism
Birk, Ian, 156–58
Bitter Lake homeless encampment, 129–30
Black Lives Matter (BLM), 20–23, 48, 51, 66; BLM Collective for CHOP, 28, 29, 31; community garden and murals at Cal Anderson Park, 277; Seattle-King County (BLMSKC), 20, 21, 52,

79; Rick Williams participating in, 159
Black people, 6; displaced by gentrification of Central District, 211–12; intergenerational trauma of, 99–100. *See also* BIPOC people; racism
Blakeney, Don, 244, 246–47
BLOCK Project, 250–52
Boren, Carsen Dobbins, 121
boundaries, 98, 218, 289
Bregel, Michelle, 177
Brettler Family Place 3 (public housing), 91, 92, 296
Bridge Care Center (ministry of Quest Church), 205–7
Bridge Program (2023), 285
Browning, Wes, 183, 184–85
Bruder, Jessica: *Nomadland*, 12, 34, 192, 211
Burgess, Tim, 131, 135
Busch, Andrew Joseph, 82–83
Butts, Francis, 105
By-Name List, 248

Cal Anderson Park: center of CHAZ/CHOP protest, 27–28, 48, 277; criminal activities at, 32, 57; final encampment sweep and park closure, 65, 118–19; history of, 27–28; homeless encampment in, 53–54, 65, 120, *photo*; mutual-aid services at, 53–54, 65, 80–81; reopened to public, 277; sexual assaults of women in, 30, 49, 57; shootings in, 277. *See also* Berge, Travis; CHAZ/CHOP; Vach, Lisa
Camphor, Franklin, 98
capitalism, 10, 23, 123, 129, 208, 260
Capitol Hill Organized Protest. *See* CHAZ/CHOP
Carlson, John, 47

Index

Farley, James A., 123
fears: homeless feared as vectors of
disease, 73–74; from homeless
women, 178; mentally ill thought
likely to be violent, 104
fentanyl, 9, 258, 274, 287
Fey, Noah, 270, 279, 281–82
"Fight for the Soul of Seattle"
(documentary), 44
First Nations peoples, 145, 150–54;
Ditidaht, 146, 152. *See also*
Indigenous people
Floyd, George, murder of, 6, 20
Fontaine, Ashley, 99
food stamps, 254
Forty-Fifth Street Youth Clinic,
223–25, 228, 229
foster care, 105, 227; Mockingbird
Family Model, 285
Foundational Community Supports program, 272
Fowle, Matt, 287, 288
Franklin, Benjamin, 33
Freedheim, Amy, 135
Freeman, Anitra Lemore, 83,
168–87; active in homeless
advocacy groups and programs,
185–86, 206, 304; background
of, 168–69, 171, 172; bipolar
condition of, 173–74; Christian
faith of, 172–73; community
health services accessed by,
175–76; exit from homelessness,
186, 286; fears accompanying
homelessness, 178; first marriage
and divorce of, 173; homelessness
of, 170–71, 175–78; lithium as
treatment for, 174–75; loss of
contact with son, 178–79; manic
episode of, 170–71; marriage to
Wes Browning, 183, 184–85; at
Noel House, 180–82; at rededication of leaves of remembrance,
299–300; self-acceptance as

starting point for change, 179,
181; social values of, 172–73;
system failures in story of,
186–87
Friday Feast, 219, 220, 237, 299

Gathering Church (formerly
U Temple), 209
GED program (UDYC), 228
gentrification, 211–12, 247
Gill, Alicia, 99
Giovengo, Melinda, 230
González, Lorena, 7
Great Depression, 7, 33, 34, 74,
123, 182–83
Great Recession, 30, 247, 284
Green, LaMont, 236, 258
gun laws (Washington State),
42–43

Harborview Medical Center:
COVID-19 measures, 8, 70,
photo; medical respite program,
275–76; MedRest Program and,
229; palliative care for homeless
patients, 276; part of disjointed
and broken systems, 107; Pioneer
Square Clinic, 126; substance
addiction treatment, 72
Harmon, Mika, 53
harm reduction approach, 2, 8, 78,
269
Harrell, Bruce, 7, 135–37, 209, 258,
279–80
Harris, Tim, 46
Hartman, Marty, 198
Harvard Implicit Association Test,
253
hate crimes, 278–79
health care: affordability of, 303;
difficult-to-discharge patients,
275; homeless due to medical
condition, 272; inadequacy
for extreme heat events, 275;

police: antibias training for, 108;
calls to defund, 52, 80, 127;
excessive use of force and killings
of BIPOC people by, 20, 94, 104,
157, 158, 286; Initiative 940,
"Police Training and Accountability in Cases of Deadly Force
Measure," 107–8; repeal of law
requiring "malice" in cases of
police killings, 108; systemic
racism of, 158
Poor Laws of British colonies, 32,
68, 125
Popsicle Place (shelter for sick
children and their parents), 198
poverty: child rates of, 254; criminalization of, 32–33, 68, 201;
mental illness linked to, 99;
mutual-aid groups and, 123;
suburbanization of, 211–12
Prefontaine Place, 126–27
privacy, 12, 175, 270, 276, 281
Pruss, Graham, 201, 203, 207–8,
210–11, 234, 259, 301–2
psychiatric deinstitutionalization,
297
PTSD (post-traumatic stress
disorder), 97, 102, 168–69
Public Health–Seattle & King
County, 8, 67, 71, 75, 78, 274
public libraries, 92–93, 107, 125,
274
Puget Sound Family Homelessness
Initiative, 256

Quinn, Bob, 220

racial justice, 20, 22
racism: adverse childhood experiences and, 172; child welfare
practices and, 99; criminalization
of homelessness and, 133; housing and zoning laws and, 6, 251;
Jim Crow laws, 33; national racial
inequality and homelessness, 287;

parks exclusion ordinance and,
127; police killings and, 104,
156–57, 158, 286; racialized disability, criminalization of, 100–101;
Seattle's homeless policies and,
52, 177; systemic, 52, 95, 99, 107,
158, 172, 178, 303; as trauma
producing mental illness, 99;
YouthCare allegations and, 236
Raikes Foundation, 236
Rankin, Sarah, 199
REACH, 117–18, 128, 131, 204, 245,
247
Real Change (newspaper), 132,
183–85
recreational marijuana, state
legalization of, 43
refugees and immigrants, 100, 196,
199, 234–35, 247
rehabilitation, failure of system to
provide, 76
Remelin, Shade Falcon, 24, 27, 83
representation, 282
resiliency, 93, 100, 154, 160, 179,
196, 202
Reynolds, Rick, 149, 199–200
RHA. *See* King County Regional
Homelessness Authority
Richmond, VA, 223
Ricky's Law (drug treatment
legislation 2016), 77–78
Ripley, Chris, 43
ROOTS Young Adult Shelter,
219–20, 222, 237, 250, 299
Ross, Sirena, 49, 55, 66, 83
Rubber Tramps, 34, 199, 211, 235
runaways, 225–27

safe parking programs / safe lots,
208–10, 234, 259
Salinas, Karen, 131
Salisbury, Omari, 21, 49, 50,
109–10
Salvation Army, 122, 126
Sanders, Charlotte, 230

Sand Point, WA, 94–97; Sand Point
Elementary School, 100
Sarey, Jesse, 20
Sawant, Kshama, 23, 79, 123,
253–55
scaling up programs, need for,
259–60
Schildt, David, 152
Scofflaw Mitigation team. *See*
Vehicle Residency Outreach
team
Scott, Mackenzie, 253
Sea-Tac Airport, homeless sleeping
at, 171, 176–77
Seattle: considered as magnet for
homeless, 69; leadership role in
addressing homelessness, 10;
reputation as progressive and
compassionate city, 3, 9, 135,
223, 225
Seattle Center, 69, 155, 159
Seattle Charter Amendment 29,
132
Seattle Children's Hospital, 107,
198
Seattle City Council, 52, 80, 106,
127–28, 254–55, 257
Seattle Indian Health Board, 152,
160
"Seattle Is Dying" (KOMO documentary), 43–44, 46–47, 56
Seattle Municipal Court's Seattle
Community Court Program,
203
Seattle Parks and Recreation, 1, 54,
66, 119, 127–28, 136, 278
Seattle Police Department (SPD):
budget cuts, 52, 79, 80; CHAZ/
CHOP area as police-free zone,
22, 52–53, 56–57; federal oversight of, 20; Navigation Team, 11,
52, 67, 68, 80, 127; protests
against, 117–18; reduced calls
from shelters during COVID-19

pandemic, 269. *See also* Lyles,
Charleena; Williams, John T.
Seattle Public Libraries, 107
Seattle Public Schools, 79, 101, 107,
130
Seattle Social Housing Public
Development Authority, 285
Section 8 housing, 94
sense of community, 197, 282
sexual assault incidents, 45, 49,
134–35
shame, 178, 194, 195, 204, 225
SHARE (Seattle Housing and
Resource Effort), 182–85, 196,
238, 286
Shaw, Debbie, 181–82, 184
shelters: in City Hall Park area,
126; closures of, 120; congregate
settings and contagious diseases,
267–68; daytime closures of,
125; family emergency shelters,
104–5; family shelters for homeless with children, 104; HOPE
Team and, 128–29; hotels used
as, during COVID-19 pandemic,
8, 25, 71–72, 269–70; as mortal
systemic neglect, 287; priority
determinations for, 128; restrictions imposed by, 73; uncomfortable environments of, 268–69;
for young adults, 219–20. *See also*
supportive housing; *specific
organizations and buildings*
Simpson, Pat, 299–300
slavery, 6, 33
smoke from wildfires, 19, 65, 117,
274
Social and Health Services Department, Washington State (DSHS),
76–77
social exclusion. *See* isolation
social housing, 132, 285
Social Housing Initiative 135
(2023), 132, 285

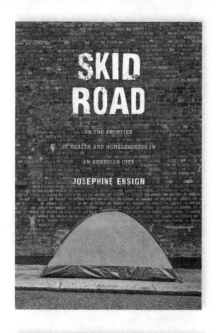
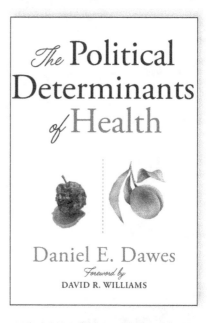
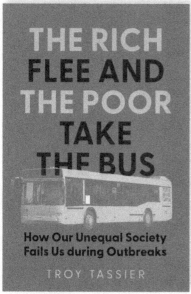